AFRICAN DEVELOPMENT REPORT
2010

AFRICAN DEVELOPMENT REPORT
2010

PORTS, LOGISTICS, AND TRADE IN AFRICA

PUBLISHED FOR THE AFRICAN DEVELOPMENT BANK
BY
OXFORD UNIVERSITY PRESS

OXFORD
UNIVERSITY PRESS

Great Clarendon Street, Oxford OX2 6DP
Oxford University Press is a department of the University of Oxford.
It furthers the University's objective of excellence in research, scholarship,
and education by publishing worldwide in

Oxford New York
Auckland Cape Town Dar es Salaam Hong Kong
Karachi Kuala Lumpur Madrid Melbourne
Mexico City Nairobi New Delhi Shanghai Taipei Toronto

With offices in
Argentina Austria Brazil Chile Czech Republic France Greece
Guatemala Hungary Italy Japan Poland Portugal Singapore
South Korea Switzerland Thailand Turkey Ukraine Vietnam

Oxford is a registered trade mark of Oxford University Press
in the UK and in certain other countries

Published in the United States
by Oxford University Press Inc., New York

British Library Cataloguing in Publication Data
Data available
Library of Congress Cataloging-in-Publication Data
Data available
ISBN 978–0-19-956605-1

Typeset by Hope Services, Abingdon, Oxon
Printed in Italy
on acid-free paper by
Legoprint S.p.A

CONTENTS

FOREWORD

This *African Development Report 2010* focuses on trade logistics in Africa, in particular maritime ports, with the objective of exploring ways to unblock bottlenecks to trade, increase competitiveness, and create sustainable economic growth for African countries. Ports are gateways for 80 percent of global merchandise trade and yet these crucial infrastructure hubs often fail to receive the attention they deserve. This report aims at bridging the existing information gap, providing detailed information on port development, institutional and regulatory aspects, and issues of managing the supply chains in general.

The report recognizes that Africa has significantly increased its trade both with emerging "new" Asian partners, such as China, and the traditional markets, i.e. the European Union and the United States. However, opportunities for enhanced market access in new as well as traditional markets continue to be hampered by trade capacity, severe supply-side constraints, and high transport costs, which severely affect the competitiveness of African economies. Maritime and dry ports are one of the critical elements in the transport logistics chain, which has a major impact on transport costs.

The remarkable growth in African trade over the last decade has put pressure on existing port capacity. As a result, many countries are challenged to transform and modernize their ports by equipping them with appropriate infrastructure to meet this growing demand, including the rise in containerized traffic.

A number of key generic messages emerge from this report, which can help to shape African port development going forward. First, "hard" physical infrastructure is of poor quality and investment in this area is very low, leading to low port efficiency and chronic congestion. Second, the connecting infrastructure networks in Africa are either dilapidated or under pressure of increased traffic, and this delays and hinders the movement of goods. Third, "soft" infrastructure is weak and African countries experience institutional and regulatory constraints in the port sector that create inefficiencies, hinder competition, and raise transaction costs. Lastly, there is the specific challenge of the 15 landlocked countries that are not only handicapped by poor logistics to the hinterland, but also by cumbersome and lengthy customs regulations and delays at borders. For these countries, median transport costs are almost 50 percent higher than the equivalent costs for coastal economies.

The *African Development Report 2010* challenges all of us and highlights the importance of strengthening private/public partnerships, exploring future cofinancing opportunities, as well as putting in place a strong policy framework to facilitate new partnerships.

At a time when the world economy is showing tentative signs of recovery from the global financial and economic crisis, boosting competitiveness will be crucial to Africa's economic growth.

I recommend this report to the readers.

Donald Kaberuka
President,
African Development Bank Group

ACKNOWLEDGMENTS

The *African Development Report 2010* was prepared by the staff of the African Development Bank. The report was guided in its overall preparation by the Bank's Chief Economist, Louis Kasekende and Mthuli Ncube. The preparation was supervised by the Director of Research, Leonce Ndikumana and the Division Managers, Peter Walkenhorst and Abdul Kamara. The report team was comprised of the Task Manager, Tonia Kandiero, Principal Research Economist Vincent Castel, Senior Research Officer, and Pauline de Castelnau, Consultant. Barfour Osei, Chief Research Economist also provided substantial inputs.

The report draws on background analysis by Jaime de Melo, Mark Pearson, Kennedy Mbekeani, Oliver Morrissey, and Lourdes Trujillo. The Report also benefited from data support from the African Development Bank's Statistics Department and from Sylvain Dika, consultant, as well as extensive comments from staff in the Departments for Research, Infrastructure, Private Sector, Policy and Compliance, Quality Assurance and Results, and NEPAD, Regional Integration and Trade. Special thanks are due to the peer reviewers, Victor Davies, Gil-Seong Kang, and Izaskun Lejárraga. In addition, the Team is very grateful for the external expert reviews by Jan Hoffmann, Bert Kruk, and Gaël Raballand, as well as comments from participants at the Global Facilitation Partnership meeting in Tunis, held on November 17–18, 2009. We are also indebted to the Kenya Ports Authority, the Port Management Association of Eastern and Southern Africa, TransNet South Africa, Tunisia Tradenet, the Office de le Marine Marchande et des Ports in Tunisia, and the Agence Nationale des Ports in Morocco for sharing insights into challenges and opportunities they face in the ports sector and related logistics.

The report team is also grateful for the editorial expertise of Sandra Jones, translation coordination from Audrey Verdier-Chouchane, and administrative support from Rhoda Bangurah, Josiane Koné, and Abiana Nelson.

LIST OF BOXES

LIST OF FIGURES AND MAPS

FIGURES

MAPS

LIST OF TABLES

ABBREVIATIONS AND ACRONYMS

ADF	African Development Fund
ADOT	average distance of trade
AfDB / ADB	African Development Bank
AFP	African Financing Partnership
AfT	Aid for Trade
AGOA	Africa Growth and Opportunity Act
AICD	Africa Infrastructure Country Diagnostic Study
AMU	Arab Maghreb Union
ATA	Air Transport Association
AU	African Union
AUC	African Union Commission
BOO	build, operate and own
BOT	build, operate and transfer
BTB	behind the border
CAR	Central African Republic
CEM	Country Economic Memorandum
CEMAC	Central African Economic and Monetary Community
CEWAL	Central–West Africa Lines
CICOS	Commission internationale du bassin Congo-Oubangui-Sangha
cif	cost, insurance and freight
COD	Central Operations Department
COMESA	Common Market for Eastern and Southern Africa
COWAC	Continent – West Africa Conference
D	depth
DB	Doing Business
DEA	Data Envelopment Analysis
DFI	Development Finance Institution
DfID	Department for International Development (UK)
DPW	Dubai Port World
DRC	Democratic Republic of Congo
dwt	deadweight tonnage
EAC	East Africa Community
ECCAS	Economic Community of Central African States
EPZ	Export Processing Zone
ESIA	Environmental and Social Impact Assessment
ESMP	Environmental and Social Management Plan
EU	European Union

FDI	foreign direct investment
FEFC	Far East Freight Conference
fob	free on board
ft	feet
FTA	free trade area
GATT	General Agreement on Tariffs and Trade
GDP	gross domestic product
GVM	gross vehicle mass
HIV/AIDS	Human Immunodeficiency virus/ Acquired Immune Deficiency Syndrome
HS	harmonized system
ICA	Infrastructure Consortium for Africa
ICT	information and communication technologies
IFI	International Financial Institution
IMF	International Monetary Fund
IMO	International Maritime Organization
IOC	Indian Ocean Commission
ISPS	International Ship and Port Facility Security
JICA	Japan International Cooperation Agency
JPC	Japan Port Consultants
L	length
LFTZ	Lagos Free Trade Zone
LI	low-income
LISCR	Liberian International Shipping and Corporate Registry
LLC	landlocked country
LLDC	landlocked developing country
LPI	Logistics Performance Index
LSCI	Liner Shipping Connectivity Index
m	meters
MA	market access
MARPOL	International Convention for the Prevention of Pollution from Ships
MDC	Maputo Development Corridor
MDG	Millennium Development Goal
MEWAC	Mediterranean — West Africa Conference
MFN	Most Favored Nation
MoU	memorandum of understanding
mtpa	million tonnes per annum
MTS	Medium-Term Strategy (AfDB)
NA	not applicable
NCTTCA	Northern Corridor Transit Transport Coordination Authority

NEPAD	New Partnership for Africa's Development
NEPAD-IPPF	New Partnership for Africa's Development — Infrastructure Project Preparation Facilitiy
NSC	North–South Corridor
NTB	nontariff barrier
NTF	Nigeria Trust Fund
NTM	non-tariff measure
ODA	Official Development Assistance
OECD	Organization for Economic Cooperation and Development
OINF	Infrastructure Department (AfDB)
ONRI	Regional Integration Department (AfDB)
OPSM	Private Sector Department (AfDB)
ORPC	Operational Resource and Policy Department
OSBP	one-stop border post
OTRI	Overall Trade Restrictiveness Index
p.a.	per annum
PA	Port Authority
PBM	Performance Based Maintenance
PIDA	Program for Infrastructure Development in Africa
PMAESA	Port Management Association of East and Southern Africa
PPI	Private Participation in Infrastructure
PPP	public–private partnership
PSA	Port of Singapore Authority
PTA	Preferential Trade Agreement
PTP	Pure Transshipment Port
PTR	Potential Trade Ratio
QUAD	Canada, EU, US and Japan
REC	Regional Economic Community
RMC	Regional Member Country
RMI	Road Maintenance Initiative
ROT	rehabilitate, operate and transfer
RTA	Regional Trade Arrangement
SADC	Southern African Development Community
SOE	state-owned enterprise
SOLAS	International Convention of Safety for Life at Sea
SSA	Sub-Saharan Africa
SSATP	Sub-Saharan Africa Transport Program
STAP	short-term action plan
TA	technical assistance

TAH	Trans-African Highway
TEU	twenty foot equivalent unit (the size of a container)
TF	trade facilitation
TIGA	Technology in Government in Africa
TIR	Transports Internationaux Routiers
TRIPS	Trade-Related Aspects of Intellectual Property Rights
TTN	Tradenet Tunisie
TTRI	Tariff Trade Restrictiveness Index
UEMOA	West African Economic and Monetary Union
UKWAL	UK-West Africa Lines
UN	United Nations
UNECE	United Nations Economic Community for Europe
UN-OHRLLS	UN Office of the High Representative for the Least Developed Countries, Landlocked Developing Countries and Small Island Developing States
UNCTAD	United Nations Conference on Trade and Development
UNECA	United Nations Economic Commission for Africa
USA	United States of America
WB	World Bank
WCO	World Customs Organization
WEF	World Economic Forum
WITS	World Integrated Trade Solution
WSS	Water Supply and Sanitation
WTO	World Trade Organization

EXECUTIVE SUMMARY

Overall, Africa's economic performance has improved markedly over the past decade, with the continent experiencing an annual rate of GDP growth above 5 percent for the period 2001–2008. However, as a result of the global financial crisis, the projected GDP growth for Africa decreased to 2.0 percent for 2009 (1.1 percent for Sub-Saharan Africa), although there are improved projections for 2010, with forecasts of 4.1 percent for both Africa and Sub-Saharan Africa (SSA).[1] In terms of its trading position, Africa's share of world trade has shown a slight improvement in recent years, rising from 2.85 percent in 2006 to 3.41 percent in 2008.

Many of the slowest-growing economies in Africa are "fragile states" that are either engaged in conflict or have recently emerged from conflict, which seriously affects their ability to engage in the world trading system and grow their economies. Geography too plays a major role in shaping the economic fortunes of African countries. Fifteen are landlocked countries (LLCs), making them both physically and economically more remote from major world markets. All these factors contribute to the much higher trade costs for Africa, as shown in Figure 1.

In a world where outsourcing is increasing rapidly, high trade costs represent a

formidable handicap, isolating countries and preventing them from reaping the benefits of globalization, as their exports become less competitive and their imports more expensive. The worldwide reduction in barriers to trade has facilitated exports for many countries; however for developing countries, international transport costs often prove to be far greater impediments to trade than the tariffs they face in developed countries. These freight costs contribute significantly to overall high trade costs for the continent and constrain growth in trade volumes.

If one looks at the factors influencing transport costs, one major element is Africa's extensive infrastructure deficit. A recent World Bank report (World Bank, 2009) concludes that poor transport infrastructure, including inefficient functioning of ports, represents a major bottleneck to sustainable growth. In SSA, a financing gap estimated at around 5 percent of GDP needs to be bridged in order to overhaul the infrastructure sector. Because the capital investments for hard infrastructure are so high, the report estimates that US$31 billion per annum will be needed to close SSA's infrastructure gap (World Bank, 2009: 15).

Seaborne transshipment is the main mode of transport for international trade, accounting for about 80 percent of the total global volume. The maritime nexus is particularly important for African countries that specialize in low-value goods, which

---

[1] AfDB, OECD, UNECA, *African Economic Outlook*, 2009.

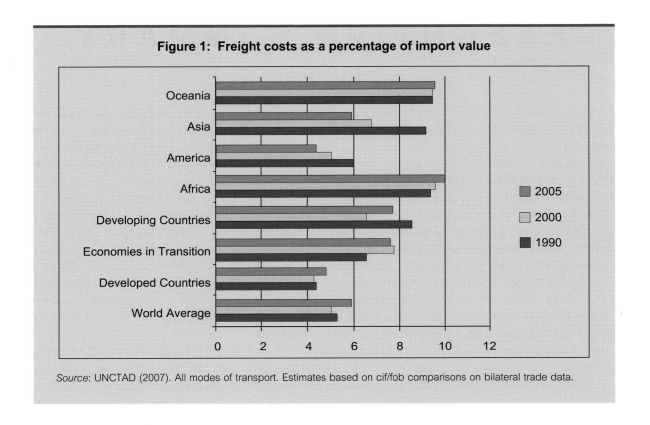

Figure 1: Freight costs as a percentage of import value

Source: UNCTAD (2007). All modes of transport. Estimates based on cif/fob comparisons on bilateral trade data.

are rarely transported by air. Improving logistics to reduce trade costs is thus essential for African countries to improve their competitiveness, and since the bulk of African trade is extra-continental and transits through ports, maritime costs are crucial. Improving efficiency in ports is one way to reduce these costs.

This report analyzes these problems — and draws the implications for the African Development Bank's activities in the transport sector — with a particular focus on ports and the maritime sector. **Chapter 1** gives an overview of Africa's trade, its policies, and the policy barriers African

exports face in destination markets. The chapter also draws on relevant international experience to situate Africa's trade costs within the broader international context. **Chapter 2** describes the "hard" infrastructure characteristics of a seaport and deals with the capacity and efficiency of African seaports, establishing the reasons for their generally poor performance. The chapter also reviews recent investments for rehabilitation and expansion of port physical infrastructure across the continent. **Chapter 3** focuses on the need for a robust institutional and regulatory framework ("soft" infrastructure), which is also needed to improve a port's efficiency and to improve the business-enabling environment and attract private sector investment. **Chapter 4** focuses on the quality of connectivity in Africa through transport networks. It analyzes the state of road, railroad, and inland waterways that link centers of production and markets. The importance of trade corridors to improve regional integration, particularly for land-locked countries, is examined. Trade facilitation measures to boost intra-African trade are also explored. **Chapter 5** draws on the key findings from previous chapters to assess the activities that the African Development Bank has undertaken in the infrastructure sector, and more specifically in the areas of ports and related logistics. The chapter then draws some key recom-mendations for future Bank interventions in the port sector.

Finally, **Chapter 6** draws on key lessons from the preceding chapters to point the way forward toward the development of regional port hubs in Africa. It highlights the basic necessities for African ports to become regional hub ports and examines the potential of their attaining this status. It also draws attention to the investment opportunities available for private sector participation in the development and modernization of African ports. The chapter then discusses possible areas of intervention on the part of IFIs, to assist African countries in the port development process.

A key premise of this report is that ports lie at the heart of the logistics supply chain, linking African countries to their trade partners (Figure 2). The infrastructure characteristics include: (i) physical or "hard" infrastructure; (ii) regulatory or "soft"

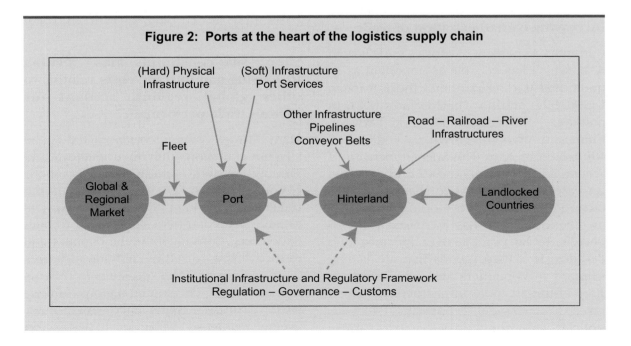

Figure 2: Ports at the heart of the logistics supply chain

infrastructure. Taken together, these elements largely determine a country's competitiveness. Because of the importance of connectivity in the trade logistics supply chain, overall trade costs are largely determined by the weakest link in the chain. This fact is acknowledged by the African Development Bank in its selection of projects in the transport sector. Good connectivity to the hinterland is recognized as a major factor in port development; it contributes to reducing freight costs, and boosts trade and economic growth.

Key Findings and Recommendations

The report's key findings and recommendations are outlined below.

Despite increased South–South trade, Africa cannot fully exploit this new opportunity without improvements in port infrastructure to accommodate the increasing containerization of trade.

Currently, 30 percent of Africa's trade is with Asia, which has become as important as its traditional trading partners, the European Union (EU) and the United States (US). In particular, the volume of trade between China and Africa has grown, exceeding US$ 100 billion in 2008. This was an increase of around 45 percent since 2007 and a tenfold increase since 2001.[2] The share of manufactured goods in developing countries' merchandise trade has increased from 20 percent to 80 percent over the past two decades. It is these goods that are largely shipped in containers and which require state-of-the-art port infrastructure. Given

that China (and Asia more generally) imports raw materials and exports manufactures — which is the opposite trade pattern to African countries — complementarities between the two regions are great and the scope for an expansion of trade is strong. However, this trade cannot sustain growth if the logistics, especially the maritime nexus, which is currently under stress with bottlenecks in many African countries, is not improved.

Intra-African trade has also grown, but at a slower pace, for a number of reasons. Among them, the lack of complementarities among African countries is well-known. Trade barriers other than tariffs, such as rules of origin that accompany Free Trade Areas (FTAs) as well as a host of behind-the-border measures, may also act as obstacles to the free flow of goods. However, this report also highlights the role that high trade costs play in curbing growth in trade volumes.

Supply-side constraints, many relating to a rising gap in trade costs relative to other global regions, account for Africa's trade performance.

Many African countries have reacted to the adverse conditions they face in the World Trading System (landlockedness, poor overall connectivity to major maritime routes) by reducing policy-imposed barriers to trade that contribute significantly to high trade costs. Consequently, the overall trade restrictiveness caused by all trade measures (tariffs and Non Tariff Measures [NTMs]) is average among developing regions; furthermore African exports face lower-than-average market access barriers in destination

---

[2] Ibid.

regions. Yet, contrary to other regions, the average distance of trade for Africa has been falling over the past 40 years, whereas it has been rising elsewhere. This pattern is broadly consistent with a relative deterioration in trade costs for Africa which is related to high transport and transport-related costs.

Of the supply-side constraints impeding trade expansion, trade costs are a crucial component. Trade facilitation measures (including those at the regional level) are key to reducing trade costs, while improvements in port efficiency exert a strong positive effect on trade volumes.

Trade costs have been shown to be greater than the costs associated with trade barriers, which represent a major source of market failure, especially for low-income countries. One way to lower these costs is to foster cooperation at the regional level, to build business contacts among neighboring countries. Regionally organized trade support institutions, which are now beginning to emerge throughout the continent, can help to identify and disseminate relevant information.

Several other trade facilitation measures (which are classified as "soft" infrastructure) can help to streamline the three phases of the logistics trade chain: the *buying process*, the *shipping process* (including ordering and preparation), and the *payment process*. Trade facilitation measures in these areas include: simplification of trade procedures and documentation, harmonization of trade practices and rules, improvements in the transparency of information and procedures, and recourse to new technologies promoting international trade (and transaction security).

However, because of the nature of the goods transported, for low-income African countries, upgrading hard infrastructure is the principal bottleneck. This is substantiated not only by the data on congestion in many African ports reported in Chapter 2, but also by the large delays in ports and along the land infrastructure due to the deficiencies in the "soft" infrastructure (e.g. road blocks and excessive red tape).

With respect to maritime transport costs, estimates derived from databases on standard-sized 20-ft Equivalent Unit (TEU) containers reveal two major factors contributing to increased freight costs: long distances and long delays in ports (one day less in shipping time to the US is equivalent to a 0.8 percent reduction in tariffs). After controlling for related factors, the elimination of market power (prevalent in African ports where competition among shipping companies is low) could increase trade volumes substantially. Controlling for a host of factors that contribute to maritime freight costs, recent large sample estimates suggest that a 10 percent increase in port efficiency would increase country-pair trade by 3 percent.

African transport infrastructure networks (including ports) are caught in a vicious circle resulting in poor quality infrastructure, low trade volumes, and low investment in hard infrastructure, especially for infrastructure connecting ports to markets (Figure 3). Measures of port efficiency throughout Africa are low on a comparative basis, but in line

with per capita income levels, suggesting a reciprocal causality between efficiency levels and per capita incomes.

Transport infrastructure networks in Africa are weak whether it is ports or the infrastructure that connects ports to the markets (roads, railroads, and inland waterways). This reflects two specific features of the African demographic landscape. First, the geographic conditions and the low population density across the continent contribute to the small scale of ports and the low density of the infrastructure linking ports to markets. The low population density also explains the lack of industrial development, as it is often cheaper to supply the sparse African population with goods imported from abroad, in spite of high transport costs (Figure 3).

A low level of hinterland and interregional trade is one factor underlying the poor level of investments (including maintenance) in infrastructures like ports, roads

and railroads, which carry high fixed costs. The dilapidated condition of much of the infrastructure results in high rehabilitation costs. Moreover, the substandard state of the infrastructure network results in delays, the slow movement of goods, and high maintenance costs. As shown in Figure 3, all of these characteristics contribute to high trade costs, which in turn lead to a low volume of trade and low per capita income. Yet, in a number of countries, the asset value of infrastructure in terms of GDP is high relative to the continent's income and hence its ability to pay for maintenance (World Bank, 2009). This is reflected in the close correlation between several indices of the efficiency of infrastructure and per capita income shown in the report.

African ports are small and often congested, while fleets visiting African ports are old. As a response, many African countries are investing in port infrastructure, often with the participation of major international container operators.

The African port situation is characterized by a large number of small ports, each with a capacity below 1 million TEUs, which is low by world standards. As shown in Figure 4, container traffic capacity is low, with only two African ports (Port Saïd and Durban) in the global top 50 league. The report's detailed review of ports by subregion suggests widespread capacity shortages across Africa, particularly in West and Central Africa. The report identifies several areas where improvements are urgently needed: (i) better subregional distribution of port facilities,

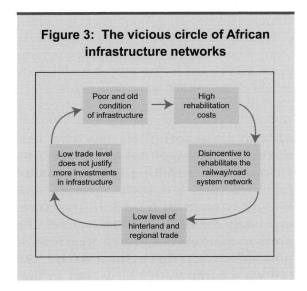

Figure 3: The vicious circle of African infrastructure networks

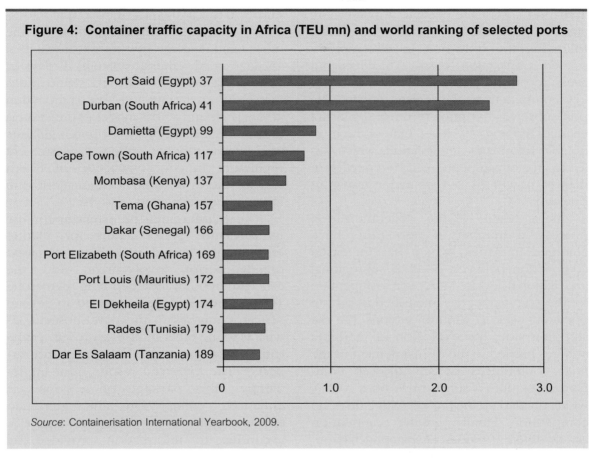

Figure 4: Container traffic capacity in Africa (TEU mn) and world ranking of selected ports

Source: Containerisation International Yearbook, 2009.

particularly on the west and east coasts; (ii) increases in capacity via the rehabilitation, upgrading and construction of improved port infrastructure such as bigger berths to accommodate large container ships; (iii) better land access to road and rail networks to reduce congestion.

A positive development is that many African countries are investing heavily in port infrastructure to meet growing demand and improve port performance. This process has been spurred by the awarding of concessions to private sector operators. This

is an approach that has been supported by the AfDB during the past several years.

Around the world, the port sector has been under pressure to contribute to a lowering of trade costs along the logistics chain. With a lag, significant progress in port reform has also taken place across Africa, but it has been uneven. Africa is shifting toward the landlord port management structure, which involves both the private and public sectors.

Transport costs have become a much more significant factor in overall trade costs following the reduction in government-related transaction costs. This has put pressure on the port subsector, which is a key component in the logistics chain. The port subsector has gone through significant changes at the global level. One of the most notable reforms is deregulation, which has led to greater competition and a reduction in market power by a few major transport operators.

As a result of the decentralization process, a number of new ports have emerged in Africa, which has increased competition between ports at subregional and national levels. Moreover, competition for the port market has intensified as private operators seek to win concessions. On the shipping side, the explosion of maritime services has led to the dismantlement of the liner conferences (which allowed companies to quote a single price on a route), which divided up the market with little or no competition. Finally, greater competition across different modes of transport has put pressure on the port subsector. If these reforms have contributed to improvements in efficiency and a reduction in the cost of maritime services, the results have been uneven, varying across subregions and countries, according to the institutional environment.

Despite these institutional reforms, many countries have not yet adopted global "best practice" methods, resulting in a great disparity across several measures of port efficiency (e.g. port costs and port transit delays). To give an example, in North Africa, the average port cost for a 20-ft container is: Euro 370 in Casablanca, Euro 210 in Rades-Tunis, and Euro 70 in Alexandria. On the other hand, average port transit delays total 15 days in Alexandria, but only 9 days in Casablanca and Tunis. The report underlines that in an environment where competition across ports and across modes of transport is increasing, it is important for port regulators to have autonomy when carrying out regulatory functions. Outside of South Africa, there is little evidence of the independent regulation of ports.

The standard reform package for the infrastructure sectors calls for market restructuring through divestiture, increased private sector involvement, and the establishment of independent regulators. This package has been applied in several African countries to the port subsector as well as to the other infrastructure subsectors (utilities, water, roads, railroads, and airports). The expected results from implementing this package of reforms are enhanced competition and increased efficiency. However, as shown in Figure 5, according to information provided by shippers, Africa still lags other regions in terms of efficiency indicators for the trade logistics chain (ports, roads, railroads, and airports).

The regional averages in Figure 5 ranked in descending order indicate a strong correlation across regions for each indicator. While North Africa ranks fourth, close behind the East Asia and Pacific region, Africa as a region ranks last, particularly for the landlocked countries in SSA.

A similar pattern emerges from Figure 6, which shows that in 2008, North Africa was the best performing subregion in the

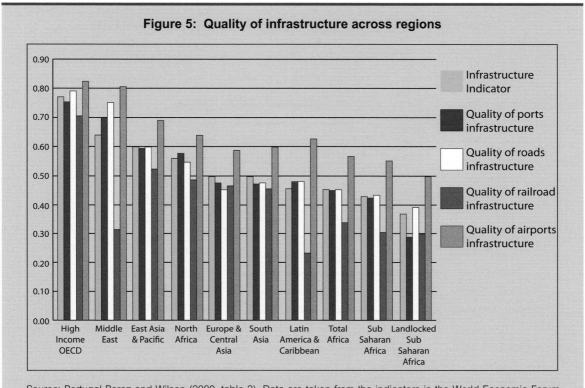

Figure 5: Quality of infrastructure across regions

Source: Portugal-Perez and Wilson (2009, table 2). Data are taken from the indicators in the World Economic Forum *Global Competitiveness Report 2008–2009* and the aggregate infrastructure index is constructed by factor analysis. *Notes*: Regions ranked by decreasing quality of overall infrastructure. The infrastructure indicator is a simple average of the 4 subindicators in the figure. The maximum value taken by the index is unity.

continent for cross-border trade fluidity indicators. For example, in Morocco in 2008 it took about 14 days for exports to clear customs procedures and 19 days for imports, compared to the Central African Republic's record of 57 days for exports and 66 days for imports. However, more recent data indicate that in 2008–2009, 14 Sub-Saharan African countries were rated as "most active" in the World Bank's global *Doing Business* league for cross-border trade policy reforms. This was in part due to

enhanced donor support for aid-for-trade initiatives (World Bank, 2010).

The report gives many examples of improvements as a result of institutional reforms. For example, Ghana, Mozambique, and Uganda reduced average processing time through customs from several weeks to only a few days and North African countries are making serious efforts to reform their customs systems in conformity with the Kyoto Convention and the agreements on international transport. However, a key

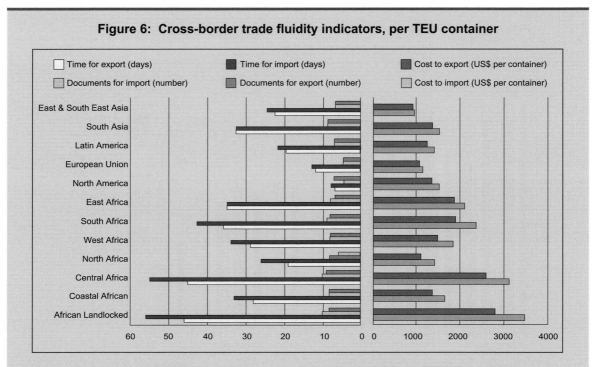

Figure 6: Cross-border trade fluidity indicators, per TEU container

Source: Time, number of documents, and costs computed from World Bank *Doing Business* data (2008).
Note: To ensure comparability across countries, these figures represent the official fees levied on a dry-cargo, 20-ft, full container load expressed in US dollars and associated with completing the procedures to export or import the goods. Costs include the costs of documents, administrative fees for customs clearance and technical control, terminal handling charges, and inland transport, and exclude tariffs as well as other trade-related taxes.

unresolved issue is how successful a regulatory reform can be in an environment with weak governance at the sectoral level.

Landlocked countries are strongly handicapped. Transit and trade corridors to improve connectivity deserve further development. Trade facilitation measures at the national, regional, and international levels are needed to relieve the plight of landlocked countries.

Africa is the continent with the highest concentration of Landlocked Developing Countries (LLDCs), 15 in total. All estimates show significantly higher trade costs for LLDCs. Estimates for a standard 20-ft container show that the median landlocked country's transport costs are 46 percent higher than the equivalent costs for a median coastal economy. Moreover, distance explains only 10 percent of the change in the transport costs between coastal and landlocked countries. Poor road infrastructure represents 40 percent

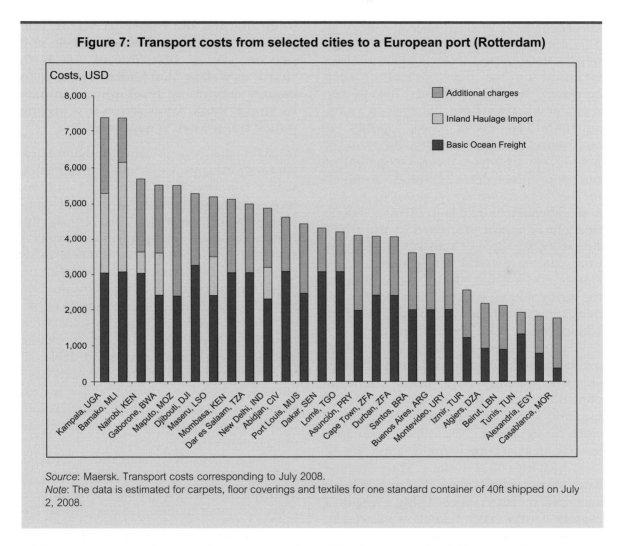

Figure 7: Transport costs from selected cities to a European port (Rotterdam)

Costs, USD

Legend:
- Additional charges
- Inland Haulage Import
- Basic Ocean Freight

Source: Maersk. Transport costs corresponding to July 2008.
Note: The data is estimated for carpets, floor coverings and textiles for one standard container of 40ft shipped on July 2, 2008.

of the transport costs for coastal countries and 60 percent for landlocked countries.

These estimates are corroborated by other findings collected for this report, including the freight charges from different global countries to Rotterdam (Figure 7), as posted on the Internet in 2008 by Maersk, a global shipper. Being landlocked imposes a large premium on overall freight costs, for shipping a standard 20-ft container carrying textiles. LLDCs pay large premia above ocean freight costs. It costs about twice as much to ship a textile container from Bamako or Kampala than from Montevideo, and only a small portion in the overall difference in costs is accounted for by ocean freight costs.

The most promising approach to improve landlocked countries' access to global markets is via transport corridors. This approach is gaining momentum and most of the transport sector strategy in Africa is based on the development of such corridors. Success depends heavily on regional infrastructure, linkages to ports, and improvements in transit logistics, as emphasized in the Almaty Program of Action. For example, the development of one-stop-border-posts (OSBPs) examined in the report are very promising. Full implementation would help LLDCs to obtain freedom of transit enshrined in the GATT Article V ("Freedom of Transit"). At the same time, the successful implementation of OSBPs necessitates "deep" cooperation at the regional level, which in turn requires the delegation of national authority to a supra-national body at the regional level.

Harmonization of safety (and other) regulations at the regional level is another area that would help all African countries, particularly the LLDCs. One important example is road safety, which is a major concern in Africa. The report examines several areas where harmonization would yield high-benefit cost ratios. These include harmonizing regulations relating to axle loads and road transit charges. Using a regional carrier's license that would allow vehicles to operate with one license, and using regional third-party vehicle insurance schemes would also reduce transport costs substantially.

The Bank considers the lack of adequate infrastructure, particularly in the transport infrastructure, as a key constraint to the growth momentum in Africa. This *African Development Report 2010* highlights an opportunity for the Bank to strengthen the transport sector, and ports in particular, through public and private sector instruments in both "hard" as well as "soft" infrastructure. To ensure maximum development impact in these Bank transactions, a strong policy framework is necessary.

In 2008, the African Development Bank Group's total approvals for the infrastructure sector amounted to US\$ 2.17 billion, representing 45 percent of its total commitments for the year. This reflects the Bank's prioritization of infrastructure as a strategic area of focus, as outlined in its *Medium-Term Strategy 2008–2012*. In respect to the ports subsector, between 1973 and 1997, the Bank embarked on 27 public sector operations and the results were positive.[3] However, after 2000 public investments in maritime transport declined. Since that time, Bank activities in ports have been supported by private sector instruments, in countries such as Senegal, Djibouti, and Egypt in order to support the private concession approach.

Going forward, given the enormous challenges presented in this report in terms of hard infrastructure requirements in African ports and other modes of transport into the hinterland (such as rail, road, and waterways), a large injection of public and private investment is required. In 2008, the Bank Group contributed US\$ 393.94 million of its own funds to cofinance projects in the transport subsector, and mobilized a further US\$ 114.41 million from external partners and

---

[3] AfDB, *2001 Review of Bank Group Operations in the Maritime Subsector.*

private sector institutions, with another US$ 243.62 million of funding from governments and local firms. The Bank should continue in this role of catalyzing investments from other major investment partners and development agencies. It should leverage all the instruments at its disposal to strengthen its key partnerships and scale up funding for infrastructure across the continent.

Further, investments in soft infrastructure, such as strong regulatory frameworks and institutions (i.e. customs) are critical to facilitate the movement of goods from ports to the hinterland. To support these operations, a revised policy framework in maritime transport and related areas is needed to guide the prioritization process and to improve the quality at entry of investments.

Finally, going forward, as many African governments and port authorities engage in ways to strengthen their overall port capacity and transshipment functions toward becoming regional hub ports, it must be underscored that investing in port capacity alone will not turn a port into a regional hub.

Consideration must be given to having a strategic location, adequate water depth, and the facilities and performance to ensure low handling costs. These enjoin governments to decide how best to foster and finance integrated port and transport facilities and associated land uses. In addition, building a conducive environment for port hubs entails determining how best to develop state-of-the-art ports, equipped with appropriate technologies and management skills. This should involve the international private sector, particularly in the container terminal

business. As African governments pursue these strategies for improving ports in Africa, they can be supported by IFIs, such as the African Development Bank, through facilitating private sector participation as well as providing finance for port development.

References

AfDB — COD. 2001. *Review of the Bank Group's Operations in the Maritime Subsector.* April.

AfDB, OECD, UNECA. 2009. *African Economic Outlook.* Paris: OECD/AfDB.

Lloyds MIU. 2009. *Containerisation International Yearbook.* 40th edition, London: Informa.

Maersk website: http://www.maersk.com/ en/Pages/Welcome.aspx, accessed in 2009.

Portugal-Perez, A. and J. Wilson. 2009. "Revisiting Trade Facilitation Indicators and Export Performance." Mimeo, World Bank.

UNCTAD. 2007. *Review of Maritime Transport, 2007.* New York and Geneva: UNCTAD.

World Bank. 2009. *Africa's Infrastructure: A Time for Transformation, Part 2 — Sectoral Snapshots.* Flagship Report: AICD Study. Washington, DC: World Bank.

———. **2010.** *Doing Business: Reforming Through Difficult Times.* Palgrave Macmillan, IFC and the World Bank, Washington.

World Economic Forum. 2009. *Global Competitiveness Report 2008–2009.* Geneva.

CHAPTER 1

Trade and Trade Costs in Africa: An Overview

Until the global financial crisis of 2008, world trade and investment flows had grown faster than world Gross Domestic Product (GDP). An important feature of the ongoing globalization was the rising share of trade in unfinished goods, reflecting the increasing importance of outsourcing in the global supply chain. These trends are likely to continue once the global financial storm is over. During the period 1976–2006, Sub-Saharan Africa's (SSA) share of world exports dropped by nearly two-thirds, from 2.9 percent in 1976 to 0.9 percent in 2006.[1] This implies that if SSA's share of world exports had remained constant since the mid-1970s, its export revenue would be almost 10 times larger than its current value.

---

[1] Figures for SSA computed from COMTRADE through the World Integrated Trade Solution (WITS) Database. For Africa, statistics from UNCTAD (2009a: 169).

In 2007, Africa's trade volume — including South Africa — stood at US$ 805 billion, which represents 2.9 percent of global trade.

Many of the slowest-growing economies in Africa are either engaged in conflict or have recently emerged from conflict, which seriously affects their ability to integrate into the world trading system. Geography too plays a major role in shaping the economic fortunes of African countries. Fifteen are landlocked countries (LLCs), making them both physically and economically more remote from major world markets, which contributes to their high trade costs. And it is these high trade costs that isolate countries and prevent them from reaping the benefits of globalization, as their exports become less competitive and imports more expensive for essentials such as fuel and spare parts. In a world where outsourcing is increasing rapidly, this is a formidable handicap. For example, in the Central African Republic and Chad, importers pay cost-insurance-freight (cif) prices that are 1.3 to 1.8 times greater than the cost of the products at point of origin. As to exports from these two countries, cif prices on arrival in Europe are 1.7 times the production cost of timber and 2.8 times that for coffee.[2]

Many African nations have reacted to these adverse conditions by reducing the policy-imposed barriers to trade, which contribute significantly to high trade costs. However, a number of additional factors — low volumes of trade, barriers in exporting markets, weak domestic institutions, and especially weak physical infrastructures along the logistics chain — serve to isolate African

countries from a successful integration into the world trading system. Indeed, African countries face some of the highest trade costs in the world and several estimates put African freight costs at twice the world average.

Seaborne transshipment is the main mode of transport for international trade, accounting for about 80 percent of the total global volume. The maritime nexus is particularly important for African countries that specialize in low-value goods, which are rarely transported by air.

With the recent growth in African trade accompanying the continent's high GDP growth experienced over the past years, ports, and more generally overall trade logistics, have grown in importance for the region in the worldwide race to increase competitiveness. Africa's real GDP growth remained above 5 percent for the period 2001–2008 (standing at 5.1 percent in 2008 — down by less than 1 percent from 2007). However, as a result of the financial crisis, this is expected to decline to 2.8 percent in real terms in 2009.

This pursuit of lower trade costs has seen the share of inventory expenditures in total trade costs drop sharply. For the United States, this change has reduced the share of inventory expenditures in total logistics expenditures from one-half to one-third over the past 20 years. As a result, transport expenditures have increased from less than half to almost two-thirds of total logistics expenditures. The same trends can be observed around the world; indeed, for many developing countries, international transport costs are now two to three times higher than the tariffs they face in developed countries.

---

[2] See World Bank (1995).

Improving logistics to reduce costs is essential if African countries are to scale up their competitiveness and participate in the prosperity created by the world trading system. Since the bulk of African trade is extra-continental and since it transits through ports, maritime costs are particularly important. This report diagnozes the problems faced by the maritime sector and makes recommendations for improvements. This chapter gives an overview of Africa's trade, its policies, and the policy barriers African exports face in destination markets. It lays the groundwork for the chapters that follow by identifying the components of trade costs, and especially of maritime transport costs, along the logistics chain. The chapter also draws on relevant international experience to situate Africa's trade costs in the broader international context.

African Trade: An Overview

The share of South–South transactions in world trade has doubled since 1990, while the share of manufactured goods in developing countries' merchandise trade has increased from 20 percent to 80 percent over the past two decades. It is these goods that are largely shipped in containers. Figure 1.1 shows the evolution of Africa's share of global trade from 2006–2008, revealing an upward trend from US$ 674 billion in 2006 to US$ 1,015 billion in 2008. This is largely due to increased demand for Africa's raw materials, particularly minerals and ores, from China and India.[3]

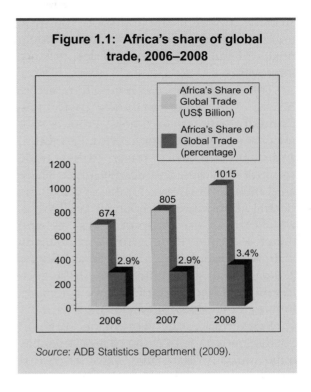

Figure 1.1: Africa's share of global trade, 2006–2008

Legend:
- Africa's Share of Global Trade (US$ Billion)
- Africa's Share of Global Trade (percentage)

Year	US$ Billion	Percentage
2006	674	2.9%
2007	805	2.9%
2008	1015	3.4%

Source: ADB Statistics Department (2009).

Whereas in 2000, Sino-African trade volume stood at US$ 10 billion, by 2008 it had increased tenfold to US$ 106 billion,[4] itself a 48 percent increase over 2007. Currently, 30 percent of Africa's trade is with Asia, which has become as important as its traditional trading partners, the European Union (EU) and the United States (US). Given that China (and Asia more generally) imports raw materials and exports manufactures — which is the opposite trade pattern of African countries — complementarities between the two regions are great and the scope for an expansion of commerce is strong. However, this trade cannot

---

[3] According to recent estimates by UNCTAD (2009a, Table 2), while global exports fell from 8.5 percent in 2006 to 2.0 percent in 2008, Africa's export position showed a reverse trend, growing slightly from 1.5 percent in 2006 to 3.0 percent in 2008.

[4] http://www.chinadaily.com.cn/china/2009-02/11/content_7463268.htm

sustain growth if the transport logistics, especially the bottlenecks in the maritime nexus of many African countries, are not improved.

Trade performance is not uniform across Africa, with some countries performing markedly better than others. From a sub-regional perspective, North Africa, East Africa, and Southern Africa enjoy higher trade volumes than West and Central Africa. There are a number of reasons for this disparity; the Central Africa subregion is largely landlocked, which increases transport costs — and therefore overall trade costs — particularly with overseas markets. Moreover, as Chapter 2 demonstrates, ports in West Africa have historically lagged in performance compared to those in the other subregions.

Furthermore, the worldwide surge in South–South trade over the past 20 years has only partially translated into a correspondingly high growth in intra-African trade flows. One reason that is frequently cited is high tariffs. However, not only have African countries lowered their MFN tariffs, but they have also established multiple Free Trade Areas (FTAs) across the continent, resulting in an elimination of tariffs for much African trade. Table 1.1 shows that intra-African trade as a share of total African trade stood at less than 10 percent for the period 2004–2006. This is well below the average for intraregional trade in other regions, both developed and developing, and indicates that trade between Africa and the rest-of-the-world is growing faster than trade within Africa.

There are several explanatory factors underlying these trends. Among them, the lack of complementarities among African

Table 1.1: Intraregional imports and exports as a proportion of total trade, 2004–2006 averages (%)

	Imports	Exports
Africa	9.6	8.7
Developing America	20.9	18.5
Developing Asia	48.1	45.5
Developed America	23.3	39.8
Developed Europe	68.1	71.4

Source: UNCTAD (2009b: 21).

countries is well-known, and this contributes to the still relatively low volume of intra-regional trade. Trade barriers other than tariffs, such as rules of origin that accompany Free Trade Areas (FTAs) may also represent a barrier. However, it is likely that the high trade costs identified in this report have played a major role in constraining growth in intraregional trade volumes.

It is worth bearing in mind that although the proportion of Africa's intraregional trade remains low in comparison with other regions, it has increased considerably over the years, albeit from a very low initial level. It was stable through to the early 1970s before falling sharply in 1978, when intra-African exports were worth only 2.9 percent of total African exports (UNCTAD 2009b: 20). Recovery began slowly in the 1980s, but picked up in the 1990s and continued on an upward trend, until it started to level off in 2007 (see Figure 1.2). This secular upward trend can be attributed to three main events. First, the adoption of structural adjustment programs in many countries opened up African economies, creating a more favorable environment. Second, the ending of apartheid in South Africa opened the way to trading opportunities with its neighbors. Finally, the intensification of Regional Trade Arrangements such as AMU in 1989, SADC in 1992, and COMESA in 1994 has led to increased regional cooperation, integration and trade. Currently, over three-fourths of intra-African trade takes place within regional trading blocs (UNCTAD, 2009b: 24), which suggests that they should be used for deeper intra-African trade.

Overall, considerable potential exists for Africa to scale up its trade flows both within the region and with the rest of the world,

especially Asia. However, as this report makes clear, to achieve this goal, a number of obstacles will need to be removed. In particular, the evidence points to supply-side constraints, many relating to a rising gap in trade costs compared to other global regions. This analysis is substantiated by the evidence on other components of trade costs reviewed in this chapter; in particular, the recent progress made by African governments in reducing tariff and non-tariff barriers (NTBs). The fact that such measures have not led to an anticipated high growth in trade volumes points to the criticality of trade costs other than policy-imposed trade barriers.

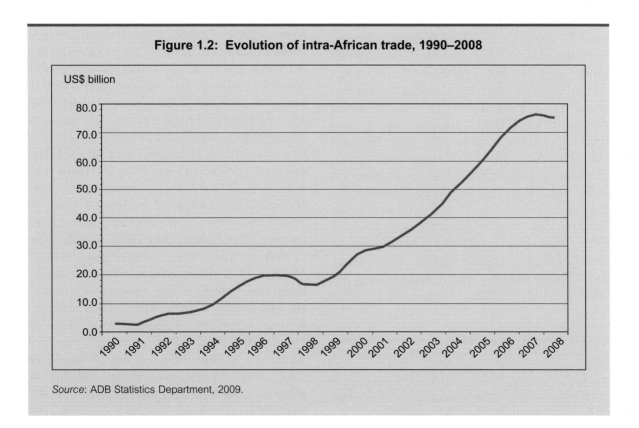

Figure 1.2: Evolution of intra-African trade, 1990–2008

US$ billion

Source: ADB Statistics Department, 2009.

The Geography of African Trade

The gravity model (see Box 1.1) is the preferred approach for analyzing the volume of trade and is especially suitable for a report that focuses on trade costs and the efficiency of trade ports. In essence, the gravity model predicts that the volume of trade between two countries i and j is proportional to the size of those countries' GDPs[5] and inversely proportional to the trade costs (TC) between the two countries:

$$T_{ij} = \frac{(GDP_i)(GDP_j)}{tc_{ij}} \approx \frac{(GDP_i)(GDP_j)}{\overline{DIST_{ij}}}$$

where trade costs are usually proxied by the bilateral distance (DIST) (relative to the average distance across all trading partners) between the trading partners. The gravity model predicts that a relative fall in border-related costs (as happened under the current wave of globalization that has reduced communication and transport costs, and barriers to trade imposed by governments) should lead countries to increase the volume of international trade relative to internal trade. This prediction is largely borne out by the data: since 1980, world production has increased by 75 percent while international trade has increased by 300 percent (Berthelon and Freund, 2008). The gravity model also predicts that a reduction in all costs related to distance (including better

information about distant markets) will lead countries to increase their volume of trade with distant partners. Conversely, if the relative costs associated with distance increase, countries will shift their trade toward closer partners. Moreover, the model predicts that the patterns of bilateral trade will depend on the evolution of trade costs between the partners relative to the evolution of all trade costs. Consequently, an all-round decrease in trade costs will not necessarily lead to an increase in bilateral trade for all countries if the trade costs between a group of countries (for example, African countries) are falling less rapidly than elsewhere.

Figure 1.3 tests this prediction by computing the evolution of the Potential Trade Ratio (PTR), that is, the average distance of trade that would be observed in a frictionless world according to the gravity model divided by the actual average distance of trade. If the gravity model is an approximate description of the determinants of aggregate bilateral trade, an increase in this ratio is then an indirect indicator that the average costs of trade are rising. As expected, Figure 1.3 shows that for the low-income (LI) group of countries (the 40 countries with the lowest per capita income), the bulk of their trade is with more distant partners. This is especially the case for the LI African group, whose average distance of partners was almost twice that of the entire sample of countries in 1970 (7,900 km vs. 4,568 km). Since potential trade, as predicted by the gravity model, has not increased significantly for the LI countries (the effect of the increasing weights of relatively close Asian partners is small), the rising PTR for these countries — especially

---

[5] For example, South Africa is a more important trading partner to Madagascar than Madagascar is to South Africa. This is predicated on the fact that in 2007, South Africa accounted for 3.6 percent of Madagascar's trade, while Madagascar accounted for only 0.1 percent of South Africa's trade share.

Box 1.1: The gravity model of trade

The gravity model of trade is used to predict the aggregate volume of bilateral trade between countries. It is especially well suited to isolate the role of various forms of trade costs from the more "fundamental" determinants of trade, such as the size of trading partners and geographic characteristics. Estimates from the gravity model are reported in several places in this report. In its most general form, the gravity model of trade stipulates that bilateral trade between two countries is given by:

$$X_{i,j} = \frac{A_i A_j}{tc_{ij}}; tc_{ij} = \left(D_{ij}\right)^\theta \prod_{m=1}^{M} \left(z_{ij}^m\right)^{\gamma_m}$$

Where A_i, A_j are the characteristics specific to each partner, invariably including the GDPs but occasionally other variables like population and country characteristics, and tc_{ij} are the trade costs between the partners that in turn are assumed to be proxied by a measure of the bilateral distance between the partners, D_{ij} and z_{ij}^m. ($m = 1,...,M$) is a set of binary dummy variables (usually invariant through time, such as sharing a common border, a common language, etc.) capturing barriers to trade other than distance. In some specifications, trade costs are augmented to include composite indices of the state of infrastructure in the trading partners. The model fits the data well, hence its popularity. Typically, the range of estimates for θ — the elasticity of trade to distance — are in the range $\theta = -1.4$ [-0.7] so that doubling the distance reduces trade by 63 percent [42 percent].

Figure 1.4 is an application of the simplest version of the gravity model, where the potential average distance of trade (ADOT^P) is predicted by a "frictionless" model of trade, i.e. one where the volume of bilateral trade depends only on the product of the trading partners' GDPs (the other relevant variables in trade costs are omitted). Taking the ratio of this potential measure to the actual average distance of trade (ADOT) gives the Potential Trade Ratio (PTR = ADOT^P/ADOT). This ratio is then a measure of changes in the costs of trade after controlling for changes in the partners' GDPs. An increase in the PTR ratio suggests that trade costs which reduce the ADOT are increasing more rapidly than potential trade, as measured by the economic size of the trading partners.

In other results derived from the gravity model reported in this report, the model is augmented to include policy-imposed barriers to trade (tariffs and the tariff-equivalents of NTBs) and indices of the quality of logistics in each trading partner (e.g. the quality of physical infrastructure) among the regressors. Also the estimation procedure exploits the possibility of zero bilateral trade flows (usually estimates of the gravity equation discard information by excluding zero trade flows, thereby biasing the estimates), an important dimension in bilateral trade flows including LI countries. In Box 1.2 below, which reports on the use of statistical analysis to measure the efficiency of ports, the estimation is at the HS-6 product level, which controls for product characteristics like weight, use of containers, and imbalances in bilateral trade.

African LI countries — means that bilateral trade is taking place with geographically closer partners. According to the gravity model, this is an indication of increasing trade costs in relative terms. Since the PTR is constant for the whole sample, this means

that it has been decreasing for high-income countries, as one would expect of falling trade costs under globalization. For African countries, the average distance of trade fell approximately 25 percent over the period. This pattern in the raw data holds up when

---

Figure 1.3: Evolution of Potential Trade Ratio in a frictionless world relative to actual average distance of trade, 1970–2005

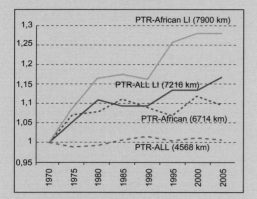

Source: Adapted from Carrère *et al.* (2009). Sample of 124 countries. Data points represent five-year averages.

Notes: The Potential Trade Ratio (PTR) is the ratio the potential average distance of trade (ADOT ^{P}) predicted by a "frictionless" model of trade (i.e. one in the volume of bilateral is given by the product of the trade partners GDP) divided by the actual average distance of trade (ADOT). An increase in the PTR ratio implies an increase in the cost of trade (see Box 1.1).
Average distance of trade in 1970 in parenthesis.

---

a full gravity model with controls (see Box 1.1) is estimated repeatedly for this sample of countries over the period 1970–2005.

Further inspection of the raw data indicates a change in the composition of trading partners, reflecting a change in the number of zero trade flows. For LI African countries, the ratio of zero trade flows, which remained stable until 1990 at around 45 percent (15 percent for the high-income countries), fell sharply by half. These new trade flows (the "extensive" margin of trade), took place with geographically closer partners. The data also show that the regionalization of trade was also generated by trade redistribution within the intensive margin (i.e. products already traded) toward closer partners.

This observed pattern could reflect a combination of changes. One would be if the closer partners were the ones who reduced their trade barriers the most, and when extending trade to new partners, the LI countries selected those countries that were closest. Another variable might be the effects of the regional trade agreements among the LI countries, especially across Africa. Then, the regionalization of trade would also reflect "deep" integration effects, as administrative and technical barriers to trade were removed more rapidly for the LI country group relative to others over the period, generating welfare-increasing new trade flows.

A less optimistic view emerges if one assumes that, over the period, a growing proportion of world trade is generated by vertical specialization and "just-in-time" production. In this case, trade costs could be viewed as a growing impediment in the supply-chain production. Then, if LI countries' trade costs (in particular distance-dependent, such as large markups in international shipping) remain high compared to other developing countries' trade costs, the observed regionalization of trade could be interpreted as a marginalization of these countries.

Landlockedness is a second geographic characteristic of Africa (distance being the first). Compared to other continents, Africa has the highest proportion of landlocked countries (LLCs). Thus 28 percent of the African population lives in landlocked countries compared to 3 percent of the population in Latin America and 2 percent in Asia. In addition, the continent lacks rivers that are navigable by oceangoing vessels. Further, Africa has a very small coastline relative to its area and there is a shortage of natural ports along the coastline. Consequently, as shown in the average distance-of-trade estimates in Figure 1.3, most African countries (especially SSA countries) are far removed from the major world markets (Europe, the United States, and now Asia).

Landlocked countries are also subject to uncertainty for delivery times at border crossings. As argued in this report, these landlocked countries should aim to become land-linked (one principal method is via transport corridors) so that they develop common infrastructures and cooperate on a regional basis to facilitate trade. Moreover, as shown at greater length in Chapter 3, landlocked LI countries face higher transport costs and this contributes to their lower volumes of trade (in the gravity trade model, bilateral trade between landlocked or island countries is always lower after controlling for other factors).

This unfavorable geography is one reason why the elasticity of distance to trade in gravity models is found to be higher for African and landlocked countries. For example, in a well-documented study based on a well-defined cargo, Limão and Venables (2001: 455) reported that the cost of shipping a 40-ft container to various destinations increases from US$ 4,620 for coastal countries to US$ 8,070 for land-locked countries. Using these "true" transport costs in a gravity model of bilateral trade, they estimated the shipping costs of landlocked countries to be 55 percent higher than those of coastal economies. Using an infrastructure index similar to the one presented in Figure 1.7 below, they also established that higher transport costs are associated with low values for their index of the quality of infrastructure.

A third characteristic of African trade, shown in Table 1.2, is that African countries mostly export primary commodities, all but a few of which (e.g. gold, platinum, diamonds, and other high-value raw materials) are transported by ship. Apparel is the only major manufactured product which is occasionally carried as air freight; most commodities are shipped in dry bulk or in general cargo (bags and pallets). Thus the bulk of African exports rely on maritime transport. At the same time, African trade is mostly inter-industry rather than intra-industry. Exports of commodities are either *dry bulk traffic* (coal, grain, and some chemicals) or *liquid bulk* (mostly oil) while most imports are for manufactures shipped under *general cargo and container* trade, with small import volumes as dry and liquid bulk. As a result, these traffic categories are unbalanced with export volumes (loadings) greatly exceeding import volumes for dry and liquid bulk, while imports exceed exports for general cargo. This imbalance raises trade costs.

A fourth characteristic, which has implications for transport costs, is that African countries receive a large share of GDP in foreign aid, which allows them to run larger trade deficits. This leads to increased

Table 1.2: Main African exports and share of total exports (2008) (mode of transport and type of shipping cargo in parenthesis)

Product	Countries	Share in total exports (%)	Product	Countries	Share in total exports (%)
Metals and Ores	Mauritania (iron ore) (1)	48.3	Crude Petroleum (3)	Angola	96.9
	Mozambique (aluminum) (1)	37.6		Cameroon	41.9
	Guinea (aluminum ore) (1)	59.2		Chad	93.8
	South Africa (platinum) (4)	15.1		Congo	86.4
	Tanzania (gold) (4)	30.4		Equatorial Guinea	76.9
	Niger (radioactive chems) (2)	22.7		Gabon	66.9
	Zambia (copper) (2)	59.3		Nigeria	87.6
	Senegal (inorganic acid) (3)	11.5		Sudan	94.5
	Morocco (inorganic acid) (3)	13.6		Algeria	66.7
				Egypt	14.8
				Tunisia	11.2
Cotton (2)	Benin	24.2	Live Animals (specialized ships)	Djibouti	18.1
	Mali	78.9		Somalia	40.7
Coffee (2)	Burundi	59.8	Cocoa (2)	Ghana	49.3
	Ethiopia	36.0		Sao Tome & Principe	66.4
	Rwanda	30.8		Togo	14.6
	Uganda	29.6			
Fish (2b)	Cape Verde	32.6	Apparel (2 or 4)	Lesotho	55.6
	Seychelles	80.2		Madagascar	49.1
Edible nuts (2)	Gambia	53.4	Tobacco (2)	Malawi	54.2
	Guinea Bissau	92.1		Zimbabwe	14.3
Sugar (1 or 2)	Mauritius	15.4	Diamonds (4)	Botswana	61.5
	Swaziland	20.8		CAR	33.5
				DR Congo	26.1
				Namibia	26.2
				Sierra Leone	49.1
Tea (2)	Kenya	16.1	Resins etc. (2 or 2b)	Eritrea	4.0
Spices (2 or 4)	Comoros	34.0			

Source: ADB Statistics Department using World Integrated Trade Solution (WITS) Database, 2009.
Notes: Type of shipping cargo (1 to 4):
1: dry bulk   2: container, but also general cargo (bags, pallets). Coffee is increasingly containerized.   2b: reefer (cold) containers   3: liquid bulk   4: air

transport costs for imports, since freight rates must also cover the cost of transporting empty containers or trucks back to their place of origin.

Trade Costs: A Classification

Trade costs — sometimes defined as comprising everything but production costs — constitute the sum of administrative barriers, trade policies (tariffs and non-tariff measures (NTMs), and transaction costs (transport and insurance costs). Trade costs

may also be analyzed along other dimensions. For example, Figure 1.4 distinguishes between border-related costs and behind-the-border (BTB) measures to identify those trade costs that are not a direct result of trade policies but that can be reduced through other channels, notably via trade facilitation resulting from cooperation, often in the context of a regional trade agreement.[6] The left-hand side of Figure 1.4 brings in another dimension. There trade costs are broken down between trade frictions that are largely

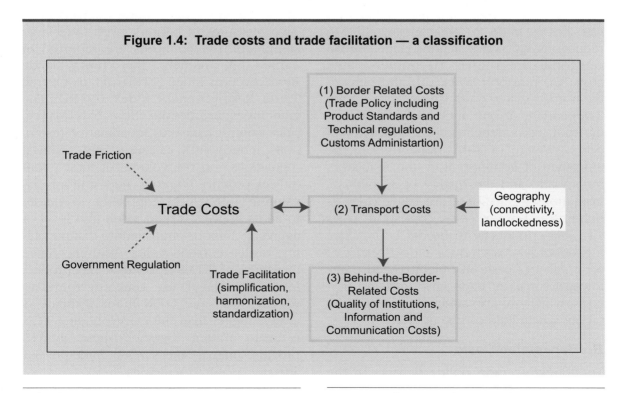

Figure 1.4: Trade costs and trade facilitation — a classification

---

[6] The terminology "BTB measure" was first used to distinguish between "deep" and "shallow" integration in Regional Integration Agreements: "deep" integration occurring when integration extends beyond the removal of protection (i.e.

integrating factor markets, combining regulatory institutions, harmonizing standards and cooperating intensively on trade facilitation, e.g. reducing "red tape" for crossing borders).

exogenous (distance, geography of trading partners, different languages) and trade costs due to government regulations, which are more directly amenable to changes in policy.

The discussion on trade costs increasingly refers to trade facilitation (simplification of trade procedures, harmonization of trade practices, and rules). These are represented separately in Figure 1.4 to signal that the implementation of trade facilitation requires some cooperation at the regional level or beyond. (The role of trade facilitation is treated below.)

The right-hand side of Figure 1.4 classifies the trade costs that are amenable to reductions via policy actions. Three broad categories are shown: (i) border-related costs; (ii) transport costs; (iii) and behind-the-border-related costs. These costs are not independent of one another. For example, transport costs depend on the efficiency of ports, which in turn depends on the efficiency of administration, the regulatory framework, and the quality of a country's institutions — all these are categorized as behind-the-border costs. Transport costs also relate indirectly to border costs, since higher border costs reduce trade. Because of economies of scale in freight-related costs, lower volumes of trade raise unit transport costs, which are also affected by geography (about which little can be done).

Border-related Costs

Traditionally, trade policy barriers in the importing country (tariffs and quotas) have been considered the most important element of overall trade costs. With the unilateral and multilateral reduction in tariffs and the quasi-elimination of quotas, non-

tariff measures (NTMs) such as technical standards and phytosanitary norms imposed by OECD countries, have come to be considered the most important policy barrier to trade. In African countries, tariffs have been sharply reduced over the past decade. As shown in Table 1.3, average tariffs in Africa are no longer the highest among developing regions. Thus one can no longer attribute the low volume of intra-African trade to closed trade regimes.

Barriers to African exports in developed countries are often cited as contributing to the continent's poor trade performance. Two measures of barriers faced by a large sample of 104 countries are reported in Table 1.3, namely the Tariff Trade Restrictiveness Index (TTRI) and the Overall Trade Restrictiveness Index (OTRI). The latter index includes the effects of NTMs (i.e. price control measures, quantitative restrictions, monopolistic measures, and technical regulations) on the volume of trade. Both indices produce the equivalent uniform ad-valorem tariff, which, if applied by a country to all its imports, would result in a level of aggregate imports equivalent to that prevailing under current policy settings. Since measures of NTMs applied at the product level (HS-6 level) are generally found to restrict trade, the OTRI index estimate is always higher than the corresponding TTRI estimate. Taken together, these indices provide summary measures of trade policies affecting a country's imports.

Table 1.3 shows the estimates of the barriers to trade on imports by developing countries across regions, and the barriers to trade imposed by the QUAD (Canada, EU, US, and Japan) on their imports. This table

Table 1.3: Tariff Trade Restrictiveness Index (TTRI) and Overall Trade Restrictiveness Index (OTRI) by region, 2003–2004*

Region	All trade	Agriculture	Manufacturing
Middle East and North Africa	21.6	32.3	19.4
	11.9	*12.1*	*11.8*
South Asia	19.5	46.4	18.2
	14.0	*31.4*	*13.2*
Latin America and the Caribbean	15.0	28.1	13.8
	5.4	*6.6*	*5.3*
Sub-Saharan Africa	14.4	24.9	12.9
	8.4	*13.8*	*7.6*
East Asia and Pacific	11.3	26.6	10.4
	5.0	*8.7*	*4.8*
Europe and Central Asia	10.1	25.9	9.0
	4.5	*10.3*	*4.0*

QUAD	All trade	Agriculture	Manufacturing
United States	6.4	18.4	5.7
	1.6	*3.8*	*1.5*
European Union	6.6	48.7	2.9
	1.4	*5.9*	*1.1*
Japan	11.4	55.8	5.7
	4.5	*31.1*	*1.1*
Canada	9.9	17.1	9.5
	5.1	*8.8*	*4.9*

Notes: Tariff Trade Restrictiveness Index (TTRI) in italics. Overall (i.e. Non-tariff-measure inclusive) Index (OTRI) in bold.
* Most recent dataset available across a large sample of countries.

is based on data for 2003–2004, which represents the most recent information available on NTMs across a large sample of countries. Compared to other global regions, Sub-Saharan Africa is in the middle both for total protection and tariffs (with an average tariff of 8.4 percent, compared to 11.9 percent for the Middle East and North Africa and 14 percent for South Asia). The averages across sectors in the QUAD show

that the restrictiveness of NTMs can be important, but especially in agriculture, a sector where African countries enjoy a comparative advantage. In the EU, the tariff equivalent of all tariff measures in agriculture (the TTRI) is only 5.9 percent, but this rises to 48.7 percent when NTMs are added (the OTRI index value). In conclusion, on average, SSA countries do not exhibit particularly restrictive trade regimes.

Table 1.4: Market access (MA) indices by income group, 2006

IMPORTERS	EXPORTERS									
	High income	Upper middle income	Lower middle income	Low income	East Asia and Pacific	Europe & Central Asia	Latin America and Caribbean	Middle East & N.Africa	South Asia	SSA
High income	**6.3**	**5.7**	**7.9**	**9.1**	**8.3**	**5.1**	**7.0**	**4.3**	**10.4**	**4.4**
	2.7	1.2	2.5	2.4	2.6	1.1	1.5	0.8	3.1	0.7
QUAD	**6.3**	**5.2**	**8.6**	**10.6**	**8.9**	**5.2**	**6.9**	**4.4**	**13.6**	**4.5**
	2.1	0.9	2.5	2.5	2.7	0.8	1.2	0.5	3.3	0.5
Upper middle income	**15.6**	**11.8**	**15.8**	**14.7**	**19.2**	**10.2**	**13.6**	**6.0**	**14.3**	**5.9**
	5.6	3.8	5.6	5.7	7.2	4.4	2.6	2.5	6.6	3.5
Lower middle income	**12.4**	**11.1**	**12.9**	**9.4**	**13.6**	**11.2**	**12.6**	**6.7**	**9.9**	**4.0**
	7.1	4.8	6.7	5.1	6.6	6.2	5.1	2.8	6.2	2.7
Low income	**18.2**	**14.3**	**19.5**	**25.4**	**22.2**	**17.7**	**15.9**	**16.3**	**16.2**	**16.3**
	10.9	8.1	12.2	12.9	13.8	6.2	9.0	0.0	10.4	12.2

Notes: MA-TTRI in italics; MA-OTRI in bold face. Importers are along rows, exporters down columns.
Source: Portugal-Perez and Wilson (2009, table 1).

What about barriers faced in export markets? Table 1.4 compares market access in destination markets across groups of countries for the year 2006, classified by per capita income (country groupings in the rows). Exporting countries are grouped either by region, or again by income-per-capita range (country groupings in the columns). Composition effects are particularly important for SSA countries, which face the lowest market access barriers (around 5 percent) in all but other low-income countries. This reflects the patterns of specialization of the SSA grouping, which has an export pattern (partly influenced by the trade policies of their partners) geared toward products that face low entry barriers in destination markets. According to these estimates, even if SSA countries have been induced (by the restrictive policies of their partners) to specialize in the export of products with low market access barriers, it does not appear that their exports face unusually high barriers (except in other low-income countries).

In conclusion, the data do not support the argument that market access is relatively less favorable for the African region in their partners' markets; even if there are some instances where trade restrictiveness in exporting markets have been found to be significant (see Oyejide *et al.*, 2000; Otsuki *et al.*, 2001).

This report argues that for African countries, the most important component of border-related trade costs amenable to policy intervention is likely to be administrative costs. These result from delays at customs, rather than from policy-imposed barriers. Customs services are responsible not only for levying tariff duties, but also for ensuring that imported goods comply with regulatory requirements, and for preventing the importation of prohibited or unsafe imports (e.g., illegal weapons or out-of-date medicines). In the case of SSA countries benefiting from duty-free access to the US market under the Africa Growth and Opportunity Act (AGOA), customs officials may also carry out physical inspections to check the conformity of shipments.

The World Bank (2008) *Doing Business* dataset reports on the procedural requirements for exporting and importing a standardized cargo of goods by ocean transport. This reveals that South Asia has the highest number of export and import procedures, closely followed by SSA (see Chapter 3, Figure 3.6). Lengthy inspections at borders create delays in customs clearance and so raise trade costs; they also increase transport costs, since transporters have to factor in the time lost due to delays. Recent estimates by Djankov *et al.* (2008) for a large sample of countries suggest that each day of delay at customs is equivalent to a country distancing itself from its trading partners by an additional 85 km. Keeping customs procedures as simple and transparent as possible helps to minimize the time needed to clear customs. As indicated in Figure 1.4, trade facilitation measures that reduce these procedures through simplification, harmonization, and standardization contribute to reducing overall trade costs.

Transport Costs

With inventory costs falling rapidly, transport costs are becoming an increasingly important element in total trade costs. Until recently, most estimates of freight rates relied on

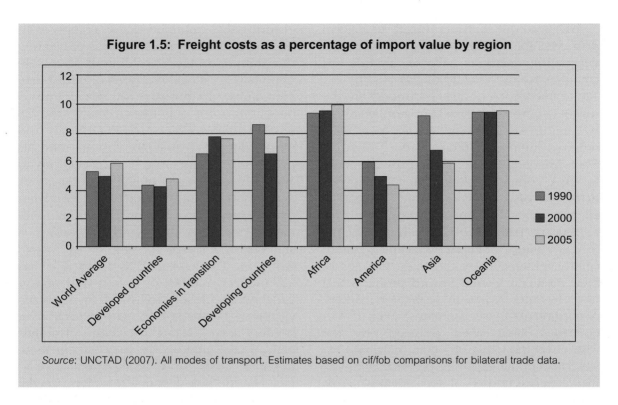

Figure 1.5: Freight costs as a percentage of import value by region

Source: UNCTAD (2007). All modes of transport. Estimates based on cif/fob comparisons for bilateral trade data.

matched comparisons of cif (cost-insurance-freight) and fob (free-on-board) trade flows, based on United Nations (UN) and International Monetary Fund (IMF) trade statistics. These estimates are used frequently because of their widespread availability for a large number of countries over time, even though their reliability has been challenged.[7]

Figure 1.5 uses these matched trade statistics to show the evolution of average freight costs across all modes of transport for various global regions and for countries at different stages of development. Several patterns emerge. First, it is clear that distance is only one component of freight costs, since Africa's trade costs are as high as those of Oceania, yet Africa is closer to its trading partners than is Oceania. Second, for both regions, trade volumes are small, suggesting that economies of scale in transport are far from exhausted. Small traffic volumes for both regions contribute to the high freight costs, which are close to double that of

[7] With the exception of a few countries that systematically report individual freight rates for each shipment (New Zealand and the US), freight rates are computed from trade data at the HS-6 level, as reported to the UN and IMF by exporting and importing countries. Hummels and Lugovorskyy (2006) discuss their shortcomings. Raballand *et al.*

(2007) discuss the shortcomings of the freight payments, notably for landlocked countries, used in Figure 1.5.

competing regions. Third, Figure 1.5 indicates that for Africa, freight costs are now as important, or more important, than the costs associated with the policy-imposed trade barriers they face in all destinations except other low-income countries. Fourth, in Africa freight costs are rising rather than falling, unlike several other regions. (For developed countries, the small increase in freight costs likely reflects the shift towards air freight for high-value products that are lighter in weight and often time-sensitive, e.g. fashion products.)

To reach a better understanding of the differences across these rough estimates, one must identify the various cost determinants of transport services. These can be grouped into the broad categories outlined in Figure 1.4, including geography (e.g. connectivity) which, though largely exogenous, is a major conributor to high transport costs in Africa. From this perspective, one may conclude that trade flows will be higher for a small Caribbean island than an equally small island in the Pacific, since Caribbean islands are located at the crossroads of the major maritime routes. Likewise, one can expect transport costs to be higher for landlocked countries, if only because freight costs for coastal countries are measured at the harbor of arrival, while for landlocked countries they are measured inland at the country's border.

Beyond the geography of African trade, high border-related costs also increase transport costs directly, as shippers have to charge for waiting time in ports. Behind-the-border costs (e.g. deficient physical infrastructure) also play their part in raising transport costs directly. Finally, Figure 1.4 shows that both border and behind-the-border costs raise transport costs indirectly because high costs reduce the volume of trade and hence reduce the demand for transport services.

With the growth in containerization, it has become easier to measure freight rates directly. Several recent studies (e.g. Limão and Venables, 2001), use the cost of shipping a standardized container between two destinations (usually the transport cost per tonne of TEU) as a measure of freight costs.[8] These studies show that differences in freight rates depend on a number of factors: distance, type and value of goods, imbalances in trade[9], economies of scale in shipping, competition, and port facilities. Some direct evidence on these costs is available for Africa and is reported in the chapters that follow. Because African countries typically transport small shipments,[10] it is instructive to consider the findings reported by Wilmsmeier and Hoffman (2008) on the cost of shipping 20-ft containers on 189 different routes in the Caribbean. These are provided in Figure 1.6, where each panel shows the correlation between the freight rate for a 20-ft container and the corresponding variable on the

---

[8] The usual yardstick is the TEU — the 20-ft equivalent unit.

[9] Because of the imbalance in the trade of LI African countries, partly resulting from the flow of foreign aid allowing for trade deficits, many shipping providers are left with empty ships or containers to return to Asia or Europe, so the freight rates for African exports are relatively low.

[10] East Asian ports service vessels in the 8,000–11,000 TEUs range, while most African ports cannot handle efficiently vessels above 2,000 TEUs.

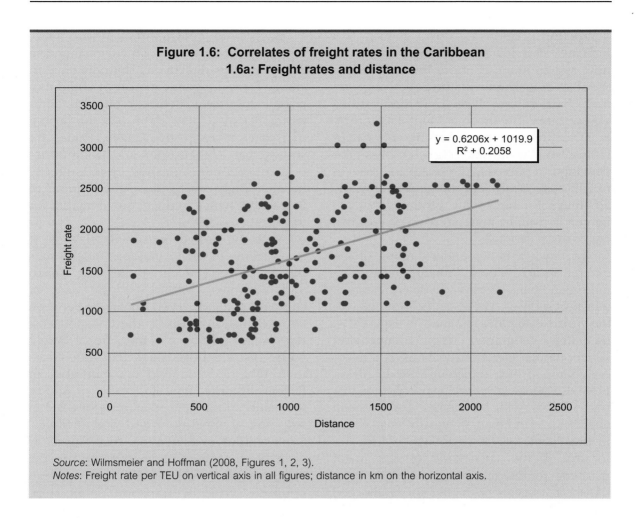

**Figure 1.6: Correlates of freight rates in the Caribbean
1.6a: Freight rates and distance**

$y = 0.6206x + 1019.9$
$R^2 + 0.2058$

Source: Wilmsmeier and Hoffman (2008, Figures 1, 2, 3).
Notes: Freight rate per TEU on vertical axis in all figures; distance in km on the horizontal axis.

horizontal axis (size of shipment, distance, time at port, and number of shippers).

Figure 1.6a confirms that long distance increases freight rates, which explains why countries often choose geographically close partners. Long delays in ports also raise freight costs, as shown by the scatter plot in Figure 1.6b. Using detailed US customs data and controlling for the choice of mode of transport (sea or air), Hummels (2001) estimates that each extra day saved in

shipping time reduces costs for manufactured goods equivalent to a 0.8 percent tariff. Applying these estimates to the data in Figure 1.6b suggests that cutting 10 days in transit time in the Caribbean would be equivalent to eliminating an 8 percent ad-valorem tariff. Finally, the significance of competition in freight rates is shown in Figure 1.6c. Each scatter plot reflects one of the contributing factors to freight costs, i.e. it is a partial correlation. The suggestion of market power in Figure 1.6c is confirmed in estimates by Hummels *et al.* (2009), who isolate the effect of market power after controlling for value of shipment, distance, and import demand elasticities. Their estimates rely on US time-series of shipping data and cross-tabulation of data for six Latin American importers (Argentina, Brazil, Chile, Ecuador, Peru, and Uruguay). They estimate that the elimination of market power would increase trade volumes by 6 percent for the US, and by 15 percent for the Latin American importers.

Behind-the-Border Costs

Trade costs are also augmented by a country's behind-the-border (BTB) costs, including its overall social infrastructure, as reflected in the quality of its governance (i.e. transparency, rule-of-law, and the business environment). Weak institutions contribute through several channels to raising trade costs. First, they lead to a lower supply of public goods, including the quality and quantity of "hard" or physical infrastructure.

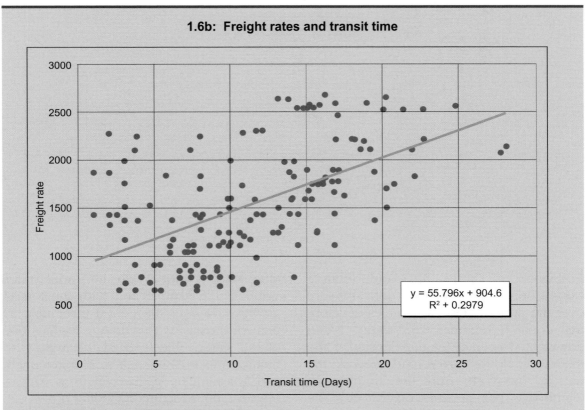

1.6b: Freight rates and transit time

$$y = 55.796x + 904.6$$
$$R^2 + 0.2979$$

Source: Wilmsmeier and Hoffman (2008, Figures 1, 2, 3).
Notes: Freight rate per TEU on vertical axis in all figures; number of days to transit on the axis.

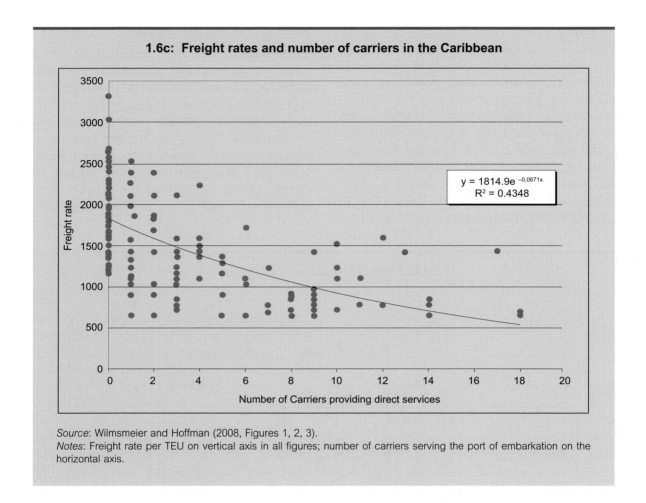

1.6c: Freight rates and number of carriers in the Caribbean

$$y = 1814.9e^{-0.0671x}$$
$$R^2 = 0.4348$$

Freight rate

Number of Carriers providing direct services

Source: Wilmsmeier and Hoffman (2008, Figures 1, 2, 3).
Notes: Freight rate per TEU on vertical axis in all figures; number of carriers serving the port of embarkation on the horizontal axis.

Figure 1.7 shows the evolution of a composite index of physical infrastructure over the period 1962–2006 across developing country regions. The index is an unweighted average of the density of the road network, the paved road network, the railroad network, and the number of telephones per person constructed. The figure shows that SSA was below average in 1962 and that its relative position in the classification of countries deteriorated over time, since it ended with the lowest index value in the sample and with the lowest growth rate over the period (around a 20 percent increase). This finding justifies one of the stated objectives of this report: to highlight the pressing need for improvement and a scaling up of investment in Africa's physical infrastructure, including ports.

Weak institutions are also reflected in a lack of "soft" infrastructure. The effects of weak institutions in many low-income

Figure 1.7: Evolution of an index of infrastructure across developing country regions, 1962–2006

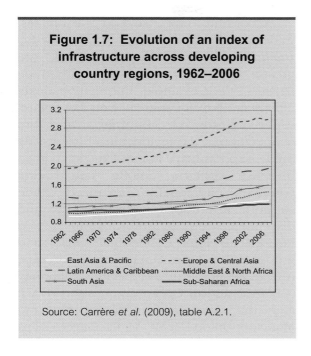

Source: Carrère *et al.* (2009), table A.2.1.

estimate that if a country with Africa's average corruption perception index of 2.8 were to improve its corruption level to Botswana's 5.9 index value, its exports would increase by about 15 percent and its imports by about 27 percent.

Trade Costs and Trade Facilitation: "Soft" and "Hard" Infrastructure

The evidence above suggests that trade costs are the most important element of overall transaction costs, and that trade costs depend largely on transport costs. Transport costs, though, are determined by many factors along the supply chain. Efficiency along the supply chain is closely linked both to the "hard" infrastructure (dock facilities, connections to railroads and trucking lines, harbor characteristics) and to the "soft" infrastructure, as reflected in the border and behind-the-border measures identified in Figure 1.4. Improvements in both types of infrastructure are required for African countries; indeed, it is difficult to estimate which of the two is more important since they are complementary and the situation will vary across countries.

That said, the evolving pattern of global trade suggests that trade facilitation is crucial. With the change in world trade patterns, 80 percent is now in manufactured goods, one-third is in unfinished goods, while about one-third is intra-company trade. With the explosion of preferential trade agreements (PTAs) and transit trade, the competitiveness of a country's export base is increasingly dependent on low transaction costs.

Trade facilitation measures relate to the three phases of the trade chain, namely: the

countries are evident at various points in the supply chain. Because of a lack of alternative sources of revenue from direct taxes, many LI countries apply relatively high border taxes in an effort to raise government revenue. The result is evasion and extortion at the border. Using data on corruption and trade policy, Gatti (2004) shows that higher trade costs — in this case, tariff rates — are indeed associated with a higher level of corruption. Similarly, Fisman and Wei (2004) report that in bilateral trade between Hong Kong and the Chinese mainland, higher tariff rates are associated with larger differences in declared values between export and import values, which points to an important evasion effect. Using a bilateral gravity model over the period 1998–2007, Musila and Sigué (2009) *buying process*, the *shipping process* (including ordering and preparation), and the *payment process*. Trade facilitation is a process that includes improvements in the following areas: (i) simplification of trade procedures and documentation (e.g. one-stop border posts [OSBPs]); (ii) harmonization of trade practices and rules (e.g. implementation of the standards in mutual recognition agreements); (iii) improvements in the transparency of information and procedures (e.g. publication of laws and regulations, inspection before shipping); (iv) recourse to new technologies promoting international trade (e.g. electronic single window implementation); and (v) transaction security (e.g. use of risk assessment techniques).

Because of the nature of the goods transported, for low-income African countries, upgrading hard infrastructure is proving to be the major bottleneck. This is substantiated by the data on congestion in many African ports reported in Chapter 2, even though part of the observed delays in ports and along the land infrastructure are due to the deficiencies in the "soft" infrastructure (e.g. road blocks and excessive red tape).

Whereas the gains from PTAs are somewhat ambiguous because of the possibility of welfare-reducing trade diversion (when inefficient partners' imports are subsidized at the expense of non-MFN partners), the trade facilitation measures described above involve only a reduction in costs and so are welfare-improving for the partners involved. This is important because the new wave of "deep" Free Trade Areas (FTAs) in Africa has gone beyond eliminating tariffs and quotas and has engaged in trade facilitation measures.

According to several estimates, trade costs (as captured by the *Doing Business* dataset of the World Bank) are greater than those associated with trade barriers.[11] For example, information deficiencies are a major source of market failure, especially for LI countries. Therefore cooperation at the regional level to provide public support helps to build and strengthen business contacts among neighboring countries. Regionally organized trade support institutions help identify and disseminate relevant information. Several Regional Economic Communities (RECs) and groupings in Africa, including the Central African Economic and Monetary Community (CEMAC), Indian Ocean Commission (IOC), and the West African Economic and Monetary Union (UEMOA), have taken steps in that direction (UNCTAD, 2007: Chapter 6). Many of the trade facilitation measures identified above, such as common standards, licenses, and trade documents, are more easily achieved at the regional than at the global level. The COMESA uniform Customs Document adopted by 15 members is one example of successful trade facilitation at the regional level.

At the same time, effective regional cooperation requires delegation of authority to a supranational body, which may prove difficult to achieve if there is a low level

---

[11] Wilson *et al.* (2004) estimate large increases in trade for APEC members from improvements in trade facilitation. Using *Doing Business* data on trade costs, Portugal-Perez and Wilson (2009) find that the ad-valorem equivalent of *Doing Business* export costs are usually greater than the ad-valorem equivalent of all trade measures (tariffs and NTMs in export markets).

of trust among trading partners, perhaps because of infrequent exchanges. As discussed in Chapter 4, for the African landlocked developing countries (LLDCs), it is essential to build the necessary trust to develop trade corridors and so boost their connectivity. Equally pressing is a successful conclusion of the World Trade Organization Trade Facilitation negotiations, launched in the July 2004 package.

In conclusion, the benefits of trade facilitation are manifold. First, trade facilitation measures are necessarily welfare-enhancing, as they cut costs rather than transfer rents (as in the case of preferential access). Second, trade facilitation enhances outsourcing and the fragmentation of the production process, which helps low-income countries to participate in the growing trade in unfinished products partly through increased foreign direct investment (FDI) inflows. The benefits of trade facilitation are further examined in Chapter 4 of this report.

Why Maritime Trade and Port Efficiency are Important

Worldwide seaborne trade has remained roughly constant in volume terms over the past several decades. Figure 1.8 shows the evolution of seaborne trade over the period 1990–2007 across regions and by type of shipments for all goods loaded (the difference between goods loaded and unloaded is small). These trends reflect the growing role of South–South trade in the global market, with the rising share of Asia-Oceania largely at the expense of the developed countries, especially since 2000. Africa's share of global trade fell during the

1990s but has recovered in recent years because of increased trade with Asia. The composition of goods loaded has not changed much at the world level, with dry cargo occupying about 70 percent of goods loaded. A major shift took place in the distribution of goods loaded across regions. Developed countries shifted away from dry cargo toward containerized cargoes, while Africa's share of crude oil shipments rose.

In order to reach a better understanding of the causative link between infrastructure (both soft and hard) and trade, one needs to examine the functioning of the port sector. Given that over 80 percent of world merchandise trade by volume is carried by sea (UNCTAD, 2008), ports and their associated infrastructure serve as critical nodes in the supply chain. The maritime sector offers the most economical and reliable mode of transportation over long distances, especially for African countries that are not yet specialized in high-value products (see Table 1.2). Ships can carry large volumes of merchandise and utilize free highways in the seas, provided that adequate physical infrastructure is available at the seaports and along the inland logistics chain to producers and consumers to avoid congestion. This makes maritime transport the backbone for facilitating international trade.

Poorly performing ports are likely to reduce trade volumes, particularly for small LI countries. As foreshadowed in this chapter and discussed at greater length in the rest of this report, myriad factors contribute to port efficiency, including dock facilities, connections to railroads and trucking lines, harbor characteristics, customs clearance

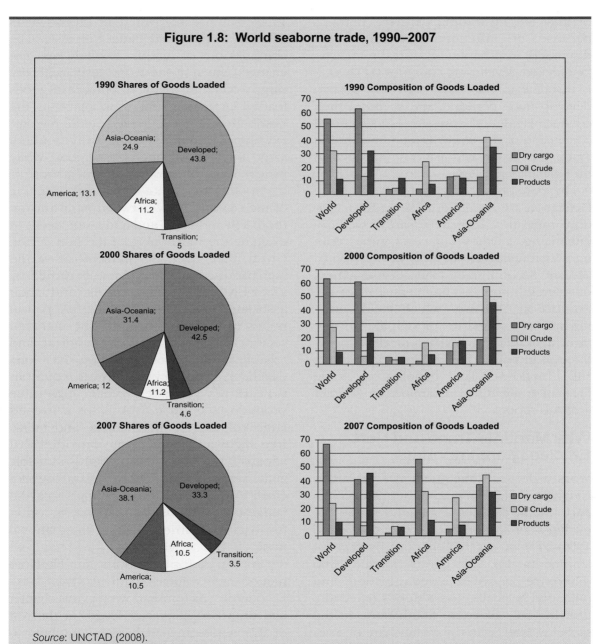

Figure 1.8: World seaborne trade, 1990–2007

Source: UNCTAD (2008).
Notes: Shares across types of cargo add up to 100% for world. In the breakdown on the composition of goods loaded, shares of each category shipment add up to 100% over the five regions.

times, and labor relations. The sheer variety of factors that influence a port's efficiency makes it difficult to attain an overview of this variable across regions. Box 1.2 summarizes results from a recent study of bilateral trade flows between 50 US ports and up to 100 ports in 40 other countries over the period 1991–2003. The study seeks to isolate port efficiency in overall maritime costs. The estimates show great disparity in port efficiency both in the US and internationally. Controlling for a host of factors that contribute to maritime freight costs, the study suggests that a 10 percent rise in port efficiency increases country-pair trade by 3 percent. Over the distribution of efficiency estimates, a change in port efficiency from the 25th percentile to the 75th percentile leads to a 5 percent increase in trade. Since all African ports are in the 25th percentile of the distribution of container shipping costs (see Chapter 4, Figure 4.9), cost reductions from improved port efficiency would increase African trade substantially.

Outline of the Report

After this introductory chapter, Chapter 2 analyzes the port situation in Africa, comparing its characteristics and performance with those in other regions. It establishes that ports lie at the heart of the logistics supply chain and compares the main characteristics of African ports: differences across subregions, capacity problems, efficiency related to small scale, etc. The chapter shows that African ports are relatively inefficient compared with those in other low-income countries and that they rank low in the Liner Shipping Connectivity Index (LSCI), which measures the geo-graphical location of ports as well as shipment volumes and other indicators of efficiency. The findings suggest that, in many instances, large productivity improvements could be achieved by improving the infrastructure at existing ports. At the same time, improvements in the regulatory environment would be necessary. Improvement of port management, often implying reform leading to the introduction of public–private partnerships (PPPs), is needed to procure the funding to carry out the capacity increases and upgrading of infrastructure identified in the chapter.

Chapter 3 deals with constraints in the "soft" infrastructure of ports: namely behind-the-border bottlenecks that increase trade costs and hamper the efficiency of ports. A review of port management structures and their recent evolution around the world shows a shift toward the landlord port model, where all but the hard infrastructure is in private hands. Albeit with a lag, Africa is joining the trend with an increased adoption of the concessioning process across ports. At the same time, the extent of private investment in physical port infra-structures has been low, reflecting a variety of factors, ranging from the size of the market to weak institutional support.

Typically, African ports are visited by small ships, implying transshipments from the port of origin before reaching destina-tion. This contributes to the higher freight costs incurred in Africa. Evidence suggests that reform packages that include regulatory reform, and that provide for independence of the regulator from government inter-ference, are likely to yield the best results in terms of port efficiency. Once these

---

Box 1.2: Estimating port efficiency by statistical analysis

Quality data on import charges and on types/volumes of cargo are needed to effectively measure port efficiency. Together, these statistical data allow the analyst to control for the composition of products, the volume of trade, and other factors affecting freight costs, so that an estimate of port efficiency can be extracted residually. Data Envelopment Analysis (DEA) uses production frontier techniques to measure port efficiency relative to a frontier. Besides requiring that data be comparable across ports, the estimates assume constant returns to scale, and do not allow for measurement error. This is why DEA estimates are viewed as limited in scope and consequently most analysts rely on applications of the gravity model.

Typically, gravity-based studies have relied on a single point in time (e.g. Clark *et al.*, 2004). However, this does not allow the analyst to control for heterogeneity across ports and time-invariant omitted variables that influence a port's overall efficiency. Several studies have also drawn on the subjective, survey-based efficiency measures of the *Global Competitiveness Report* for countries rather than ports (firms rank a country's port efficiency on a scale from 1 to 7) (World Economic Forum, 2000).

Drawing on data over the period 1991–2003 provided by the US National Data Center of the Army Corps of Engineers, Blonigen and Wilson (2008) use reliable data on import charges on bilateral trade at the commodity HS-6 level along with distance measures and port-to-port distances. For each time period and product, they regress import charges on weight, value, distance, percentage of shipments in containers, a measure of trade imbalance and fixed-effects that control for all time-invariant factors (observed and unobserved) connected with each country-pair. These high-quality data coupled with controls produce precise estimates, even though they do not control for changes in product composition at the port level over time.

In their study, Blonigen and Wilson show that: (i) a 10 percent increase in distance raises freight costs by 1.3 to 2.1 percent and (ii) weight and product value lead to an increase in import charges. These results are in accordance with those of previous studies. Containerization reduces import charges, more so for high-value products. The study also finds that imbalanced trade raises costs, but not by much.

Fixed effects for the US and foreign ports give estimates for the average efficiency of a port relative to the excluded port (Oakland for the United States and Rotterdam for foreign ports), after controlling for all the other factors affecting import charges mentioned above. For US ports, only 13 out of 50 are within 5 percent of the efficiency of Oakland. For foreign ports, they estimate an average improvement of 1.4 percent per year relative to Rotterdam. The only African port in the sample, Durban, is estimated to have port charges 15 percent above those at Rotterdam.

Overall, Blonigen and Wilson's estimates suggest that a 10 percent rise in port efficiency increases trade between a country-pair by 3.2 percent. Over the distribution of estimates, they find that a change in port efficiency from the 25th percentile to the 75th percentile leads to a 5 percent increase in trade. However, these estimates do not take account of the fact that increased port efficiency is likely to lead to increased trade in new products as well as in existing products. Taking that into account, new products would raise the value of the estimates.

---

measures have been put in place, private shipping companies will be more likely to visit these ports. Moreover the more conducive environment for private investment will induce the participation of key development actors to help finance the hard physical infrastructure essential to relieve the congestion bottlenecks identified in Chapter

2. Overall, the change to a more privatized environment still has a long way to go in Africa compared to the rest of the world, but many African nations have begun to commit in earnest to this process.

Chapter 3 also suggests several precautionary steps that need to be taken in port reforms. First, the privatization process should not take place without a clear vision of the objectives that the public sector is trying to achieve. Second, close coordination between the different institutions involved (port institutions, customs, transport ministries, labor unions, etc.) is needed to define how their respective roles and responsibilities will evolve to result in an overall gain for all parties. Third, other efficiency-enhancing factors such as pro-competitive policies and arrangements, better coordination of the various agencies operating at ports, and a simplification of documentation requirements and single-window processing should be encouraged.

Chapter 4 deals with the hinterland infrastructure (roads, railroads, and inland waterways) that connects ports to markets and which impacts the overall costs of trade. The chapter also deals with the transit corridors that are essential to link the landlocked developing countries (LLDCs) to the other African countries, to ports, and to global export markets. For all African countries, but especially those in SSA, the efficiency of ports is hampered by poor connectivity with the hinterland because of the substandard physical condition of roads, railroads, and waterways, which deliver poor quality service. As a result, and especially because there is little competition across modes of transport, ports can be

"held hostage" to deficient infrastructure. An estimated financing gap of 5 percent of GDP in SSA needs to be closed in order to overhaul the infrastructure sector. The chapter also points out that the improvement in corridors can only be made effective by "deep" regional integration.

The chapter establishes that trade facilitation measures are the single most important policy action to reduce transport costs. However, without international coordination and recognition of the need for an appropriate regulatory environment, their effectiveness will not achieve full potential. This is particularly the case for the trade facilitation negotiations currently underway through the auspices of the World Trade Organization (WTO). If successful, these negotiations, which aim at implementing the Freedom of Transit obligation of Article V of GATT 2004, will go some way toward improving the situation of the 15 landlocked countries in SSA.

Chapter 5 looks at the African Development Bank Group's support to projects and programs aimed at enhancing the capacity and efficiency of ports in Africa (including hinterland connectivity). The initial finding is that the Bank considers the lack of adequate infrastructure, and in particular the lack of transport infrastructure, to be a key constraint to the growth momentum in Africa. In the area of ports specifically, the Bank Group has made significant public investments over the last decades. More recently, the Private Sector Department has been instrumental in supporting the port concession process in several African countries. This is in line with some of the key findings in this report, in particular the need to increase private participation in the port sector to improve efficiency. Going forward, given the enormous challenges presented in this report in terms of hard infrastructure requirements in African ports and other modes of transport into the hinterland (such as rail, road, and waterways), a large injection of public and private investment is required. The scaling up of support to this vital sector is in line with the Bank's Medium-Term Strategy 2008–2012, with its strong emphasis on infrastructure. The Bank continues to play a major role in this area, not only by allocating it a large proportion of funding from its own resources, but also by catalyzing investments from other major investment partners and development agencies.

Furthermore, investments in soft infrastructure, such as robust regulatory frameworks and institutions (i.e. customs), are crucial to facilitate the movement of goods between ports and the hinterland. To support these operations, a revised policy framework in maritime transport and related areas is needed to guide the prioritization process and to improve the quality at entry of investments.

Finally, Chapter 6 examines the issues surrounding the development of regional port hubs in Africa. Many African countries are aiming to modernize their ports and develop them into regional hubs. However, the continent can support only a few regional hubs and the key issues of *how* African ports can transform themselves into regional hubs, and *where* such hub ports should be located, is of critical importance and are considered in the chapter. The chapter examines both the physical and policy considerations that governments must take into account in developing regional hub ports. It also examines the contributions IFIs can make towards the development of the port hubs. Governments have put in place large-scale investment programs, which provide avenues for private sector participation in the development of the ports. At the same time, for the ports to become regional hubs, the governments need to pay attention to the location, water depth, and the facilities and performance of the port to ensure low handling costs. As complementary measures, policies must be put in place to foster and finance integrated port and transport facilities and associated land use. Moreover, in order to develop state-of-the-art ports and to equip them with appropriate technologies and management skills, the involvement of the international private sector is essential and this could be enhanced through the landlord port model. Also, the dredging of African ports, many of which are characterized as too shallow for the latest generation of container ships, could be a frontline area of intervention for the private sector and development partners alike.

References

Arvis, J.F., G. Raballand, and J.F. Marteau. 2007. "The Costs of Being Landlocked: Logistics Costs and the Supply Chain." Working Paper Series No. 4258, Washington, DC: World Bank.

Berthelon, M. and C. Freund. 2008. "On the Conservation of Distance in International Trade." *Journal of International Economics,* 75: 310–20.

Blonigen, B.B. and W.W. Wilson. 2008. "Port Efficiency and Trade Flows." *Review of International Economics*, 16 (1): 21–36.

Bora, S., A. Bouët, and D. Roy. 2007. "The Marginalisation of Africa in World Trade." IFPRI Research Brief No. 7, Washington, DC: International Food Policy Research Institute.

Brun, J.-F, C. Carrère, P. Guillaumont, and J. De Melo. 2005. "Has Distance Died? Evidence from a Panel Gravity Model." *World Bank Economic Review,* 19 (1): 99–120.

Carrère, C., J. de Melo, and J. Wilson. 2009. "The Distance Effect and the Regionalization of the Trade of Developing Countries", CEPR DP No. 7458, London: Centre for Economic Policy Research.

Clark, X., D. Dollar, and A. Micco. 2004. "Port Efficiency, Maritime Transport Costs and Bilateral Trade." *Journal of Development Economics*, 75 (2): 417–50.

Collier, P. and J.W. Gunning. 1999. "Explaining African Economic Performance." *Journal of Economic Literature*, XXXVII: 64–111.

Djankov, S., C. Freund, and C.S. Pham. 2008. "Trading on Time." *Review of Economics and Statistics*, November.

Fisman, R. and S. Wei. 2004. "Tax Rates and Tax Evasion: Evidence from 'Missing Imports' in China." *Journal of Political Economy,* 112: 471–500.

Gatti, R. 2004. "Explaining Corruption: Are Open Countries Less Corrupt?" *Journal of International Development,* 16: 851–61.

Hummels, D. 2001. "Time as a Trade Barrier", Global Trade Analysis Project Working Paper No. 18.

Hummels, D. and V. Lugovskyy. 2006. "Are Matched Partner Trade Statistics a Usable Measure of Transportation Costs?" *Review of International Economics*, 14 (1): 69–86.

Hummels, D., V. Lugovskyy, and A. Skiba. 2009. "The Trade Reducing Effects of Market Power in International Shipping." *Journal of Development Economics*, 89 (1): 84–97.

Jones, C., O. Morrissey, and D. Nelson. 2008. "African Trade Policy in the 1990s: Political Economy or Technocratic Reforms?" Centre for Research in Economic Development and International Trade Working Paper, University of Nottingham, UK.

Kee, H.L., A. Nicita, and M. Olarreaga. 2009. "Estimating Trade Restrictiveness Indices." *Economic Journal,* 119 (534): 172–99.

Kumar, S. and J. Hoffman. 2002. "Globalisation: The Maritime Nexus." In Prof. C. Th. Grammenos (ed.), *Handbook of Maritime Economics and Business.* London: Informa UK.

Limão, N. and A.J. Venables (2001). "Infrastructure, Geographical Disadvantage, Transport Costs and Trade." *World Bank Economic Review*, 15: 451–79.

Musila, J. and S. Sigué. 2009. "Corruption and International Trade: An Empirical Investigation of African Economies." *The World Economy*, September.

Otsuki, T., J.S. Wilson, and M. Sewadeh. 2001. "What Price Precaution? European Harmonization of Aflatoxin Regulations and African Groundnut Exports." *European Review of Agricultural Economics,* 28 (3): 263–84.

Oyejide, T.A., E.O. Ogunkola, and S.A. Bankole. 2000. "Quantifying the Trade Impact of Sanitary and Phytosanitary Standards: What is Known and Issues of Importance for Sub-Saharan Africa." Paper presented at the workshop on "Quantifying the Trade Effect of Standards and Regulatory Barriers: Is it Positive?" held at the World Bank, Washington, DC, on April 27, 2000.

Portugal-Perez, A. and J. Wilson. 2009. "Why Trade Facilitation Matters to Africa." *World Trade Review,* 8 (3): 1–38.

Radelet, S. and S. Jeffrey. 1998. "Shipping Costs, Manufactured Exports and Economic Growth." Mimeo, Cambridge, MA: Harvard Institute for International Development.

Sanchez, R., J. Hoffmann, A. Micco, G. Pizzolitto, M. Sgut, and G. Wilmsmeier. 2003. "Port Efficiency and International Trade: Port Efficiency as a Determinant of Maritime Transport Costs." *Maritime Economics and Logistics,* pp. 199–218.

Schiff, M. and A. Valdes. 1992. "The Plundering of Agriculture in Developing Countries." Washington DC: World Bank.

Tadesse, B. and B. Fayissa. 2008. "The Impact of African Growth and Opportunity Act (AGOA) on US Imports from Sub-Saharan Africa." *Journal of International Development,* 20: 920–41.

Teravaninthorn, S. and G. Raballand. 2008. "Transport Prices and Costs in Africa: A Review of the Main International Corridors." Washington, DC: World Bank.

UNCTAD. 2006. *Landlocked Developing Countries: Facts and Figures.* New York and Geneva: UNCTAD.

———. **2007.** *Review of Maritime Transport, 2007.* New York and Geneva: UNCTAD.

———. **2009a.** *Review of Maritime Transport 2009.* New York and Geneva: UNCTAD.

———. **2009b.** *Economic Development in Africa, Report 2009. Strengthening Regional Economic Integration for Africa's Development.* New York and Geneva: UNCTAD.

Wilmsmeier, G. and J. Hoffman. 2008. "Liner Shipping Connectivity and Port Infrastructure as Determinants of Freight Rates in the Caribbean." *Maritime Economics and Logistics,* 10: 131–51.

Wilson, J., C. Mann, and T. Otsuki. 2004. "Trade Facilitation and Economic Development: A New Approach to Measuring the Impact." World Bank Policy Research Paper No. 3324. Washington, DC: World Bank.

World Bank. 1995. *Improving African Transport Corridors.* Operations Evaluation Department Précis, no. 84. Washington, DC: World Bank.

World Economic Forum. 2000. *Global Competitiveness Report,* Cambridge MA: Harvard University.

CHAPTER 2

Port Development in Africa

With approximately 80 percent of world merchandise trade carried by ships, maritime transport remains by far the most common mode of international freight transport. It is the backbone to facilitating international trade, offering the most economical and reliable way to move goods over long distances. Ships can carry large volumes of merchandise and use free highways in the seas, which only require infrastructure investments at the seaports. For all countries,

how ports perform is an essential element of overall trade costs, as identified in Chapter 1. This is especially the case for Africa, as 15 of its countries are landlocked and face severe infrastructural and trade facilitation problems. For the landlocked nations, ports — together with the inland waterway and land infrastructures (railroads and highways) — constitute a crucial link to the outside world and to the global marketplace. Consequently, high transport-related costs represent a fundamental constraint to these LLDCs' global competitiveness and their sustained economic growth.

It is generally recognized that the African continent lacks natural ports, while its artificial seaports have been poorly developed (UNCTAD, 1999; Wood, 2004; Hoyle, 1999). African ports became more congested following the rise in GDP growth and levels of global trade witnessed in most African countries in the years leading up to the global financial crisis of 2008. Indeed, over the last decade, the amount of cargo transiting through Africa's ports has tripled, but containerization is still low and the inland transportation linkages remain weak (World Bank, 2009). Nonetheless, as discussed in this and the following chapters, governments are now demonstrating the political will necessary to confront this challenge, in a drive to improve port and other infrastructure. For example, several ports have introduced, or renovated, container and cargo transshipment and bulk terminal (for coal, oil, food and mineral) facilities. This has greatly improved port performance and efficiency, for example in Egypt following the regulatory reforms of 2000.[1]

---

[1] Before the reforms in early 2000, the World Bank (1998) reported that customs and other clearance procedures at Egyptian ports delayed cargoes by 5–20 days, compared to 1–2 days in more efficient ports. This resulted in high storage costs and damage to cargo, which overall were costing the Egyptian economy about US$1 billion per annum. After the reforms of 2000, Egypt developed one of the most efficient ports in Africa: the time to export decreased from 27 to 10 days between 2006 and 2009, and the time to import from 29 to 25 days over the same period (*Doing Business* website of the World Bank).

This chapter assesses port development and performance throughout Africa (Annex 2.1 gives a detailed description of seaports across the continent). It establishes the areas where improvements in port logistics and, more generally, infrastructure, are urgently needed. However, port development in its broadest sense covers not only the development of infrastructure and superstructure, but also environmental concerns. Africa has some 40,000 km of coastline, extending over 32 countries. Port development and activities should not have a harmful environmental impact on land, nor lead to a deterioration in the marine environment through pollution. The African Development Bank Group has an Environment Policy in place to mitigate the potential negative impacts of its projects and programs, including those in the infrastructure sector, and to mainstream environmental and sustainability safeguards throughout the project cycle (see Box 5.2). In this way, the Bank seeks to ensure that all its port development projects conform to international best practice, including the International Maritime Organization (IMO) Convention on Marine Pollution (MARPOL 73/78).

Following this introduction, the next section of this chapter describes the *infrastructure characteristics* of a seaport, which can be divided into two categories or assets: (i) its physical or "hard" infrastructure and (ii) its organization or "soft" infrastructure. The analysis helps to situate African ports within a global context. The subsequent section deals with the capacity and overall efficiency of African seaports, which are generally shown to be among the least efficient in the world, although on a par with ports in other low-income countries in other global regions. African ports' poor performance can be attributed to a range of factors, principally: geography (poor connectivity); inadequate physical infrastructure resulting in congestion; and weak institutional development (reforms and institutional development are covered in Chapter 3). We then turn to the recent investments for regeneration and expansion in port physical infrastructure. Conclusions and recommendations close the chapter.

What Is a Seaport?

A port lies at the heart of the logistics supply chain, linking a country with its trading partners (Figure 2.1). This is especially the case for Africa, which relies on maritime shipping as its principal mode of transportation for both primary and manufactured goods destined for export. Ports are an infrastructure facility allowing goods to be loaded/unloaded, stored, and transferred for inland delivery via other transport modes, such as trucks, trains, or inland waterway vessels. Ports usually have deepwater channels or berths, as well as storage facilities, which determine how much cargo the port can handle and the type and capacity of vessels it can receive.

With the exception of some export processing zones (EPZs) that are located in the vicinity of ports, cargo and merchandise leaving ports come from the hinterland via the infrastructures identified in Figure 2.1. To function properly, the links between ports and the hinterland must operate smoothly to avoid bottlenecks in the ports'

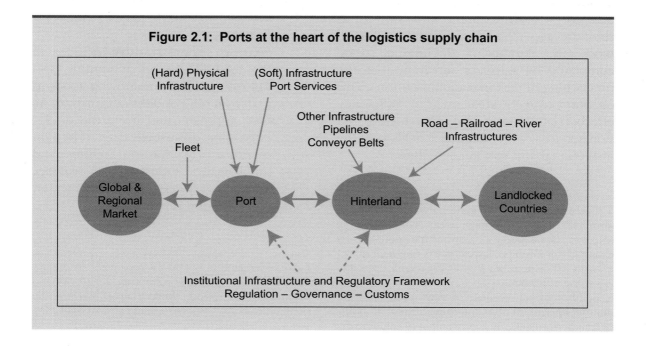

Figure 2.1: Ports at the heart of the logistics supply chain

entrepôts and to minimize dwell times.[2] The quality of a port's physical infrastructure and related services is an important determinant of its overall efficiency. However, as also indicated in Figure 2.1, equally important in this regard is the institutional and regulatory infrastructure.

Hard and Soft Infrastructure in Seaports

To function efficiently and to maximize its potential, a port needs two types of assets: (i) the "hard" physical infrastructure (seaport infrastructure and superstructure facilities for loading and unloading) and (ii) the "soft" infrastructure, which includes all the administrative and customs services necessary to facilitate the transit of goods, plus the supportive information and communications technologies (ICT). The overall efficiency of a port therefore depends directly on the quality of both its hard and soft infrastructure as well as the institutional framework (the number of documents to be completed by shippers and importers; the functioning of customs administration). This chapter concentrates on the efficiency effects related to the hard infrastructure and port services, while Chapter 3 deals with the institutional and soft infrastructure.[3]

- **Seaport infrastructure** provides oceangoing vessels with the necessary facilities to come within reach of the land. It comprises deepwater channels and berths where the ships and other floating craft can tie up alongside, in order to load/unload goods. Harbors require a sufficient depth of water to receive large ships; the size and design of berths vary according to their purpose. For instance, container berths are designed to service containerized cargoes. The hard infrastructure mentioned in Figure 2.1 is essential to the overall efficiency of a port, as it ensures access to intermodal transportation through connections to roads, railroads, and inland waterways. A seaport also needs inside railroad terminals or lines, and road access to the major transport corridors.

- **Seaport superstructure** includes all the facilities aimed at loading and unloading ships, and moving goods to and from other modes of transport. As they approach and leave the docks, large ships are usually moved in tight quarters by harbor pilots and tugboats. The superstructure provides ancillary services like fuel, water, cleaning, and repair services.

---

[2] "Dwell time" is the time cargo remains in a terminal's in-transit storage areas, while awaiting shipment (for exports) or onward transportation by road/rail (for imports). Dwell time is one indicator of a port's efficiency: the higher the dwell time, the lower the efficiency.

[3] Although all aspects of port efficiency are interdependent in the determination of a port's overall performance, it is convenient to examine the

factors identified in Figure 2.1 separately. Therefore Chapter 3 focuses on the role of the regulatory and institutional framework, while Chapter 4 covers the behind-the-border aspects of trade costs (connecting ports to markets).

PORT INFRASTRUCTURE

Berth at the cargo terminal of the Port of Alexandria

Storage area at the International Container Terminal in El Dekheila, Port of Alexandria

Source: Alexandria Port Authority.

Source: Alexandria Port Authority.

Post-Panamax cranes to unload/load container ships

Reachstacker handling containers

Source: Port Management Association of Eastern and Southern Africa, PMAESA.

Source: Port Management Association of Eastern and Southern Africa, PMAESA.

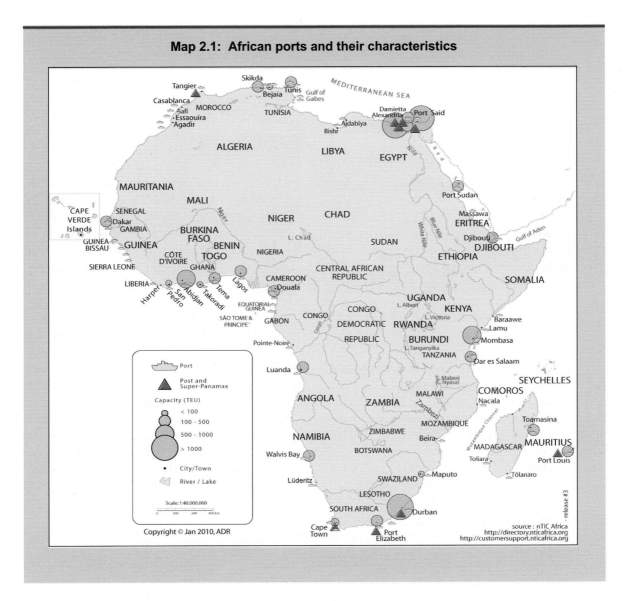

Map 2.1: African ports and their characteristics

- **Port administration** organizes and oversees the movement of ships and goods. When ports handle international traffic, customs facilities are also part of the port assets. The administration services include regulation of consignees, import/ export documents and permits, phytosanitary certificates, and administration of taxes. As part of the port administration, information and communication technologies contribute to the speed with which goods transit through ports. This includes information systems, electronic databases, and platform management software.

Categorization and Location of African Seaports

Ports are categorized based on their functions and the type of goods they handle, e.g. general cargo ports, hub ports, feeder ports, bulk ports, transshipment terminals, dedicated oil terminals, and river ports (see Map 2.1). These are discussed individually below in Box 2.1.

Capacity and Efficiency of African Ports

African ports often work beyond their capacity limits. Indeed, capacity shortfalls are reported for all Sub-Saharan maritime trading areas (Cameron, 2008). This is partly due to the fact that demand for resources such as oil — which have also led to growing economic activity — have scaled up the demands being placed on ports. However, port capacity and port logistics have not kept up with increasing traffic across most of Africa, causing severe challenges such congestion. As detailed in Box 2.2, this congestion is attributable to several factors, including deficient physical infrastructure, malfunctioning regulatory systems, and poor management. These factors translate into poor port efficiency, raising trade costs in Africa.

African ships are usually old and small relative to evolving global shipping standards, which are shifting toward containerization and increased size. As Table 2.1 shows, by the end of 2005, the average age of the merchant fleet of African countries was 11.8 years, including those with open registry; and 20.5 years without a maritime open registry.[4] By comparison, ships registered in developed economies are the youngest (average age: 9.7 years in January 2008), followed by developing countries (12.3 years) and transition economies (15.5 years) (see Annex 2.2). Furthermore, in 2005 none of the 35 countries that controlled over 95 percent of the world merchant fleet was African (UNCTAD, 2006). In 2007, Africa accounted for only 0.58 percent of the world merchant fleet.

The small number of shipping operators in Africa hinders the development of synergies and stifles competition.[5] The national lines, which offer containerized transportation services, run fleets that usually comprise small and old vessels. Companies generally use multipurpose vessels, as exports (agricultural, natural resources) are usually shipped unprocessed. This situation further contributes to the marginalization of Africa from international markets.

---

[4] "Open registry" is a national ship registry — under a national flag — open to ships of all nations, regardless of nationality.

[5] Hummels *et al.* (2009) estimate that, after controlling for other factors such as costs related to cargo size, eliminating market power for ships en route to the US from Latin American ports would increase trade volume by 15 percent for Latin American countries. One can surmise that gains in trade volumes would be even higher for Africa, as fewer ships call on African ports.

Box 2.1: Types of ports according to function

General Cargo Ports are medium-sized ports (including container terminals) with a large enough volume to attract frequent direct vessel calls. Volumes are typically between 2–10 million tonnes p.a. and 100,000–500,000 TEUs p.a. Examples of general cargo ports include Port Elizabeth in South Africa and Walvis Bay in Namibia. Most general cargo ports have ambitions to expand into regional hubs.

   Hub Ports are large regional ports, with high volumes of direct large-vessel calls. They service a large catchment area, which also serves the smaller regional ports by transshipping containers and general cargo in smaller vessels. Typical examples are Durban in South Africa and Port Said in Egypt. These two ports are ranked among the 60 largest ports in the world in terms of container volume throughput (over 2 million TEUs p.a.).

   Feeder Ports are normally smaller ports with limited vessel calls and depth restrictions. They are unable to attract many direct vessel calls because of the small volumes of trade they handle (generally less than 100,000 TEUs p.a.). These ports are mostly fed by smaller coastal services from the regional hub ports. The Mozambican and Angolan ports and many of the West African ports are typical examples. The feeder service and the double handling of containers add to the overall logistics costs.

   Bulk Ports are mainly dedicated to handling large volumes of bulk materials, accommodating capesize vessels,[6] with depths of 18–25 m, generally without dedicated container terminals. Typical examples are Richards Bay (coal) and Saldanha Bay (iron ore) in South Africa and Port Saco in Angola and Buchanan in Liberia, both handling iron ore.

   Transshipment terminals or ports are large container terminals where cargo is transferred from one carrier to another, or from one type of vessel to another. Examples of transshipment terminals include the ports of Algiers, Durban, Mombasa, and Djibouti. Transshipment terminals handle very large container vessels (above 6,000 TEUs), which very few African ports can handle. Vessels of more than 15,000 TEUs are now in service and these vessels require a quayside depth of 16–18 m (such as Singapore port, and Salalah in Oman). The new port of Ngqura in South Africa, with a depth of 16 m, has been developed as a transshipment port and will receive large vessels from the east and transship to smaller vessels for the East and West African coasts.

   Dedicated oil terminals handle crude oil which is most often transported in large capesize vessels of 120,000 to 150,000 dwt, which require greater water depths than can be provided at any of the African ports currently. Oil tankers are mostly handled at offshore moorings which are linked to landside storage tanks via submarine pipelines. This is the case for the ports of Durban in South Africa, Dar es Salaam in Tanzania, and Cabinda in Angola. Some ports, such as Cape Town in South Africa, have dedicated tanker basins.

   River Ports are generally small and isolated, and do not serve oceangoing vessels. One notable exception is Matadi port in the Democratic Republic of Congo (DRC), which is 150 km from the coast and serves as the country's main port, but with restricted depth. There is currently a project proposal for the development of a port on the Zambezi/Shire River waterway to serve Malawi, which will require dredging of sections of the river system. However, this development is subject to an economic feasibility study and a positive outcome of an environmental impact assessment.[7]

---

   [6] "Capesize vessels" are very large bulk carriers between 80–150,000 dwt, which used to be unable to transit the Suez Canal and were therefore forced to sail around the Cape of Good Hope to and from Europe. Now those vessels can transit through the Suez Canal as long as they meet the draft restriction (18.91 m/62 ft as of 2008).

   [7] The Shire–Zambezi Waterway Project is described in Box 4.1.

Box 2.2: Port congestion in Eastern and Southern Africa

According to the Port Management Association of Eastern and Southern Africa (PMAESA), the factors leading to port congestion in Eastern and Southern Africa are:
- Increased container traffic volumes not consistent with infrastructure development, thus growth outstrips available capacity;
- Long container dwell times, caused by inter alia, poor off-take by rail and the use of ports as storage areas;
- Lack of adequate capacity and poor hinterland transport infrastructures, especially rail and road;
- Inadequate technology and aging, unsuitable equipment and vessels;
- Poorly integrated supply chains;
- Low productivity levels;
- Capacity constraints, for example insufficient container storage space;
- Poor planning such as overbooking of cargo by shipping lines, leading to cancelations and rollovers;
- Bunching of vessels and unscheduled arrivals;
- Changes in routing patterns, causing vessels to make shorter rotations;
- A change in container size from 20 ft to 40 ft;
- Resistance to change in management styles;
- Lack of communication between stakeholders;
- Cumbersome regulatory systems, decentralized documentation processes coupled with bureaucratic clearance procedures;
- General poor planning by the various cargo interveners.

Source: PMAESA (2008).

Table 2.1: Age distribution of African merchant fleet compared to those of other regions

Type	World Total	Developed Economies	Transition Economies	Developing Economies	African Countries including Open Registry[1]	African Countries without Open Registry[1]
Bulk carriers	12.7	11.9	17.8	12.7	14.0	18.0
Container ships	9.0	8.6	10.6	8.9	6.9	12.3
General cargo	17.1	13.4	20.0	17.6	17.3	22.1
Oil tankers	10.1	7.5	11.2	11.0	11.2	21.4
Other types	14.7	13.1	11.8	15.5	17.2	21.2
All	11.8	9.7	15.5	12.3	11.8	20.5

Note: (1) Data for African countries for year-end 2005; data for other countries at January 1, 2008.
Source: UNCTAD (2006; 2008).

Table 2.2: Port capacity and value of trade in Africa

Country	Total TEU Capacity	Ranking (1 to 16)	Trade: Imports + Exports (US$ mn)	Ranking (1 to 16)
Algeria	189,848	13	87,794	3
Angola	407,609	5	58,057	4
Cameroon	200,254	12	6,727	12
Djibouti	294,902	10	531	16
Egypt	4,755,879	1	56,324	5
Ghana	513,204	4	12,268	10
Kenya	585,367	3	13,070	9
Libya	44,202	16	54,720	6
Mozambique	62,516	15	6,000	15
Namibia	144,993	14	6,442	13
Nigeria	235,846	11	95,550	2
Senegal	375,876	6	6,123	14
South Africa	3,781,403	2	158,234	1
Sudan	359,537	7	17,654	8
Tanzania	301,579	9	7,508	11
Tunisia	349,507	8	34,009	7
China	*101,963,351*		*1,760,430*	
Brazil	*6,798,200*		*287,217*	

Sources: WTO database; Containerisation International Yearbook, 2009.
Note: Brazil and China given for comparative purposes.

African Regional Port Situation

The African port situation is characterized by large number of small ports, each with a capacity of less than 1 million TEUs. As shown in the detailed review of ports by subregion presented in Annex 2.1, capacity shortages are widespread, particularly in West and Central Africa.

It is important to note that countries with higher port capacity have higher trade capacity. However, the types of commodity that the country trades in terms of imports and exports also matters (Table 2.2). For example, Egypt is ranked number 1 in Africa in terms of port capacity and South Africa is ranked number 2. However, the value of trade in South Africa is higher than Egypt due to the type of exports, which are mainly expensive minerals such as platinum and gold. Moreover, the value can also be driven by the number of ports that the country services. In the case of South Africa, landlocked economies such as Botswana, Lesotho, Swaziland, Malawi, Zimbabwe, and Zambia depend on its ports, and this explains South Africa's higher trade volumes.

Egypt and South Africa have the highest port capacity in the continent, with Port Said in Egypt as the leading port (see Annex 2.1 for more details). Given that most of the countries in Africa start from a lower base in terms of port capacity, the industry has substantial economic and investment prospects going forward. The *Drewry Report* forecasts an annual growth rate of 2.5 percent in the African port subsector over the next six years, which is close to the global rate. In North Africa, in addition to Egypt's massive investment in the port subsector, other countries such as Morocco and Algeria have also scaled up their investments with the aim of transforming their ports into major transshipment hubs. Similarly, in the Southern Africa subregion, South Africa continues to expand in terms of port capacity to meet its growing demand both nationally and regionally. For example, the new deepwater Port of Ngqura became operational in 2009 to accommodate the latest generation of container ships. Other countries in the subregion, including Namibia and Mozambique, have also embarked on investment and rehabilitation activities in their port subsectors.

In Eastern Africa, the terminal in Djibouti offers the most modern facilities (i.e. for Panamax ships[8]) but needs further investment to increase capacity, particularly to accommodate the high transit volumes from Ethiopia. One of the major concerns in East Africa is the safety risk due to growing attacks by Somali pirates in the Indian Ocean. Port performance in major East African ports such Mombasa in Kenya and Dar es Salaam in Tanzania has a lot of potential but congestion is still rife due to low investment in infrastructure and poor connection to the hinterland.

In West and Central Africa, an infrastructure deficit also continues to hamper port performance and efficiency. This is mainly due to a lack of concrete programs for the transportation sector, leading to a lower prioritization and investment to support the sector. However, in 2009, investments by the French company, Bolloré, in Pointe Noire in the Republic of the Congo, will increase substantially the port capacity there, allowing it to service other parts of the region. Ports in Nigeria have also gone through reforms (see Box 3.3), although congestion there remains a concern.

Capacity: Global Comparisons

World container port throughput grew by an estimated 11.7 percent to reach 485 million TEUs in 2007 (UNCTAD, 2008), with Chinese ports accounting for approximately 28.4 percent of this volume. In 2007, Singapore was the busiest port, followed by China and Hong Kong (Table 2.3). Port Said in Egypt and Durban in South Africa were the only African ports to rank in the top 50 container port traffic league in 2007.

Only 13 African countries are ranked among the top 62 developing countries in

---

[8] "Panamax" ships are the largest ships that can pass through the locks of the Panama Canal (specifically used for dry bulk and container vessels). Panamax ships can measure up to 956 ft long (for container ships), 105 ft wide, 190 ft from the waterline, and up to 39 ft below the waterline. Weight can vary, but based on these measures should average between 65,000–69,000 tons. Ships too large to transit the canal are called "post-Panamax."

Table 2.3: Selected leading ports in the world by volume of containerized cargo, 2007

Global rank	Port	Country	Region	Capacity (TEUs mn)
1	Singapore	Singapore	Asia	27.93
2	Shanghai	China	Asia	26.15
3	Hong Kong	China	Asia	24.00
4	Shenzhen	China	Asia	21.09
5	Busan	South Korea	Asia	13.27
6	Rotterdam	Netherlands	Europe	9.65
13	Los Angeles	United States	USA	8.35
25	Jawaharal Nehru	India	Asia	4.06
36	Manila	Philippines	Asia	2.87
37	Port Said	Egypt	Africa	2.78
42	Santos	Brazil	South America	2.53
41	Durban	S Africa	Africa	2.51
47	Kingston	Jamaica	Caribbean Basin	2.16
50	Melbourne	Australia	Asia/Pacific	2.14

Source: Containerisation International Yearbook, 2009.

terms of container port traffic (Table 2.4). Total containerized cargo volume for the whole of Africa was estimated at just over 15 million TEUs, which is almost half the volume handled by the largest ports in Singapore and China. In Latin America, Port Santos in Brazil has the largest port capacity, although still lower capacity than Port Said in Egypt. However, the total volume for the whole of Brazil is higher than that of Egypt.

Containerization has been growing rapidly in Africa at a pace of more than 10 percent annually. However, container traffic to and from Africa remains marginal compared to overall global traffic. For example, commodities to the Far East or Europe are still carried in break-bulk[9] from African ports. As a reference, Africa's share of container traffic has ranged from 0.6 percent to 0.85 percent of total global volumes over the last 10 years.

In addition, African ports record the highest rate of empty containers shipped out. Algeria, Angola, Libya, and Nigeria have the highest proportion, ranging from 85–100 percent. For Cameroon, Egypt, Ghana, South Africa, and Sudan the shipped cargo is between 63 percent and 100 percent full,

---

[9] "Break-bulk" is loose, non-containerized cargo stowed directly in a ship's hold, in small, separable units. Loose cement, grain, ores, etc. are termed "bulk cargo," whereas cargo shipped in units (bags, bales, boxes, cartons, pallets, drums, sacks, etc.) is "break-bulk."

while Kenya and Tanzania ship 42–53 percent full. This is a reflection of three main factors that characterize the African shipping industry: (i) its high volumes of unprocessed exports, which do not require containerization; (ii) its low volume of manufactured exports, and (iii) its heavy dependence on manufactured imports. This reflects a fundamental trade imbalance for the continent. Nonetheless, strenuous efforts are being made in countries like South Africa (i.e. Durban port — Pier 1), which is

Table 2.4: Container port traffic for selected developing and African countries, 2006–2007 (million TEUs)

Developing Country Rank		2006	2007	% Change 2006/07
Selected Developing Countries:				
1	China	84.02	101.96	21.36
2	Singapore	25.61	28.76	12.32
5	Malaysia	13.42	15.12	12.68
7	UAR	10.97	12.83	16.96
8	Brazil	6.28	6.80	8.20
12	Indonesia	4.04	6.11	51.23
18	Mexico	2.68	3.07	14.58
20	Argentina	2.43	2.58	5.90
22	Jamaica	2.15	2.19	2.02
25	Dominican Republic	1.86	2.05	10.40
47	Trinidad and Tobago	0.47	0.52	10.51
Selected African Countries:				
13 (1)	Egypt	4.53	4.76	4.94
16 (2)	South Africa	3.55	3.78	6.45
43 (3)	Côte d'Ivoire	0.51	0.54	7.00
44 (4)	Kenya	0.48	0.59	22.12
45 (5)	Ghana	0.48	0.51	7.71
49 (6)	Angola	0.38	0.40	7.00
50 (7)	Tanzania	0.30	0.33	10.78
51 (8)	Mauritius	0.36	0.41	15.19
52 (9)	Sudan	0.33	0.36	10.05
54 (10)	Djibouti	0.22	0.29	33.24
56 (11)	Cameroon	0.20	0.19	–3.76
60 (12)	Madagascar	0.09	0.11	21.55
62 (13)	Namibia	0.08	0.14	74.14

Source: Containerisation International Yearbook, 2009.

Table 2.5: Deployment of ship-to-shore gantry cranes by region and outreach, 2008

	Africa	World	Eastern Europe	North America	South America	South Asia
Panamax	57	1744	71	236	63	48
16–18 rows	31	949	10	131	24	27
18–20 rows	25	698	12	105	22	49
20–22 rows	12	415	0	87	0	4
22+ rows	26	803	0	59	0	0

Source: Drewry Shipping Consultants (2009).

investing in terminals that handle containers only. The use of containers not only facilitates the movement of goods and lowers trade costs, but also addresses security issues such as theft.

In terms of operational performance, one of the major challenges facing the continent is raising the finance to invest in equipment that can handle the world's largest container ships. This means accommodating not only vessels that are currently in service but also the future generation of vessels that might be deployed in the coming years. Table 2.5 gives the number of Panamax and "super post-Panamax"[10] quayside gantry-cranes and their outreach in Africa compared to the rest of the world. Africa has lagged behind in terms of large investments in this type of equipment. For example, Africa has 57

Panamax cranes, which represents only 3 percent of the global total and 24 percent of the number in North America.

Efficiency Indicators for African Ports

Several indices are used to measure the various factors contributing to port performance, some based on subjective indicators (ordinal rankings on a scale), some based on cardinal indicators (e.g. dwell times). Several factors are taken into account when producing these efficiency indices: physical infrastructure; management and services; governance; regulations; customs and institutional framework. According to the indicators in Table 2.6, African ports have a medium efficiency (between 3.72 and 4.63 on a scale of 7, with 7 being the best and 1 the worst) but they have the worst customs clearance, especially in Sub-Saharan Africa (more than 11 days). In the discussion below, the focus is on three specific indicators: turnaround time; dwell time; and Liner Shipping Connectivity Index (LSCI).

---

[10] The latest generation of "super post Panamax" vessels has a width of about 22 container rows, compared to "post Panamax" vessels, which accommodate 18 container rows.

Table 2.6: Efficiency indicators of selected leading ports by volume of containerized cargo, 2006

Region	Port Efficiency (7=best, 1=worst)	Customs Clearance (days)	Container handling charges (US$/TEU)
North America	6.35	3.50	261.7
Europe (except East)	5.29	4.00	166.7
Middle East	4.93	NA	NA
East Asia and the Pacific	4.66	5.57	150.5
East and South Africa	4.63	12.00	NA
North Africa	3.72	5.50	NA
Former Soviet Union	3.37	5.42	NA
Eastern Europe	3.28	2.38	NA
Latin America	2.90	7.08	251.4
South Asia	2.79	–	NA
West Africa	NA	11.7	NA

Source: World Economic Forum (1999), World Bank surveys, Camara Maritima and Portuaria de Chile (1999), and LSU-National Ports and Waterways Institute (1998).
Note: Efficiency variables per region are not directly comparable because the availability of countries is not the same.

(i) Efficiency Indicator: Turnaround Time

Primary measures of port performance are the average turnaround time per ship, and the tonnage handled per ship-day in port. The ship turnaround is the rate at which cargo is handled and the duration that cargo stays in port prior to shipment or post discharge. It is calculated from the time of the ship's arrival to the time of its departure. Traditionally expressed in days, it is now common to express turnaround time in hours. The port authority (PA) would normally compile statistics giving monthly and annual average turnaround times. The average turnaround time per ship is determined by dividing the total hours by the total number of ships calling at the port.

In its basic form, ship turnaround time does not mean much, as the length of stay is influenced by a number of factors: the volume of cargo, the facilities made available, and the composition of the cargo itself. Thus, it becomes necessary for the port to further break down the basic ship turnaround time according to type of ship: tankers, bulk carriers, container vessels, and general cargo vessels. These may be subdivided further into domestic trade, regional trade, and oceangoing vessels.

In compiling data to determine ship turnaround time or the tonnage handled per ship-day (or ship-hour), a port would normally split total time in port into "time at berth" and "time off the berth." Within each of these and for each service activity, the amount of delay (idle time) would be recorded as well as the reasons for the delay. In particular, the ratio between waiting time for berth and the time spent at berth, known as the *waiting rate*, is a significant indicator of possible congestion status.

(ii) Efficiency Indicator: Dwell Time

The assessment of a port's performance from the point of view of the exporter/importer focuses primarily on the *dwell time* of cargo in port, measured in terms of the number of days that a tonne of cargo remains on port. A high dwell time is generally an indication that all is not well with the port. The importance of dwell time also varies with the nature of goods.

Capacity and productivity constraints in African ports add to transport costs, by increasing both the port charges and the time in ports (which can be considered as a deadweight loss).[11] When a port cannot handle the largest ships, shipping companies may prefer to use other major handling ports. If cargo or containers need to be transferred to smaller vessels to serve smaller ports, this raises unit costs. As many SSA countries have relatively small ports in terms of cargo-handling capacity, this will increase their freight costs.

As shown in Table 2.7, in Africa dwell time is relatively high (measured in days, whereas in high-performing ports it is typically hours), berth productivity is fairly low, and costs are high. Mombasa appears to be one of the most efficient ports, with only 5 days' dwell time, high berth productivity (60 moves per hour) and the lowest costs (US$ 90 per TEU). With 29 berths and 73 percent capacity utilization, it also has scope to expand operations. This is also supported by Al-Eraqi *et al.* (2008) in a study that evaluates the location efficiency of ports in East Africa and the Middle East. In Kenya, however, the general finding is that most of the ports should improve their efficiency levels at least 1.5 times through bigger berths, improved handling equipment (e.g. post-Panamax ship-to-shore gantry cranes) to speed up the loading/offloading of cargoes, and other infrastructure in order to reduce congestion and waiting time.

South African ports, especially Durban (although it is at full capacity) are relatively efficient but other African ports face problems. Dar es Salaam and Toamasina have relatively low berth times and moderate berth efficiency, but very high costs. This may explain the low capacity utilization, especially as they have relatively few berths.

A number of ports have moderately high costs (not the highest, but above the South African benchmark) and, even if berth productivity is relatively good, high dwell times. Dwell times are particularly high in Port Sudan in the Sudan, Matidi in DRC (which also has low productivity), Tema in Ghana, and Lagos in Nigeria, although berth productivity is often reasonably high. The major problem in these ports is poor turnaround times; in such cases, increasing efficiency could increase capacity utilization and reduce costs. Dakar in Senegal seems to be the most efficient of the West African ports. According to Scheck (2007), the

---

[11] For discussion see Standard Bank (2008), who report that container handling costs in Africa are often three times higher than in European ports. Moreover, shipping companies have noted that African costs, in particular slow and cumbersome customs procedures, are increasing faster than revenue (Scheck, 2007).

Table 2.7: Efficiency indicators for selected African ports, 2006

	Dwell Time (days)	No. of Berths	Moves per Hour	Capacity Utilization (%)	Cost (US$/TEU)
East Africa					
Kenya: Mombasa	5	29	60	73	90
Madagascar: Toamasina	9	6	22	35	184
Mozambique: Maputo	22	2	22	40	155
Tanzania: Dar es Salaam	7	11	20	45	275
Sudan: Port Sudan	28	17	20	78	150
Southern Africa					
Angola: Luanda	12	11	14	77	320
Namibia: Walvis Bay	8	8	8	60	110
South Africa: Cape Town	6	34	36	70	121
South Africa: Durban	4	57	45	100	121
West Africa					
Benin: Cotonou	12	11	NA	70	180
Cameroon: Douala	12	18	40	70	220
Congo, DR: Matidi	26	10	7	75	120
Ghana: Tema	25	14	40	60	168
Nigeria: Lagos	22	42	28	60	155
Senegal: Dakar	7	52	10	80	160
North Africa					
Morocco: Tangier	NA	1	NA	NA	NA
Algeria: Bejaia	NA	21	NA	NA	NA
Tunisia: Rades	NA	7	NA	NA	NA
Egypt: Port Said	NA	20	NA	NA	NA

Sources: Ocean Shipping Consultants (2007) for SSA; International Containerisation Yearbook, 2009 and the World Port Source website: http://www.worldportsource.com/index.php.
Notes: Dwell time is in average container days; Berths gives number of docks; and productivity is the average container moves per hour (mph); Capacity Utilization (CU) is percentage capacity utilization for containers and cost is for imports per TEUs (usually the same for exports, except in South Africa where it is US$243).

average wait time in Africa is 4 days and berth productivity is 25 moves per hour, whereas in Europe it is 2 days' waiting time and berth productivity of 40 moves per hour.

For shipping lines, port efficiency and cost are major factors in deciding whether or not to call at a port. Kenya and South Africa appear to be most efficient and among the lowest-cost ports; Namibia is relatively low-cost but not as efficient. Thus, it is likely that large container ships would only call in Kenya and South Africa, and perhaps Senegal in West Africa. In this regard, there would be an incentive to transfer cargoes to smaller vessels to serve smaller ports, contributing to higher costs and lower capacity utilization elsewhere. Although there are evident problems with costs in Madagascar and Tanzania, in general Eastern and Southern Africa are better served by port infrastructure than is West Africa.

Dwell time, unlike ship time in ports, identifies areas where improvements may be sought. However, it does not provide a breakdown according to the various procedures that need to be completed before cargo can be shipped or delivered. Failure to address dwell time contributes to high congestion levels, which acts as a constraint to the competitiveness of African ports. Notteboom (2006) calculated that in East Asia, the time spent in port averages 20 percent of the total transport time, whereas in Africa this ratio increases to over 80 percent. The shipping company Delmas calculated that in 2004, 146 days were lost on the weekly service between Europe and Africa because of congestion, which translates into an estimated loss to the shipping companies of US$ 5 million. In Lagos (Nigeria) in 2003, the average cost was higher than in Felixstowe (UK) (Palsson *et al.,* 2007).

(iii) Efficiency Indicator: Liner Shipping Connectivity Index (LSCI)

UNCTAD's Liner Shipping Connectivity Index (LSCI) is a measure of a country's level of integration into the existing liner shipping network. It captures liner shipping services to a country's port(s) using five components: (i) the number of ships; (ii) the container carrying capacity (in TEUs) of those ships; (iii) maximum ship size; (iv) number of services; and (v) the number of companies that deploy container ships on services to and from a country's ports. The LSCI can be considered a proxy of the accessibility to global trade. The higher the index, the easier it is to access a high capacity and frequency global maritime freight transport system and thus effectively to participate in international trade. Therefore, the LSCI can be considered both as a measure of a country's connectivity to maritime shipping and as a measure of trade facilitation.

The countries with the highest overall LSCI rankings are those most actively involved in trade. The export-oriented economies of China and Hong Kong (China) rank first, followed by the transshipment hub of Singapore. Large traders such as the UK, Germany, and the US are also in the top 15. As shown in Table 2.8 below, the best-connected countries in Africa in the 2009 LSCI were Egypt (ranked 1st in Africa; 17th internationally), Morocco (2nd in Africa, 23rd internationally) and South Africa (3rd in Africa; 29th internationally). At the other end of the scale, Guinea Bissau, Eritrea, and Somalia were the worst connected. Over the period 2007–2009, Morocco dramatically improved its LSCI ranking, from 9.0 in 2007 to 38.4 in 2009. This was the result of major investments in the sector. Other countries also improved their ranking in the 2009 index (e.g. Egypt, South Africa, Nigeria, Côte d'Ivoire, Ghana, and Djibouti) while others (e.g. Sudan, Senegal, Tanzania, and Guinea Bissau) witnessed a decline.

Table 2.8: UNCTAD Liner Shipping Connectivity Index, 2007–2009

	2007		2008		2009	
	LSCI	Int. Rank	LSCI	Int. Rank	LSCI	Int. Rank
Top Six Countries (in 2009)						
China	127.9	1	137.4	1	132.0	1
Hong Kong, China	106.2	2	108.8	2	104.5	2
Singapore	87.5	4	94.5	3	99.5	3
Netherlands	84.8	5	87.6	5	88.7	4
Republic of Korea	77.2	8	76.4	10	86.7	5
United Kingdom	76.8	9	78.0	7	84.8	6
Selected Developing Countries						
Malaysia	81.6	7	77.6	9	81.2	10
Sri Lanka	42.4	19	46.1	19	34.7	26
Mexico	31.0	25	31.2	26	31.9	31
Brazil	31.6	24	30.9	27	31.0	33

	2007	2008	2009		
	LSCI	LSCI	LSCI	Int. Rank	African Rank
African Countries					
Egypt	45.4	52.5	52.0	17	1
Morocco	9.0	29.8	38.4	23	2
South Africa	27.5	28.5	32.1	29	3
Nigeria	13.7	18.3	19.9	50	4
Côte d'Ivoire	15.0	16.9	19.4	53	5
Ghana	15.0	18.1	19.3	54	6
Djibouti	10.5	10.4	18.0	58	7
Senegal	17.1	17.6	15.0	63	8
Mauritius	17.2	17.4	14.8	64	9
Togo	10.6	12.6	14.4	68	10
Namibia	8.4	11.1	13.6	69	11
Benin	11.2	12.0	13.5	70	12
Kenya	10.8	11.0	12.8	72	13
Cameroon	11.6	11.1	11.6	73	14
Congo	9.6	11.8	11.4	74	15
Angola	9.9	10.2	11.3	75	16

cont.

	2007	2008	2009		
	LSCI	LSCI	LSCI	Int. Rank	African Rank
Tanzania	10.6	10.5	9.5	83	17
Libya	6.6	5.4	9.4	84	18
Mozambique	7.1	8.8	9.4	85	19
Sudan	5.7	5.4	9.3	86	20
Gabon	8.6	8.9	9.2	88	21
Madagascar	7.8	7.8	8.6	91	22
Algeria	7.9	7.8	8.4	96	23
Guinea	8.5	6.4	8.3	97	24
Gambia	4.7	5.0	7.5	103	25
Mauritania	7.9	7.9	7.5	104	26
Tunisia	7.2	7.0	6.5	107	27
Sierra Leone	5.1	4.7	5.6	111	28
Liberia	4.5	4.2	5.5	112	29
Cape Verde	2.5	3.6	5.1	115	30
Comoros	5.5	5.2	5.0	117	31
Seychelles	5.3	4.5	4.9	118	32
Dem. Rep. of Congo	2.7	3.4	3.8	137	33
G. Bissau	5.1	5.3	3.5	143	34
Eritrea	–	3.3	3.3	145	35
Somalia	3.1	3.2	2.8	149	36

Table 2.8: cont.

Countries such as South Africa, Morocco, and Egypt are geographically well positioned as major hubs in Africa, which has contributed to their higher LSCI ranking.

Countries at the bottom of the index include small island states, which rely on small feeder service connections to a regional hub, and landlocked countries, which have only inland waterways connections serviced by small ships. The composition of the worst connected countries (which are mostly in Africa) changes more frequently than the best connected countries, as the overall numbers

of companies and services are very low. A withdrawal of one service provider or one service can therefore strongly impact the overall ranking. This is particularly relevant for small island countries such as Comoros, Seychelles, Cape Verde and São Tomé and Principe.

While African least developed countries (LDCs) have seen improvements in the TEU capacity in general, there is still a large gap between their capacity and that of developed countries. The two LDCs with the biggest TEU capacity are Senegal (128,496

TEUs) and Angola (100,000 TEUs), while the comparable figure for China, Germany, the United Kingdom, and Singapore is more than 1 million TEUs.

Investments for Rehabilitation and Expansion

Many African countries are investing in port infrastructure to meet growing demand and improve port performance, while major international container operators are also eager to invest. Several examples suggest that port development is taking place, even if it is too early to see the results. In Egypt, in 2000, significant reforms and investments in port infrastructure elevated that country to premier position in terms of port capacity in Africa. South Africa has followed with the opening of Pier 1 container terminal in Durban in 2007, which is highly automated to address capacity and productivity constraints. Ngqura, another container terminal in South Africa, became operational in 2009. Namibia also invested heavily in the Walvis Bay port and is seeking to attract private sector participation. Morocco is among the few African countries with equipment to handle Panamax vessels and the government plans a US$ 2.5 billion public investment in the ports subsector.

Investments are also underway in other parts of Africa. Equatorial Guinea aims to double its port capacity and transform the country into a major shipping hub. The port project and associated infrastructure will cost around US$ 4.5 billion and is due to be completed in 2011. Côte d'Ivoire is planning to spend over US$ 60 million to upgrade the port of Abidjan into a regional trans-shipment hub for West Africa — an

improvement that would help redress the current imbalance across the continent. Mozambique's Nacala Development Corridor is planning to invest US$ 150 million to upgrade its port, rail, and road infrastructure over the next five years to raise capacity to 4 million tonnes. The Djiboutian port of Doraleh, under a concession contract to DP World, has already raised US$ 400 million to develop a container terminal. The Kenya Ports Authority has ambitious plans for more investments in Mombasa. The Democratic Republic of Congo, through a concession contract, has also made significant investments in the port of Pointe Noire, which will increase capacity in the region. For the most part, these investments come from large foreign investors.

The investments cited above, underway or planned, show strong dynamism that should yield large economy-wide benefits. For example, the new container terminal at Pointe Noire (Congo Brazzaville) is expected to boost permanent employment in the port to reach 1,000 employees by 2018 (compared to just 230 permanent jobs at present). In parallel, the site will generate nearly 200 jobs during the execution of the infrastructure works.

Assessing the full benefits of these investments will require more data on port performance that is currently lacking, especially for African ports. Using East Asia as a case in point, the cost of expanding port capacity in that region to a total of 36 million TEUs would cost about US$ 1.4 to 2.9 billion p.a. at the financial rate of return of 10 percent (Abe and Wilson, 2009). The total consumer surplus due to the expansion would amount to US$ 8 billion a year. Such gains warrant further large capital injections into the port subsector in the region.

Summary: The Way Forward for African Ports

The growth in global trade over the past decade, together with increasing container-ization and an improved policy framework in Africa (see Chapter 1), have boosted demand for African port capacity. With 80 percent of the volume of world trade carried by maritime vessels, the importance of ports in the logistics supply chain is paramount. However, trade imbalances, congestion, low productivity/efficiency, and low connect-ivity to other regions impede Africa's full integration into the world trading system. To illustrate the logistical problems facing the ports in the region, it has been estimated that the share of total transport time spent in port (dwell time) may be up to four times higher in Africa than in East Asia. To remedy the inefficiencies, the infrastructure and services of African ports need to be improved along the dimensions identified in this report. In particular, the following critical areas of action need to be addressed:

(i) Regional imbalances. Two regions that are most lacking adequate port facilities are the west coast (from Equatorial Guinea to Namibia) and the east coast (from Tanzania to South Africa). As a result, ports such as Durban and Dar es Salaam have come to serve as the main points of entry for numerous landlocked countries in the region, creating congestion risks and bottle-necks. Lack of seaport choice also increases the level of dependence for landlocked countries on the usually poor hinterland transport facilities. Imbalances also result in weak links in the chain of ports called upon by liners, since it is the weakest link that determines the type of vessel used for multi-port deliveries.

(ii) Capacity. Congestion, delays in expansion plans, the need for rehabilitation, upgrading or new construction are systemic problems that plague many African ports. With the economic downturn and reduced demand for many primary commodities, the problems of congestion and delays have eased for the moment. Although capital financing is likely to be more difficult to obtain given the liquidity constraints, the current environment provides an opportunity to implement the planned improvement projects with less disruption to normal port activities.

(iii) Size and Container Accom-modation. Spurred by the growth in containerized cargoes, the need for ports to offer increased berth size and state-of-the-art container-handling activity has expanded. However, most African ports do not have the capacity to handle gearless ships and port equipment is often inadequate or poorly maintained. As a result, most African ports cannot receive ships exceeding 2,500 TEUs, even though ships of up to 15,000 TEUs are now sailing the major international routes. Many smaller African ports are unable to justify the acquisition of expensive equipment such as quayside gantry cranes, and must rely on mobile

cranes and ships' cranes (geared vessels). This prevents ports achieving the desired international benchmarks for container movements per hour (40 per hour in the region), which in turn affects the cost competitiveness of the port.

(iv) Other Infrastructure. Longer berth lengths, wider ship turning circles, and deeper access channels alongside berths for modern ships are needed.

(v) Land Access. Land access, for both road and rail, is restricted in many African ports since the latter are generally surrounded by densely developed areas. Resulting delays and congestion in both the delivery and removal of cargoes to and from the port affect port capacity and increase costs. In some cases, greenfield sites may be called for, rather than trying to heap more facilities onto an already overcrowded port infrastructure.

The analysis in this chapter suggests that, in many instances, large productivity gains can be achieved by improving existing ports. At the same time, improvements in the regulatory environment are also necessary. Improvements in port management, often implying reform leading to the introduction of public–private partnerships (PPPs), may be needed to provide the necessary funding to carry out major rehabilitation and expansion. These regulatory and institutional aspects are covered in Chapter 3. Furthermore, since ports are part of the larger trade logistics chain, reforms need to go beyond improving the efficiency of ports alone and work toward integrating the ports more

efficiently into the broader economy. As argued in Chapter 4, this means guaranteeing well-functioning, multimodal (road, rail, inland water, and air) transport links between ports and the hinterland.

References

Abe, K. and J.S. Wilson. 2009. "Weathering the Storm: Investing in Port Infrastructure to Lower Trade Costs in East Asia." World Bank Working Paper No. 4911. Washington, DC: World Bank.

Al-Eraqi, A.S, C.P. Barros, A. Mustaff, and A.T. Khadar. 2008. "Evaluating the Location Efficiency of Arabia and African Seaports using Data Envelopment Analysis (DEA)." Working Paper, School of Economics and Management, Technical University of Lisbon.

Drewry Shipping Consultants Ltd. 2009. *Annual Review of Global Container Terminal Operators 2009.* London: Drewry Publishing.

Hoyle, B. 1999. "Port Concentration, Inter-port Competition and Revitalization: The Case of Mombasa, Kenya." *Maritime Policy and Management,* 26 (2): 161–74.

Hummels, D., V. Lugovskyy, and A. Skiba. 2009. "The Trade Reducing Effects of Market Power in International Shipping." *Journal of Development Economics*, 89 (1): 84–97.

Lloyds MIU. 2009. *Containerisation International Yearbook.* 40th edition. London: Informa.

Notteboom, T.E. 2006. "The Time Factor in Liner Shipping Services", *Maritime Economics & Logistics*, 8: 19–39.

Pálsson, G., A. Harding, and G. Raballand. 2007. "Port and Maritime Transport Challenges in West and Central Africa." SSATP Working Paper No. 84. Washington, DC: World Bank.

PMAESA. 2008. "Consultative Workshop on Port Congestion in the PMAESA region", Mombasa.

Scheck, J. 2007. "Port Infrastructure in Africa", Presentation at the 5th Intermodal Africa 2007 Conference, Durban, South Africa, March 29–30, 2007.

Standard Bank. 2008. *African Infrastructure Survey — Harnessing Local Opinion and Insight.* Research Economics, Africa Hardcover.

UNCTAD. 1999. *UNCTAD's Contribution to the Implementation of the United Nations New Agenda for the Development of Africa in the 1990s: African Transport Infrastructure,* *Trade and Competitiveness.* Report No. TD/B/46/10. New York and Geneva: UNCTAD.

——. **2006.** *Landlocked Developing Countries: Facts and Figures.* New York and Geneva: UNCTAD.

——. **2008.** *Review of Maritime Transport, 2008.* New York and Geneva: UNCTAD.

——. **2009.** *Transport Newsletter*, No. 43, Second and Third Quarters 2009, Geneva.

Wood, G. 2004. "Tanzanian Coastal and Inland Ports and Shipping: Crises and Policy Options." *Maritime Policy and Management,* 31 (2): 157–71.

Wood, G. and P. Dibben. 2005. "Ports and Shipping in Mozambique: Current Concerns and Policy Options." *Maritime Policy and Management,* 32 (2): 139–57.

World Bank. 2009. *Africa's Infrastructure: A Time for Transformation, Part 2 — Sectoral Snapshots.* AICD Report. Washington, DC: World Bank.

Annex 2.1: Overview of African Port Facilities, Capacity, and Infrastructure by Subregion and Country

This annex discusses the main ports in Africa in terms of their infrastructure, facilities, and capacity. For the purposes of this review, the ports are divided into six subregions:

   i. **North Africa**: Algeria, Egypt, Libya, Mauritania, Morocco, and Tunisia;
   ii. **East Africa**: Djibouti, Eritrea, Kenya, Somalia, Sudan, and Tanzania;
   iii. **Southern Africa**: Angola, Democratic Republic of Congo, Mozambique, Namibia, and South Africa;
   iv. **Central Africa**: Cameroon, Congo, Equatorial Guinea, and Gabon;
   v. **West Africa**: Benin, Côte d'Ivoire, Gambia, Ghana, Guinea, Guinea Bissau, Liberia, Nigeria, Senegal, Sierra Leone, and Togo;
   vi. **Island Countries**: Mauritius, Madagascar, Comoros, São Tomé and Principe, Seychelles, and Cape Verde.

The two premier ports serving the continent are Port Said in Egypt and the port of Durban in South Africa (see Table 2.9 for a listing of Africa's top container ports in 2007). Excluding these two, port capacities across the continent are generally patchy, and in need of improvement and development.

(i) Ports in North Africa

The North Africa subregion includes Algeria, Egypt, Libya, Mauritania, Morocco and Tunisia, which are all middle-income countries, except for Mauritania. Egypt has the largest capacity and is home to some of Africa's biggest and most sophisticated ports. The ports in the other North African countries are relatively small and have adequate facilities to handle the low volume of traffic. In all the ports, cranes are connected to national rail networks, supporting an efficient movement of goods.

In **Egypt**, the *Port of Alexandria* has witnessed significant reforms since 2002, which have improved its performance. The port has two main container terminals: the Alexandria Container Terminal and the Alexandria International Container Terminal. The Alexandria Container Terminal has a storage capacity of 11,000 TEUs and is scheduled to benefit from sophisticated handling equipment, including post-Panamax gantry cranes. The new infrastructure is expected to reduce the average waiting time for ships. The terminal has a rail connection to support the movement of goods. The Alexandria International Container Terminal has a smaller storage capacity of 7,000 TEUs.

Table 2.9: Africa's top container ports, 2007

Port	Country	TEUs handled 2007 (000s)	Post and Super Panamax facilities
Port Said	Egypt	2,768.9	Yes
Durban	South Africa	2,511.7	Yes
Damietta	Egypt	1,195.6	Yes
Cape Town	South Africa	874.6	Yes
Mombasa	Kenya	585.4	No
Abidjan	Côte d'Ivoire	507.1*	No
Tema	Ghana	458.1	No
Dakar	Senegal	424.5	No
Port Elizabeth	South Africa	415.9	Yes
Port Louis	Mauritius	413.8	Yes
El Dekheila	Egypt	453.2	Yes
Luanda	Angola	407.6*	No
Alexandria	Egypt	385.0	Yes
Rades	Tunisia	383.2	No
Port Sudan	Sudan	342.2	No
Dar es Salaam	Tanzania	334.1	No
Lagos	Nigeria	235.8	No
Djibouti	Djibouti	221.3*	No
Douala	Cameroon	217.7	No
Walvis Bay	Namibia	145.0	No
Toamasina	Madagascar	112.4	No
Skikda	Algeria	100.0	No
Maputo	Mozambique	80.4	No
Bejaia	Algeria	70.8*	No
San Pedro	Côte d'Ivoire	58.5	No
Takoradi	Ghana	55.1	No
Tanger-Med	Morocco	NA**	Yes

Source: Containerisation International Yearbook, 2009.
* 2006 data.** no data available at time of survey in 2008

The container terminal at *Damietta* is the biggest in Egypt, with a storage capacity of 30,000 TEUs. The terminal benefits from rail connections to Cairo and other parts of the Nile delta and Upper Egypt. Two additional super post-Panamax cranes and other sophisticated machinery have been ordered. There are plans to dredge and extend the existing container channels and a new terminal is expected to be opened by the end of 2009.

The *Port of El Dekheila* has two container terminals: Dekheila Container Terminal and Dekheila International Container Terminal. Both ports have state-of-the-art, post-Panamax equipment capable of handling high volumes of cargo. The Dekheila Container Terminal is served by rail tracks, making it more efficient to move goods. There are also plans to acquire super post-Panamax gantry cranes for Dekheila.

Port Said is the busiest port in Africa and serves as a major hub. It has two main container terminals: Port Said Container Terminal and the Suez Canal Container Terminal. Port Said Container Terminal has state-of-the-art handling equipment including post-Panamax cranes, which are set to increase in number. The terminal has one rail terminal to facilitate the movement of goods. The Suez Canal Container Terminal is the busiest in Africa, with the largest number of super post-Panamax, ship-to-shore equipment in Africa. The terminal is also linked to a rail line. *Sokhna Port* also has post-Panamax equipment. Recent reforms in Egypt in the port subsector have led to significant investments which have boosted performance, so that

Egypt now surpasses South Africa in terms of global rankings in container traffic.

Morocco is geographically located on one of the main liner shipping routes. From 2004–2007, its Liner Shipping Connectivity Index was in the range 8.50–9.40, but this has risen dramatically in recent years, to reach 30 in 2008 and 38 in 2009 (see Table 2.7). Now Morocco is ranked 23rd at the global level, according to the LSCI. Data for recent years show that the port of *Casablanca*, which accommodates over 70 percent of Moroccan maritime trade volumes, has absorbed most of the country's trade increase. The largest ongoing project in the port subsector is in Tangier, where the *Tanger-Med* port has the biggest capacity in the country (3.5 million TEUs). This multipurpose port entered into operation in July 2008 and is primarily intended for transshipment, and part of the traffic will also service the hinterland. The project Tanger Med II is currently under development and consists in an expansion of the container terminal capacity of the Tanger Med I to 8 million TEUs.

Algeria has two main ports: *Algiers* and *Bejaia*, which provide services to the neighboring landlocked countries of Mali and Niger. The ports are located within easy access of the major markets of Europe and the United States. The two ports are relatively small but are well equipped to handle the small volume of cargo in and out of the port. Algiers, as a transshipment port, had benefited from the recent concession process to Dubai Ports. Bejaia is the larger and busier of the two ports. Rail facilities are available under gantry cranes connected to national rail network. Bejaia has two main

limitations: first, the length and the depth of its berths restrict the size of vessels that can access the port. Second, the port does not operate 24 hours per day.

Tunisia has seven ports, handling more than 95 percent of its international trade, and over 1,300 km of coastline. The main port is the *Port of Rades*, which handles 350,000 TEUs per annum. To attract large container ships, in early 2007 the government launched a deepwater port project at Enfidha, 17 meters deep and able to accommodate 80,000-tonnes vessels. This will enable Tunisia to attract large ships passing through the central Mediterranean, which are estimated at 10.3 million TEUs. In addition, this port will boost Tunisia's trade with the European Union, which accounts for 80 percent of all of its foreign trade, 97 percent of which is conducted by sea. The Tunisian coastline has the potential to become a strategic location for transshipment between the EU and the entire Maghreb region. With this new deepwater port, the goal is to capture a flow of 3 million additional containers per annum by 2020.

Libya has two main ports, *Benghazi* and *Tripoli*. The Port of Benghazi operates only for 12 hours, which limits operations. The Port of Tripoli is also limited in terms of operating hours.

Table 2.10: North Africa — port infrastructure, capacity, and facilities

Port	Country	Berths types and dimensions (m)	Terminal Facilities		Railroad Facilities	Dwell Time (days)
			Total Area (000m²)	Storage TEUs (000s)		
Algiers	**Algeria**	10 ro-ro [D(7.10)] 3 container [D(11)]	175	5.6	Quays connected to national rail network	NA
Bejaia		4 container/ro-ro [D(12); L(500)]	90	9.0	Gantry cranes connected to national rail network	NA
Oran		General cargo for geared vessels	410	3.0	Quays have rail links	NA
Alexandria (Container Terminal)	**Egypt**	3 container [D(14); L(520)] 1 ro-ro [D(14); L(160)]	163	11.0	Rail link to terminal	NA
Alexandria (International Container Terminal)		1 container [D(12); L(180)]	110	7.0	Rail link to terminal	NA
Damietta		4 container [D(14.5); L(1,050)]	1,000	30.0	Rail connections to Cairo and other parts of the Nile Delta and Upper Egypt	NA
El Dekheila (Container Terminal)		4 container [D(12-14); L(1,040)] 50m ro-ro ramp	380	20.0	Rail link to terminal	NA
El Dekheila (International Container Terminal)		2 container [D(12); L(512)]	190	NA		
Port Said (Abba Quay)		1 container/ro-ro [D(13.7); L(250)]	375	NA	NA	NA
Port Said (Container Terminal)		1 container [D(14); L(970)]	467	24.0	One rail terminal	NA
Port Said (Suez Canal Container Terminal)		4 container [D(16.5,); L(1,200)]	600	24.0	300m rail line	NA

(cont.)

Table 2.10: cont.

Port	Country	Berths types and dimensions (m)	Terminal Facilities		Railroad Facilities	Dwell Time (days)
			Total Area (000m²)	Storage TEUs (000s)		
Sokhna	**Egypt**	1 container [D(17); L(750)]	180	24.2	3,000m rail line	NA
Benghazi	**Libya**	1 general cargo [D(8.5); L(1,228)]	4,400	24.4	NA	NA
Tripoli		3 Container [L(11)] ro-ro facilities available	210.1	NA	NA	NA
Nouadhibou	**Mauritania**	1 general [D(8); L(128)] 1 general [D(7); L(110)]	NA	NA	Rail linked	NA
Nouakchott		3 general/container [D(9-10.3); L(107)]	NA	NA	NA	NA
Casablanca (Container Terminal)	**Morocco**	3 container [D(12); L(380)] 1 ro-ro [D(8);L(160)]	45	5.0	Available	NA
Casablanca (Mole Tarik/ Ro-Ro Terminal)		5 container [D(7.5-8.2);L(500)] 3 Ro-ro [D(8.2);L(300)]	19	3.0	Available	NA
Tanger-Med		1 container [D(18);L(400)]	390	35.0	NA	NA
Tangier		1 container [D(16);L(800)] 1 ro-ro [D(6.5);L(173)] 3 general [D(9);L(308)]	460	NA	2 rail tracks	NA
Rades	**Tunisia**	1 container	325	NA	NA	NA

Key: D= Depth; L = Length; Ro-ro = Roll on/roll off vessel.
Sources: Containerisation International Yearbook 2009 — based on survey conducted in 2008; Africa Infrastructure Country Diagnostic Report (World Bank, 2009).

(ii) Ports in East Africa

The East African subregion is composed of Djibouti, Eritrea, Kenya, Somalia, Sudan, and Tanzania. Port Sudan is the largest port in terms of total area, while Djibouti is the largest in terms of storage capacity. Kenya has the busiest port (Mombasa) which provides the major export gateway to landlocked countries in the subregion. The Djibouti terminal offers the most modern facilities but needs more investment to meet the high transit demand from Ethiopia.

One of the major concerns in East Africa is the safety risk due to growing attacks by Somali pirates in the Indian Ocean. Insecurity in the Somali waters has led to a rise in the cost of shipping insurance, which has resulted in high freight costs. In 2008, shipping companies reported that they had handed over about US$ 80 million in ransom payments to Somali pirates.

In **Kenya**, the *Port of Mombasa* is the busiest port in East Africa. It services Uganda, Rwanda, Burundi, Southern Sudan, and the eastern gateway for the Democratic Republic of Congo. The port handles containers, general cargo, dry bulk, and liquid bulks. The container terminal has a storage capacity of 7,272 TEUs and benefits from a rail link to the city of Mombasa, although there is a greater dependence on road transport. The strongest growth has been noted in the container sector. However, the port struggles to cope with heavy throughput traffic which has often resulted in chronic congestion. According to the Kenya Ports Authority, Mombasa is approaching saturation point. The port was designed to handle 20 million tonnes per annum and reached 16.4 million tonnes in 2008. This is projected to rise eventually to 30 million tonnes per annum by 2030.[12] The container terminal was designed to handle 250,000 TEUs per annum, whereas in 2008 its throughput was 615,733 TEUs.

Furthermore, the terminal's performance is constrained by its small storage capacity and depth, which limit the size of vessels using the port. The available equipment cannot load/unload cargoes fast enough to avoid congestion. Lack of modern advanced handling equipment, such as super and post-Panamax ship-to-shore gantry cranes, has also led to congestion and delays. Two major challenges experienced by the port in Mombasa are: (i) poor hinterland connectivity due to substandard and unreliable rail services as well as poor road infrastructure and missing links and (ii) the inability of road transporters to cope with demand. In view of the compelling need for greater capacity, in 2009 the Kenya Ports Authority submitted to the National Environment Management Authority (Nema) an environmental impact assessment study report on dredging works aimed at accommodating post-Panamax containers to boost Mombasa's competitiveness. Once the navigation channel is completed, this would allow large oil tankers to dock, thereby reducing the cost of crude oil imports, as currently Kenya has to use a large number of smaller vessels, which increases freight costs.[13]

---

[12] Kenya Ports Authority website, Nov. 30, 2009. http://www.kpa.co.ke/InfoCenter/News/Pages/MombasaPortsRemainsARegionalHub.aspx

[13] *Daily Nation* online (Nairobi), November 4, 2009.

Table 2.11: East Africa — port infrastructure, capacity, and facilities

| Port | Country | Berths types and dimensions (m) | Terminal Facilities | | Railroad Facilities | Dwell Time (days) |
			Total Area (000m²)	Storage TEUs (000s)		
Djibouti	**Djibouti**	2 stern-ramp ro-ro [D(11.5); L(250)] 2 Container [D(9.5-12); L(400)]	220	12.0	3 on-dock 600m rail tracks for intermodal container traffic. Rail-link dockside to Ethiopia.	NA
Assab	**Eritrea**	7 general cargo/ container/side/ quarter-ramp ro-ro 2 stern-ramp ro-ro L: 145m	360	2.6	NA	NA
Mombasa	**Kenya**	5 container [D(11);L(586)]	220	7.3	Rail link to Mombasa	5
Port Sudan	**Sudan**	2 container [D(12.6); L(427)]	1,200	10.0	Available	28
Dar es Salaam	**Tanzania**	1 container [D(11.5); L(549)]	180	7.0	Terminal for inland rail movements	7
Mtwara		2 multipurpose	15	NA	NA	NA

Key: D= Depth; L = Length; Ro-ro = Roll on/roll off vessel.
Sources: Containerisation International Yearbook 2009; data based on survey conducted in 2008; Africa Infrastructure Country Diagnostic Report (World Bank, 2009).

Sudan's main port is *Port Sudan*, which also services landlocked Chad. The port handles containers, general cargo, dry bulk, and liquid bulks. Port capacity has reached its maximum and to address this situation, two container berths are under construction. The *Port of Suakin*, 45 km from the Port of Sudan, has been identified as the site for future expansion to reduce the pressure on Port Sudan.

Tanzania's biggest port is *Dar es Salaam*; the others being Mtwara and Tanga. The port of Dar es Salaam has three deepwater berths and handles containers, general cargo, dry bulk, and liquid bulks. Over 95 percent of Tanzania's cargo transits through the port, as well as transshipment cargo to and from Zambia, Malawi, DRC, Burundi, and Rwanda. The port is witnessing large increases in the general cargo sector as well as consistent growth in dry and liquid bulk traffic. The strongest growth has been in the container sector, where transit, transshipment, and national gateway traffic is handled. According to Wood (2004), problems of competitiveness are at least partially due to under-investment, management failures, skills shortfalls, and difficulties in interfacing with the railroad network.

The **Djibouti** Container Terminal has the capacity and facilities to accommodate larger volumes of cargo than it is currently handling. The 20-year concession granted in 2000 to Dubai Ports International, a subsidiary of Dubai Ports Authority, has enabled the port to acquire the most advanced equipment on the east coast of Africa (e.g. two post-Panamax, ship-to-shore gantry cranes). The port has three rail tracks for intermodal container traffic, and a rail link from the dockside to the Ethiopian capital. Djibouti's port subsector is of strategic importance beyond its borders, in particular as a gateway for Ethiopian cargo, which accounts for around 70 percent of Djibouti's throughput. However, the port's full potential has not been achieved due to inadequate capacity of the port's container terminal facilities. The main challenges to be addressed by Djibouti port authority are: (i) low availability of rail wagons and locomotives, (ii) delays in cargo deliveries, (iii) congestion in the port terminal, and (iv) high costs to importers/exporters.

(iii) Ports in Southern Africa

The Southern Africa subregion includes Angola, Mozambique, Namibia, and South Africa. South Africa has the largest and most developed ports, with Durban as the second busiest port in the continent. The ports in Mozambique handle goods for the neighboring landlocked countries of Malawi, Zambia, and Zimbabwe, thanks to developed railroad networks; however they are in urgent need of capacity development.

Angola's two main ports are *Lobito* and *Luanda*. Lobito is the smaller of the two, with two general cargo berths and very basic cargo-handling facilities. The port is linked to the national railroad network. The port of Luanda is Angola's main port. There is congestion in most cargo-handling sectors and the scope for volume development is constrained by lack of capacity. The port has the potential to service Zambia and DRC, however, this is not possible due to the poor road and rail networks. In response, the Angolan government has devised an action plan to address the following constraints: inadequate infrastructure, lack of handling equipment, low productivity, poor management, high labor-intensive processes, heavy administrative clearance processes, and lack of use of information technology in ports.

Mozambique's ports are of strategic importance to the neighboring countries of Malawi, Zimbabwe, Zambia, Swaziland, and South Africa. The majority of the country's ports have strong rail connections beyond its borders. *Maputo* offers rail connections to South Africa, Zimbabwe, and Swaziland. Similarly, the *Port of Beira* has rail connections to Zimbabwe and marginally to Malawi and Zambia, while the *Port of Nacala* connects to Malawi.

The *Port of Maputo* is Mozambique's largest port and handles cargo to and from

Table 2.12: Southern Africa — port infrastructure, capacity, and facilities

Port	Country	Berths types and dimensions (m)	Terminal Facilities		Railroad Facilities	Dwell Time (days)
			Total Area (000m²)	Storage TEUs (000s)		
Lobito	**Angola**	2 general cargo	40	3.0	Linked to national railroad	NA
Luanda		TC1: 2 container TC2: 2 container [D(10.5); L(450)] TCG2: 2 general cargo/container [D(10.5); L(450)]	227	NA	NA	12
Beira	**Mozambique**	4 container [D(11); L(645)]	200	3.6	3 rail tracks	20
Maputo		1 container [D(11.5); L(300)]	80	1.5	2 rail tracks	22
Nacala		2 container [D(14); L(335)] + [D(12); L(37)]	84	1.8	2 rail tracks	NA
Walvis Bay	**Namibia**	3 container [D(12.8); L(503)] 2 general [D(10.6); L(574)] 2 general/ro-ro (for geared vessels) [D(12.6); L(349)]	45	1.9	NA	8
Cape Town	**South Africa**	5 berths [D(15.5); L(1300)]	970	12.0	Rail transfer facility with rail-mounted yard gantry	6
Cape Town (Container Terminal)		6 container [D(10.7-14); L(1,554)]	970	12.0	Rail transfer facility with rail-mounted yard gantry	NA
Durban (Container Terminal)		7 container [D(11.2); L(1,900)]	1,122	14.5	3 rail tracks each 760m equipped with 45t rail-mounted gantry cranes	4

(cont.)

Table 2.12: cont.

Port	Country	Berths types and dimensions (m)	Terminal Facilities		Railroad Facilities	Dwell Time (days)
			Total Area (000m²)	Storage TEUs (000s)		
Durban (Container Terminal Pier 1)	**South Africa**	1 container [D(11.9); L(180)] 1 container [D(11.9); L(180)] 1 container [D(11.8); L(180)]	120	3.5	3 railway lines, 50 rail wagons per line. 2 reach stackers and 2 rail-mounted gantry cranes	NA
East London		7 berths [D(10.7); L(1,204)] 6 berths [D(10.7); L(1,206)]	38	1.5	Direct rail-link to all major cities and neighboring countries	7
Port Elizabeth		2 container [D(12.2); L(635)]	22	3.1	2 lines which accommodate 25 rail wagons per line	6
Richards Bay		3 multipurpose [D(14.4); L(540)] 3 multipurpose [D(14.2); L(644)] 1 multipurpose [D(18.7); L(200)]	21,570	NA	NA	NA

Key: D= Depth; L = Length; Ro-ro = Roll on/roll off vessel.
Sources: Containerisation International Yearbook, 2009 — survey conducted in 2008; Africa Infrastructure Country Diagnostic Report (World Bank, 2009).

South Africa, Swaziland, and Zimbabwe. It is southern Africa's nearest port to the rapidly developing mega-markets of Asia and is the closest deepwater port to the capital Johannesburg. The port has small storage capacity of 1,504 TEUs, which is inadequate for its needs.

The *Port of Beira* is Mozambique's second port after Maputo. It links directly to Zimbabwe and Zambia by road and rail networks, and to Malawi by road only. However, the Sena rail line linking Beira with Malawi and the Tete Province is currently being rehabilitated. The port has a storage capacity of 3,654 TEUs. It has more facilities for loading and offloading than the port of Maputo, with three rail stacks. The *Nacala harbor* serves its own hinterland and landlocked Malawi to the west, to which it is connected by rail. It has the potential to service Zambia through Malawi. Because of it natural deep water and sheltered position, Nacala has no restrictions on ship movement or size.

With the ending of the civil war and significant reforms in the country, there are now positive opportunities for coastal shipping in Mozambique, although the capacity for developing inland shipping appears to be very limited (Wood and Dibben, 2005). Future growth depends on local participation, training and skills development, and the broader social, economic, and transport infrastructure.

South Africa now has eight major ports: Durban, Richards Bay, Cape Town, Mossel Bay, East London, Port Elizabeth, Saldanha, and Ngqura. South African ports play an important role for the landlocked economies of the subregion, including Botswana, Lesotho, Swaziland, Malawi, Zimbabwe, and Zambia. South African ports are equipped with modern facilities including super post-Panamax, post-Panamax, and Panamax ship-to-shore container equipment, and the ports are linked to the rail network.

The *Port of Durban* is South Africa's main general cargo and container port. It is the second busiest port in Africa and is strategically placed on the world shipping routes. The Durban Container Terminal storage capacity of 14,5000 TEUs has state-of-the art handling equipment with super post-Panamax and post-Panamax and Panamax ship-to-shore container equipment. The upgrading and re-equipping of port infrastructure are well advanced,

including the widening and deepening of the port entrance and channels to enable much larger, later-generation ships to use the port facilities. Meanwhile congestion on the roads outside port terminals has become a major problem. To address this challenge, the Port of Durban opened another port terminal, Pier 1, which handles containers only. This terminal is highly automated, which has improved productivity and reduced congestion at the port of Durban. The increased use of containers has also reduced theft of goods at the harbor.

The Port of Cape Town is another busy container port, second in South Africa to Durban. The emerging oil industry in West Africa has also become a significant factor for the port's repair and maintenance facilities. The harbor and Table Bay are subject to strong winds during the months of April to September, and this can sometimes disrupt cargo-handling and ship refits in the port.

Richards Bay is South Africa's biggest dry bulk port, built in 1976 as one of the world's leading coal export platforms but has since expanded into other bulk and break-bulk cargoes. Currently, Richards Bay handles 60 percent of South Africa's seaborne cargo, making it South Africa's leading port in terms of volume handled. The port is the largest in area in South Africa, with total land and water surfaces of 2,174 ha. and 1,443 ha. respectively.

The Port of East London has a car terminal on the West Bank, which includes a four-storey parking facility connected by dedicated road to the adjacent DaimlerChrysler factory. The terminal has a theoretical design throughput of 50,000 units a year with 2,800 parking bays. The parkade can be expanded to 8 storeys to increase the throughput to 180,000 vehicles a year and the provision of a third berth is also possible. The multipurpose terminal on the East Bank handles an increasing volume of containers and is geared for 90,000 TEUs a year — many for the motor industry. However, the port lacks gantry cranes.

Port Elizabeth container terminal has three berths and is equipped with one post-Panamax and one Panamax ship-to-shore container gantry. The port has adequate rail and road links with other parts of the country. The container terminal can load railroad trains directly under the gantry cranes, without containers having to be double handled, thus speeding up delivery to inland destinations. The terminal has three quayside gantry cranes and is supported by a number of straddle carriers. Motor vehicle components constitute a large proportion of the container traffic at Port Elizabeth. Plans are underway to replace the Panamax with post-Panamax cranes.

It is important to note that the investment in the new deepwater port of *Ngqura* has been influenced by the need to support the activities of the Coega Industrial Development Zone, which generate both dry and liquid cargo. In this regard, ports not only play their central role in the logistics chain but also help to support industrial policies that facilitate trade. The Port of Ngqura is expected to be fully functional by year-end 2009, and will be serving the latest generation of container ships.

Although South Africa is ranked highly in terms of performance, there are still some areas in need of improvement. These targets are stated in Transnet's[14] strategic goals, and are expected to be met between 2009 and 2012. Expected outcomes include: sustained infrastructure capacity provision ahead of growth demand; integrated planning of port infrastructure; safe and secure world-class port system; competitive and efficient port system that drives volume growth; and human capital development. Box 2.3 presents recent highlights in the development of port terminals in South Africa.

In **Namibia,** *Walvis Bay* is the main port. It is a general cargo port and is being aggressively marketed as an alternate port of choice to South African ports. There are good roads and rail connections with the rest of Namibia while the Trans Kalahari Corridor links the port with Botswana and Johannesburg in South Africa. The port has a total of nine berths, handles in excess of 2 million tonnes of cargo annually, and is attracting a greater number of shipping lines as regular callers. In October 2009 the Namibian Ports Authority invested in a N$100 million deal to purchase new equipment to improve port performance. The new rubber-tired gantries (cargo-moving cranes) will improve storage capacity by 42 percent. Furthermore, the system will reduce costs by about 10 percent compared to a conventional stacker system.

In Southern Africa it is important to note that many ports in postconflict areas still suffer from the legacy of a lack of infrastructure development and investment, even though the conflicts may have ended more

---

[14] Transnet is a state-owned organization operating and controlling major transport infrastructures within South Africa.

Box 2.3: South Africa: recent highlights in the development of port terminals

Eight Specialized Port Terminals
- Durban, Richards Bay, Cape Town, Mossel Bay, East London, Port Elizabeth, Saldanha and Ngqura (the latter became operational in 2009)

Highlights in 2009
- All ports have been dredged to promulgate depth
- The process of widening and deepening the entrance channel at Durban port underway; to be completed by June 2010
- Expansion of the Cape Town Container Terminal on track
- Operationalization of Port Ngqura
- Capital investment of Rand 4.2 billion

Strategy
- Creating infrastructure capacity ahead of demand
- Improving port efficiency
- Managing the port position as a gateway for trade

Focus Areas in 2009/2010
- Growing real estate revenue and cost containment
- Delivering infrastructure and capacity improvements ahead of demand
- Building human capital through talent management and training

Key Risks
- Not providing adequate infrastructure, which could impact revenue
- Non-compliance with legislative requirements
- Risks of non-compliance with safety policies
- Inadequate skills
- Global economic environment resulting in low volumes.

Source: Transnet Limited Annual Report 2009

---

than 10 years earlier. In Angola, port development effectively ceased at the outbreak of civil war in 1975, at a time when containerization was being introduced in other African ports. Major upgrading has therefore been necessary, and severe congestion has plagued the port operations at Luanda for many years. In addition, civil unrest has had an effect on the transport and transit corridors servicing the ports. Corridors that used to be relatively efficient were closed for many years in the 1970s and 1980s (such as Lobito, Nacala, Maputo, and Beira) because of civil war. This resulted in the decline of the ports concerned as well as the economic decline of landlocked countries that relied on these ports. For example, the World Bank estimates that for Malawi, by the late 1980s, additional transport charges since the closure of the corridors passing through Mozambique (Beira and Nacala in particular) caused cumulative losses of more than US$ 75 million. Postconflict countries such as

Table 2.13: Central Africa — port infrastructure, capacity, and facilities

Port	Country	Berths types and dimensions (m)	Terminal Facilities		Railroad Facilities	Dwell Time (days)
			Total Area (000m²)	Storage TEUs (000s)		
Douala	**Cameroon**	1 container (for geared vessels) [D(11.5); L(220)] 1 container ro-ro (for geared vessels) [D(11.5); L(220)]	170	13.0	Terminal connected to CAMRAIL (capacity 2x44 TEUs)	NA
Matadi	**DRC**	2 container (for geared vessels) [D(7.6–8.9); L (350)]	40	2.8	2 rail tracks	25
Pointe Noire	**Republic of Congo**	2 general cargo (for geared vessels); L 520. Ro-ro facilities available	20	NA	NA	18

Key: D= Depth; L = Length; Ro-ro = Roll on/roll off vessel.
Sources: Containerisation International Yearbook, 2009 — survey conducted in 2008; Africa Infrastructure Country Diagnostic Report (World Bank, 2009).

Mozambique should be commended for their efforts to scale up investments in ports.

(iv) Ports in Central Africa

The Central Africa subregion includes Cameroon, the Democratic Republic of Congo, the Republic of Congo, Equatorial Guinea, and Gabon. The subregion has some of the least developed ports in Africa. The port of Douala in Cameroon is the most developed.

Douala is the largest port in **Cameroon,** handling over 95 percent of the commercial traffic, and having a storage capacity of 13,000 TEUs. The port services the surrounding landlocked countries of Central African Republic and Chad. The port has fairly low depth, which restricts the size of vessels that call on the port. The terminal is connected to the Cameroon Railway. Even though Doula has emerged as one of the most efficient ports on the west coast of Africa, it has limited capacity.

The **Democratic Republic of Congo**'s main port is *Matadi*. This is a small port, situated on the left bank of the River Congo halfway between the Atlantic Ocean and Kinshasa. The port is connected by two rail facilities. The main concern is congestion due to poor infrastructure and space.

The **Republic of Congo**'s main port is *Pointe Noire,* which has ambitions to become a premier deepwater port in Central Africa. The port only operates at certain times during the day (0700–1200 hrs and 1430–1700 hrs), which limits its efficiency. Nonetheless, Pointe Noire is undergoing significant infrastructure works such as refurbishing and extending existing quays, purchasing the latest equipment such as gantry cranes, and developing a logistics area next to the port. A new container terminal in the port of Pointe Noire became operational on July 1, 2009 as a major transshipment hub and also for hinterland import and export in the Congo basin. This provides access to the principal transport corridors of the subregion, in particular serving the DRC, the CAR, and the north of Angola.

(v) Ports in West Africa

The West Africa subregion includes Benin, Côte d'Ivoire, Gambia, Ghana, Guinea, Guinea Bissau, Liberia, Nigeria, Senegal, Sierra Leone, and Togo. The major ports are Abidjan, Tema, Dakar, and Lagos. Abidjan is recovering from loss of business due to internal conflict. Sierra Leone and Liberia have also come out of conflict and the ports are in need of rehabilitation. West Africa counts numerous ports but to date there is no comprehensive regional strategy to organize the flow of ships and connect the sea to the hinterland. According to the Port Management Association of West and Central Africa, an infrastructure deficit continues to hamper port performance and port efficiency. This is mainly due to a lack of concrete programs for the transport sector, leading to lower prioritization of resources to the ports subsector.

Cotonou port in **Benin** is situated along the Gulf of Guinea. The port is rail-linked but has limited capacity to handle high volumes of cargo. The depth only accommodates small vessels. The port handles containers, general cargo, dry bulk, and liquid bulks. It also provides transshipment to the neighboring countries of Burkina Faso and Niger. The Port of Cotonou is operating beyond its capacity and is in need of rehabilitation.

Abidjan and *San Petro* are the main ports for **Côte d'Ivoire**. Abidjan port is the bigger of the two but with very basic handling equipment that cannot be used for large vessels or for high-volume loading and offloading. However, in 2008 the government initiated the Ile Boulay expansion project for Abidjan, which aims to double the handling capacity to 3 million TEUs per year. Ile Boulay will eventually have a 1,500 m wharf length, a draft of 15 m, and will cover an area of 60 ha.[15]

The *Port of Banjul* is the **Gambia**'s main seaport, handling 90 percent of its foreign trade. Senegal, Guinea Bissau, and Guinea are the three main destinations for re-exported cargoes through the Port of Banjul, which is strategically located close to major shipping routes. The port can accommodate large vessels but lacks rail facilities. Container traffic has seen an average 11 percent annual growth rate in recent years and now handles over 30,000 TEUs each year. Containers (although 90 percent are empties) form the largest export.

The *Port of Tema* is **Ghana**'s busiest seaport. It handles transshipped and transit cargo goods destined for the hinterlands/landlocked countries of Burkina Faso,

---

[15] Port Autonome d'Abidjan, http: www.paaci.org. See also:
http://www.winne.com/specialevents/2009/ene/port.php

Table 2.14: West Africa — port infrastructure, capacity, and facilities

Port	Country	Berths types and dimensions (m)	Terminal Facilities		Railroad Facilities	Dwell Time (days)
			Total Area (000m²)	Storage TEUs (000s)		
Cotonou	**Benin**	1 ro-ro 6 general 1 container [D(11); L(220)]	65	NA	Available	12
Abidjan	**Côte d'Ivoire**	2 container [D(11.5); L(200)] 2 container [D(12.5); L(440)] 1 ro-ro [D(12.5); L(200)]	250	6.0	Available	NA
San Pedro		1 general [D(11-12); L(581)] 1 general [D(9); L(155)]	100	NA	NA	NA
Banjul	**Gambia**	5 general/ container/ro-ro [D(10); L(750)] (max vessels L: 182.9m)	38.9	NA	None	NA
Takoradi	**Ghana**	5 multipurpose [D(9-10); L(714)] 1 ro-ro	390	1.8	Rail line 100m from the port	NA
Tema		2 container [D(11.5); L(566)] 1 container [D(10); L(200)] 2 container [D(10); L(366)] 7 multipurpose [D(8); L(1,281)]	254	5.0	None	25
Conakry	**Guinea**	2 general [D(8); L(340)] 3 multipurpose [D(8.5-10); L(550)] 1 container [D(10.5); L(269)]	480	5.0	NA	NA
Monrovia	**Liberia**	4 general [D(9.14); L(609)]	45	NA	NA	NA

(cont.)

Port	Country	Berths types and dimensions (m)	Terminal Facilities		Railroad Facilities	Dwell Time (days)
			Total Area (000m²)	Storage TEUs (000s)		
Lagos — Container Terminal	**Nigeria**	4 container [D(10.5); L(1,001)]	50	14.6	Available	NA
Lagos — Old Apapa Quays		20 berths [D(9); L(2,459)]	1,200	2.0	Linked to national rail system	NA
Lagos — Tin Can Island		7 general/ro-ro [D(10)] 2 ro-ro [D(9.5)]	NA	NA	None	NA
Calabar		3 general [D(11)] 4 General [D(8)]	NA	NA	None	NA
Onne		1dcontainer [L(250)] 1 ro-ro [D(5.7); L(250)]	200	NA	NA	30
Port Harcourt		13 berths [D(7.6); L(1,390)]	470	NA	NA	NA
Warri		5 general [D(11.5); L(1,250)] 8 general [D(6.5); L(1,500)] 1 ro-ro [D(11.5); L(250)]	NA	NA	None	NA
Dakar	**Senegal**	20 ro-ro [D(8-12); L(3,463)] 15 container/ro-ro [D(8-11.6); L(2,562)]	11	NA	NA	7
Freetown	**Sierra Leone**	1 container [D(8.84); L(174)] 2 container [D(9.6); L(331)]	85	1.1	NA	NA
Lomé	**Togo**	2 container [D(11-12); L(250)]	80	NA	Linked to the national rail system	NA

Key: D= Depth; L = Length; Ro-ro = Roll on/roll off vessel.
Sources: Containerisation International Yearbook, 2009 — survey conducted in 2008; Africa Infrastructure Country Diagnostic Report (World Bank, 2009).

Mali, and Niger. Tema has encountered substantial congestion problems that look set to continue over the short-term at least. It has a storage capacity of 5,000 TEUs. The port lacks modern handling equipment suitable for large vessels, to facilitate faster turnarounds. In addition, the port does not have rail facilities. The future plan is to develop a second container terminal and dredge to increase the depth of the port. *Port of Takoradi* is Ghana's second port and is situated on the Gulf of Guinea (Atlantic Ocean) in the south of the country. The port has a storage capacity of 1,784 TEUs. Ghana Railways Corporation is 100 m from the port. Takoradi port is gearing up for further upgrades and increased private sector participation. The future plans include construction of two new container berths and rehabilitation of port access roads.

Guinea's main port is *Port of Conakry*. This is a small port with a storage capacity of 5,000 TEUs.

The *Port of Lagos* is **Nigeria**'s primary seaport. The other ports are *Calabar, Onne, Port Harcourt,* and *Warri.* Port of Lagos is split into three main divisions: Lagos Port, Old Apapa Port, and Tin Can Island. Lagos handles significant volumes of trade from neighboring Benin, Niger, and Cameroon. The terminal handles imports of consumer goods, foodstuffs, motor vehicles, machinery, and industrial raw materials. Lagos, Apapa, has traditionally played the role of the major public port in Nigeria. Lagos Port Complex (port of Lagos) is located at the Apapa area of Lagos, South West Nigeria. Apapa Port's operational area consists of standard berthing area, cargo handling, stacking areas, and storage facilities.

Ports in Nigeria have undergone significant reforms. However, congestion is still a concern. As the economy has continued to grow since the booming oil times, there is a need to develop port capacity to keep up with demand. According to the Nigerian Ports Authority, the main challenge for Nigeria is to scale up investment in ports in order to meet changes in vessel sizes and architecture.

Dakar is the principal port serving **Senegal** and the surrounding landlocked countries. The Port of Dakar handles container, general cargo, dry and liquid bulk traffic. Growth in the container sector is constrained by lack of available capacity and facilities to speed up the loading/offloading processes to ensure faster turnarounds.

(vi) Island Countries

These include the **Cape Verde Islands** and **São Tomé and Principe** in the Atlantic Ocean and **Madagascar, Mauritius,** and the **Seychelles** in the Indian Ocean. The other island countries have smaller ports and do not handle large vessels, which also reflects the size of their economies. The general observation is that the larger the economy, the busier the port. Unlike the island countries in the Caribbean (which have relatively larger economies), the African island countries (with the exception of Mauritius) are visited by few shipping lines. This increases the cost of shipping.

Port Louis in **Mauritius** is located on an important trading route between Africa and Asia and is the busiest port among the island countries. In 2007 it handled 413,828 TEUs and ranked as one of Africa's 10 busiest ports. The Mauritius Container Terminal is the largest, covering an area of 274,500 sq m. The port is able to handle post-Panamax vessels; it has 5 post-Panamax ship-to-shore gantry cranes. According to the *Enabling Trade Index 2009*, Mauritius has the highest score (33) in Africa. However, the poorest score is in the quality of transport services, which leads to delays in shipping.

Madagascar's main port is *Toamasina*, which has a storage capacity of 2,300 TEUs.

In 2007 the port of Toamasina handled 112,427 TEUs. The port facilities are just adequate to handle the volume of cargo considering the size of the economy. The other smaller islands (Seychelles, Cape Verde Islands and São Tomé and Principe) handle even less cargo, also reflecting the sizes of their economies.

Annex 2.2: African Merchant Fleet, by Flag of Registration and Type of Ship, as of January 2007 (dwt 000s)

Flag	Oil tankers	Bulk carriers	General cargo	Container cargo	Other types	Total
Algeria	26	234	75	0	442	777
Angola	8	0	12	0	26	47
Benin	0	0	0	0	0	0
Cameroon	69	0	3	0	6	79
Cape Verde	4	0	13	0	6	23
Comoros	243	224	480	5	57	1,010
Congo	0	0	0	0	1	1
Congo (DR)	2	0	1	0	14	17
Côte d'Ivoire	1	0	0	0	4	5
Djibouti	0	0	3	0	1	4
Egypt	345	778	332	58	134	1,646
Equatorial Guinea	1	0	6	0	13	19
Eritrea	3	0	19	0	3	25
Ethiopia	0	0	125	0	0	125
Gabon	1	0	4	0	3	8
Gambia	5	0	5	0	2	12
Ghana	5	0	15	0	67	87
Guinea	0	0	0	0	9	9
Guinea-Bissau	0	0	0	0	2	2
Kenya	8	0	2	0	6	16
Libya	13	0	62	0	24	99
Madagascar	17	0	18	0	6	32
Mauritania	0	0	1	0	24	25
Mauritius	0	8	15	0	43	66
Morocco	113	0	41	90	122	365
Mozambique	0	0	11	0	17	27
Namibia	0	0	4	0	52	56
Nigeria	384	13	28	0	99	524
São Tomé & Principe	1	7	32	0	2	42
Senegal	0	0	2	0	17	18
Seychelles	111	0	4	0	30	145
Sierra Leone	105	7	232	5	23	372
Somalia	2	0	5	0	4	10
South Africa	10	0	0	30	70	110
Saint Helena	0	0	0	0	1	1

Flag	Oil tankers	Bulk carriers	General cargo	Container cargo	Other types	Total
Sudan	1	0	26	0	1	29
Togo	0	0	4	0	8	12
Tunisia	67	26	3	0	25	122
Tanzania	14	0	23	0	2	39
Total	1,548	1,299	1,606	187	1,367	6,007
World fleet	382,975	367,542	100,934	128,321	62,554	1,042,328
Percentage of world fleet:						
Africa	0.40	0.35	1.59	0.15	2.19	0.58
Developing countries of Asia	21.97	25.00	29.06	16.45	16.09	22.69
Developing countries of S. America	2.28	1.39	4.27	0.52	4.39	2.07
Developed countries	20.37	12.40	17.14	28.43	31.71	18.92

Source: UNCTAD (2008).

CHAPTER 3

Reforms and the Regulatory Framework of African Ports

With the growth in world trade spurred by the reduction in government-imposed transaction costs (e.g. customs levies and tariffs), transport costs have become a much more significant factor in overall trade costs, as outlined in Chapter 1. This change has put pressure on the port subsector, which is a key component in the logistics chain.

Consequently, over the last 50 years, the port subsector has gone through significant changes at the global level. One of the most notable reforms is deregulation, which has led to more competition. Prior to the reforms, competition between ports was almost nonexistent, and featured a few major transport operators who controlled the bulk of operations from port-to-port. As a result of the deregulation, competition across ports has increased across several dimensions.

First, a number of new ports have emerged in Africa as part of the decentralization process and this has increased competition between ports at subregional and national levels. Second, competition for the port market has intensified as private operators seek to win concessions. Third, on the shipping side, the explosion of maritime services has led to the dismantlement of the liner conferences[1] that divided up the market with little or no competition across liners. Fourth, greater competition across different modes of transport has put pressure on the port subsector. If these reforms have contributed to improvements in efficiency and a reduction in the cost of maritime services, the results have been uneven, varying across subregions and countries, depending on the institutional environment.

This chapter focuses on institutions and on the role of the regulatory framework in increasing the efficiency of maritime services. Weak institutions have a negative impact on trade through several channels.

First, poor management contributes to delays at the *port level,* as it slows the loading and unloading of cargo. Weak institutions also increase delays at the *border,* when cumbersome customs procedures slow the movement of goods at entry and exit. High taxes and customs fees, sometimes accompanied by extortion along the import–export chain, characterize those countries with a weak regulatory framework.[2] Third, they can lead to inefficient *regulation and control* of the fleet, leading to substandard safety levels and labor rights which ultimately cause delays and affect trade adversely. All these inefficiencies contribute to high trade costs along the logistics chain. A key issue is whether regulatory reform can be successful in an environment with weak governance at the sectoral level.

Although institutional reforms have taken place in the African port subsector, many countries have not yet adopted global "best-practice" methods, resulting in a great disparity across several measures of port efficiency. To give an example, in North Africa, average port costs on 20-ft containers amount to Euro 370 in Casablanca, Euro 210 in Rades-Tunis, and Euro 70 in Alexandria. On the other hand, average port transit delays total 15 days in Alexandria, but only 9 days in Casablanca and Tunis (Kostianis, 2005).

---

[1] A liner conference is an agreement between two or more shipping companies to provide a scheduled cargo and/or passenger service on a particular trade route under uniform rates and common terms. Since October 2008, the EU has banned liner conferences for shipping companies serving EU ports by abolishing the Far East Freight Conference (FEFC), following the example of their American counterparts. This decision implied the banning of certain activities, in particular price fixing and capacity regulation.

[2] Empirical evidence in Kandiero and Wadhawan (2003) shows that trade performance as measured by trade openness (trade to GDP) will yield optimal benefits if the quality of institutions (i.e. less corruption in customs) in developing countries is improved substantially.

Before designing and carrying out any port reforms, a detailed and complete assessment of the objectives that the public sector is seeking to achieve should be drawn up. The participation of the private sector, even if deemed beneficial or resulting in improvements in port efficiency, should not be considered as an end in itself. Indeed, reforms to increase port privatization should be a means to achieve precise and clear public interest objectives, taking into account economic and social needs. In this context, the objectives of port sector reform could range from expanding/ modernizing container-handling capacity, to stimulating economic growth, to reducing government expenditures on the sector, so that limited public funds can be channeled to other more pressing social needs. Private participation in port services, and more generally, in the infrastructure sector, is but one of the many instruments available to solve specific problems and to achieve explicit public interest objectives.

This chapter reviews the reforms in the port subsector in Africa, focusing on the regulatory framework and several efficiency indicators of port services. It also compares trade costs in Africa with those of other regions. The analysis encompasses port management models that range from fully state owned to fully privately owned (the latter being when the private sector owns the hard infrastructure as well as delivering port services). In view of fact that the quality of governance varies across countries and that ports deliver both public goods and private services, there is a need to adopt appropriate ownership and regulatory structures, which are likely to be country-specific.

This chapter then moves on to discuss broad trends in port reforms across African subregions, contextualizing these within the categories of port management models presented previously. We then turn our attention to trends in the reform of the regulatory framework: the institutions, the regulation of the fleet, and port management. The final section of the chapter situates these African reforms within the global framework, using several indicators ranging from perceptions by business to more comparable and standardized measures drawn from aggregate indicators. The comparisons show that progress is being made, although more efforts are required to compete on a global scale.

Institutional Set-up of Port Management in Africa

Globally, 80 percent of container traffic is handled by commercial global operators, such as Dubai Ports, Hutchison, Port of Singapore Authority (PSA), and International Container Terminal Services Inc. (ICTSI), who won concessions to invest and operate the world's major common-user container ports under the "landlord" scheme. In Africa, however, as discussed below, about 50–70 percent of traffic is still handled by public/ government operators in tool ports or public service ports. It was observed that in a considerable number of African ports, public sector ownership of the port infrastructure and superstructure, together with direct involvement of the ministry in the provision of port services, has generally been responsible for inefficiency and non-profitable performance. Two major generic reasons were highlighted in the *Bank Review of the Maritime Sector in Africa* (AfDB, 2001):

    (i) Regulation of tariff structures for ships and other services at levels below the cost of providing such services and some cases, even below the break-even point; and

    (ii) Overstaffing of the Port Authorities (PA), resulting in government subsidy in regard to both recurrent and capital expenditures. This issue will be discussed in the next chapter.

Several factors have contributed to this situation:

- A large number of African ports are too small to be commercially attractive to private investors;
- Commercial and political uncertainties in several African countries, which are linked to the institutional and political environment, further deter private investment;
- Many African ports operate in a monopolistic environment, while complex cross-border procedures effectively limit inter-port competition.[3] This makes it difficult for the public sector to privatize the port services, since strong public regulatory institutions are needed to control these natural monopolies;

---

[3] For instance, traders from Tanzania will mostly use Dar es Salaam while those from Kenya use Mombasa only. This differs from the situation in Europe, where a lot of German cargo uses Rotterdam (the Netherlands), the largest port for Norwegian cargo is Gothenburg (Sweden), and Polish cargo transits mostly through Hamburg.

- Ports may face opposition to reforms from trade unions and vested interests, who oppose private sector investments that might reduce direct employment in their ports.

Alternative Forms of Port Administration

Port reform is complicated by several unique characteristics. First, ports provide a combination of public goods (e.g. the coastal protection works necessary to create port basins) and private goods (e.g. cranes, quays, and other "hard" infrastructure). The public goods are indivisible and nonrival, which excludes private sector involvement, thereby justifying public intervention for their provision. This is important since these public goods create positive externalities (increases in trade and trade-related services) and social benefits over and above the market price that would be paid by private commercial operators. Also, ports are increasingly integrated into global logistics chains and the public benefits they provide are taking on regional and global attributes. This complicates the administration of ports, which is in the hands of the port authority (PA[4]) — a governing body, generally public, which plays a coordination role, ensures the proper use of common facilities, and takes care of safety issues as well as the general design of port facilities (see Box 3.1).

Three types of organizational models accommodate this diversity: the *landlord*

---

[4] PA is interchangeably referred to as "Port Authority," "Port Management," or "Port Administration," each definition describing the functions carried out by the PA.

Box 3.1: The role of the Port Authority

The term Port Authority (PA) was defined in 1977 by a commission of the European Union (EU) as a "State, municipal, public, or private body, which is largely responsible for the tasks of construction, administration and sometimes the operation of port facilities and, in certain circumstances, for security." The PA can be created at different government levels: national, regional, provincial, or local. The most common form is the local port authority. In this case, the PA is an authority administering only one port. However, in some African countries national port authorities still exist, as in Tanzania and Nigeria.

In principle, the role of the PA should be confined to the provision of infrastructure (and superstructure, depending on the PA model) and the coordination of port services. Often though, the PA has broad regulatory powers relating to both shipping and port operations. It is also responsible for applying conventions, laws, rules, and regulations (e.g. relating to public safety and security, the environment, navigation, and healthcare) and it can be assigned police powers (World Bank, 2007). The PA can also publish port bylaws, with rules and regulations concerning the behavior of vessels in port, use of port areas, and other issues. The PA also provides the investment planning and financing, or technical and economic regulation of the private operators.

Statutory powers of a national port authority

As stated in the UNCTAD *Handbook for Port Planners in Developing Countries* (based on the assumption that operational decisions will be taken locally), a national port authority should have the following statutory powers:

- *Investment*: Power to approve proposals for port investments for amounts above a certain level. The criterion for approval would be that the proposal was broadly in accordance with a national plan, which the authority would maintain.
- *Financial policy*: Power to set common financial objectives for ports (for example, required return on investment defined on a common basis), with a common policy on what infrastructure will be funded centrally versus locally, and advising the government on loan applications.
- *Tariff policy*: Power to regulate rates and charges as required and to protect the public interest.
- *Labor policy*: Power to set common recruitment standards, a common wage structure, and common qualifications for promotion; and the power to approve common labor union procedures.
- *Licensing*: When appropriate, power to establish principles for the licensing of port employees or agents.
- *Information and research*: Power to collect, collate, analyze, and disseminate statistical information on port activity for general use, and to sponsor research into port matters as required.
- *Legal*: Power to act as legal advisor to local port authorities.

Source: World Bank (2007)

---

port; the *tool port*; and the *services port* (public or private) models. As shown in Table 3.1, regardless of the model selected, the physical infrastructure (berths, etc.) is both owned and managed by the PA. However, depending on the model chosen, the superstructure and equipment (cranes, etc.) may be owned/managed by either the PA or by the private operator, as detailed below.

In the ***services port*** model, the infrastructure, superstructure and services are all managed by a PA which could be public (*public services port*) or private (*private services port*). In the ***tool port*** model, a public PA owns the superstructure and equipment, while the private sector operates the facilities through licenses or management contracts. This tool port model is usually adopted for medium and small ports where, because of the small volume, the private sector lacks incentives to invest in infrastructure.

In the ***landlord port*** model, the PA owns the facilities to avoid the risk of monopolization of essential assets by private firms. The PA then either rents or awards in concession these facilities to private operators, leaving as many activities as possible in the hands of the private sector (Matto *et al.*, 1999; Trujillo and Nombela, 2000).

Until the 1980s, private sector involvement in ports was negligible owing to the combination of restrictive labor practices, centralized control by the government, and an unwillingness to invest in infrastructure. On occasion, investments in infrastructure were not aligned to the needs of foreign trade and shipping.

A first shift occurred with the recognition that the role of the public sector should be restricted to the provision of public goods. A second occurred with the outsourcing of public services to the private sector. Port governance successively evolved through a nationalization period, when national planification was prevalent and public ownership of economic activities was widespread, to a period where both public and private port operations were involved. The most recent wave of privatizations has seen a shift toward the landlord port model,

Table 3.1: Main types of organizational structures for Port Authorities (PAs)

Organizational type	Infrastructure	Superstructure & Equipment	Services
Landlord port	PA owned PA managed (1)	Privately owned Privately managed	Privately managed
Tool port	PA owned PA managed	PA owned Privately managed	Privately managed
Public Services port	PA owned PA managed	PA owned PA managed	PA managed
Private Services port (2)	PA owned PA managed	PA owned PA managed	PA managed

Source: Estache and Trujillo (2008a).
Notes: (1) In some cases privately managed; (2) In this case the Port Authority is a private organization.

which is dominant in terms of TEU movement. This has come to be the preferred model at the international level for its efficiency and productivity (especially for large and medium ports).

In Africa the public services port is the dominant port management model. When a government contemplates a shift away from a public services port to a private services port, it needs to determine what risks the public sector can afford to bear and what risks it can shift to the private sector. This is because port operations require several categories of long-lived assets, some of which are more amenable to private investments than others. Charges for infrastructure equipment (on-dock storage and transshipment facilities) can be awarded through competition, whereas charges for breakwaters, channels and turning basins are essentially a public good with a high marginal benefit and a low marginal cost, so that a private operator would make a monopoly profit by charging a price based on user benefits. Should this last category of high-cost infrastructure be placed in the hands of private operators (as it would under the private sector model, as indicated in Figure 3.1), the private sector investors would face a high-risk tradeoff between their ability to set prices independently without regulatory constraint when considering their very long-term investment decision. This explains why countries with weak governance may fail to procure the hoped-for investment from the private sector in a reform that concessions services of long-lived assets to the private sector.

The tradeoff shown in Figure 3.1 may help explain the patterns of public–private

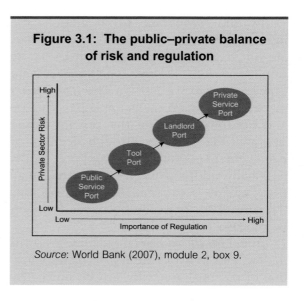

Figure 3.1: The public–private balance of risk and regulation

Source: World Bank (2007), module 2, box 9.

involvement in the port subsector across Africa, which are displayed in Table 3.2. Investing in high-cost and long-term infrastructure carries high risks for the private sector, in the absence of an independent and autonomous regulatory framework (such an institutional framework is considered as "best-practice" for the port subsector). Consequently, in Africa one observes few instances of landlord and private services ports where the superstructure and equipment are privately owned.[5]

Port Reform in Africa

Much progress has been made in the last decade toward institutional reform in the infrastructure sector, with ports achieving the greatest success after telecommunications and

---

[5] The World Bank Port Reform Tool Kit (June 2003) discusses choices and options for reforms in the port subsector.

Table 3.2: Port management models and regulatory agencies in selected African countries

Country	Management Model	Agency responsible for regulation
Djibouti	Management concession	Ministry of Transport
Sudan	Service port	Sudan Sea Ports Corp.
Kenya	Service port	Ministry of Information, Transport, and Communications
Tanzania	Part landlord, part service port	Tanzania Ports Authority
Madagascar	Part landlord, part service port	NA
Namibia	Service port	Namibian Ports Authority
South Africa	Service port	Transnet National Ports Authority
Angola	Part landlord, part service port	Ministry of Transport, Merchant Marine and Ports Division
Democratic Republic of the Congo	Service port	NA
Congo (Brazzaville)	Service port	Port Autonome de Pointe Noire
Cameroon	Part landlord, part service port	National Ports Authority
Nigeria	Landlord model	Nigerian Ports Authority
Benin	Service port	Port Autonome de Cotonou
Ghana	Landlord model	Ghana Ports and Harbor Authority
Côte d'Ivoire	Part landlord, part service port	The Autonomous Port of Abidjan
Senegal	Part landlord, part service port	Direction of Ports and the Interior Maritime Transport
Cape Verde	Service port	NA

Source: Cameron (2008); Ocean Shipping Consultants (2008).

ahead of roads and railroads, where private sector financing has been low. Institutional reform in the infrastructure sector in general, including ports, has placed emphasis on the quality of governance in state-owned enterprises (SOEs) of which many remain, particularly in the port subsector.

Disparities in economic and institutional development across African countries make it difficult to pick out a standard "African" model of reform. Table 3.2 shows that the public–private partnership (PPP) takes many forms which vary from region to region and even within the same country. According to

a 2001 UNCTAD survey,[6] some 24 of the 34 ports in the sample featured private sector

---

[6] In 2001, UNCTAD carried out a survey of 50 African ports across all regions, entitled "Expériences de la participation du secteur privé dans les ports africains" [The experience of African ports with private sector participation]. The objective was to obtain an idea of the involvement of the private sector in port management and development and in privatizing services. The replies (34 relating to 46 ports) came from either the port authorities or the responsible ministry, even for ports that were privately managed. The results of the survey alluded to here were not published.

participation while seven ports had plans to bring in private operators by 2005 (UNCTAD, 2003). Yet in Africa, where a single port is a natural monopoly, it is tempting for the government to maintain direct ownership control and operation, which allows the port to cross-subsidize other government activities.

Further, transit operations account for quite a large share of total activity. The port of Djibouti, which absorbs 75 percent of shipments currently destined for Ethiopia, is a notable example (UNCTAD, 2003). Regional competition for the lucrative transshipment business provides the impetus for reforms leading to a public–private partnership. According to the 2001 UNCTAD survey, when entering into partnership with the private sector, the main objectives of African port authorities were to: enhance the productivity, efficiency, and quality of their services (45 percent); modernize their infrastructure (17 percent); reduce port costs (20 percent each); and attract private investors (17 percent).

Overall, private participation in ports has been quite successful in 24 countries in SSA, with 26 container terminal concessions investing a total of US$ 1.3 billion since the mid-1990s. More importantly, before examining the varied regional experience, it is useful to keep in mind one of the findings of the recent Africa Infrastructure Country Diagnostic (AICD) study (World Bank, 2009). This concludes that even though the private concessions approach has not substantially bridged the financial gap in infrastructure needs, it has made a significant contribution to improving operational performance, leading to the recovery of funds lost to various sources of inefficiency.

Subregional Trends

The participation of the private sector has generally been initiated through the award of concessions to operate the port services and terminals, rather than through the sale of public port assets (Trujillo and Tovar, 2007). Concession contracts can take diverse forms, depending on the port size, initial conditions, and the type of service considered. The types of contract include: BOO (Build, Operate, and Own); BOT or ROT (Build/Rehabilitate, Operate, and Transfer); joint-ventures; leasing; licensing and management contract (Trujillo and Nombela, 2000; Guasch, 2007).

The use of concession contracts has emerged as the preferred method for private sector participation, rather than selling seaports' hard infrastructure assets to the private sector. The recent Word Bank (2009) AICD report concludes that there is great potential to continue granting concessions. For example, the port of Maputo in Mozambique has been fully privatized on a 15-year renewable concession basis (DP World/Grindrod).

It is now common practice for container terminals to be concessioned out to international operators, such as DP World (Djibouti, Dakar, Algiers, and Maputo), AP Moller (Walvis Bay, Luanda, Lagos, and Tema) and Hitchinson (Dar es Salaam and Mombasa). South African ports are the major exception to this trend, as the government there has decided to keep container terminals under state control (Transnet Port Terminals).

General cargo and special terminals are also often privately operated, particularly the stevedoring and warehousing operations. Large dedicated bulk terminals are also most often privately operated, particularly when linked to a single customer or consortium. The large iron ore terminal at Saldanha Bay in South Africa, handling more than 40 mtpa, is, however, operated by Transnet Port Terminals, with Transnet also being responsible for the provision and operation of the 800-km dedicated rail line.

The highest rates of private sector participation are recorded in North and East Africa (41.7 percent) and in South Africa (37.5 percent). In East and Southern Africa, this reflects the political commitment by the governments of the Southern African Development Community (SADC), who have dedicated financial and technological resources and expertise to modernize and increase the efficiency of their national and regional transportation systems. SADC also recognized the need to create a liberal environment conducive to the development of a partnership with the private sector for operations and investments in the port subsector (UNCTAD, 2003; Cameron, 2008).

In West Africa, the privatization process is following two divergent paths (Harding *et al.*, 2007). The first has led to the establishment of the statutory port companies, who offer shares. Shares are at present owned only by Treasuries, but equity participation by others is being opened up. The second path follows the continental trend toward the concessioning of specialized terminals. For example, in Senegal stevedoring services have been transferred to the private sector in Dakar port, which has progressively evolved toward a landlord port system (Trujillo and Nombela, 1999).

Implications of Privatization

Notwithstanding growing participation by the private sector, especially in port operations and services, in Africa the public sector still plays a major role in the seaport system (Baird, 2000). In the vast majority of African countries (and elsewhere), the public sector retains a central role in seaport planning, regulation, development and investment through the PA, marine department, or other agencies. In many respects, governments seem unwilling to fully privatize the industry, preferring to retain control over what is deemed to be a strategic national asset. This is despite the fact that private sector participation in port operations in Africa has generally been seen as successful, because it is almost always financially viable, with pricing influenced by a largely captive market.

As a result, the landlord port model has not been widely adopted in Africa and the involvement of international private operators remains very low. So far, only Nigeria and Ghana have moved toward partial or complete adoption of the landlord port model, while several francophone countries have adopted a hybrid model. According to the review conducted by Ocean Shipping Consultants in 2008, this trend is striking. Of the 17 African countries included in their study, nearly half retained the public services port model, while nine countries had begun to privatize certain areas by concessioning out to the private sector key container facilities (Ocean Shipping Consultants, 2008).

One important consequence of privatization is that the government expenditures are lowered as the role of public sector involvement is reduced. Consequently, some of the costs are transferred to the private sector, which will, ultimately, boost government revenues through concession agreements and taxes (World Bank, 2007). In general, the private sector also offers greater opportunities in terms of responsiveness and adaptation to the services required from the shipping companies. In addition, privatization favors the transfer of technical know-how for more efficient terminal management (Gillen and Cooper, 1995). On the other hand, the seaport industry has large capital needs, especially in the context of reduced public subsidies. Consequently, private financing has become a very important opportunity for many countries. Indeed, total investments from the private sector for container terminal concessions in SSA has reached US$ 1.3 billion since the mid-1990s, which has gone some way toward bridging the infrastructure financing gap.

Studies on the impact of privatization on African port efficiency indicate improvements across several measures of productivity (Al-Eraqi *et al.*, 2007; Clark *et al.*, 2004; Valentine, 2000). Enhanced productivity has been achieved mainly at container terminals where private investment has occurred. In container terminals, an increase in traffic and greater efficiency in services as well as enhanced intraregional competition were observed from the very first year of private-sector involvement (UNCTAD, 2003; Foster, 2008). Certain ports, however, are still suffering from the effects of substandard practices and poor performance (delays, missing goods, etc.) of other services such as

customs and security, and from the deficiencies of overland transportation such as railroads and roads. The case of the Apapa Container Terminal in Lagos, Nigeria, described in Box 3.2, illustrates how such problems can impact efficiency.

As we have seen, not only can private sector participation improve productivity, but it can also open the way to the adoption of modern technologies and management practices that have revolutionized the world markets for shipping and cargo handling. The mobilization of private capital and management skills could also improve efficiency and help to develop a logistics system in terminal operations and other areas in the port structure (World Bank, 2009).

In spite of this overall positive assessment of private sector participation, the relationship between ownership structure and performance is complex, as it goes beyond "hard" infrastructure to encompass "soft" institutional reform (Gonzalez and Trujillo, 2009; Brooks and Cullinane, 2006; Estache and Trujillo, 2008). For example, prior to moving toward a more privatized type of management, the culture of performance measurement might be lacking; this may need to be introduced by private operators. Second, the privatization process is predicated on there being a robust regulatory and governance framework in place. Research suggests that deregulation may have a negative impact on efficiency in the short term, as there are costs incurred in moving from a regulated to a deregulated environment. Third, privatization of the port subsector usually generates numerous deregulations and reforms in peripheral

---

Box 3.2: Obstacles to port efficiency: the case of the Apapa Container Terminal, Lagos

Lagos port has long been notorious for inadequate facilities and congestion. As part of a broader program of port reform in early 2006, the Nigerian PA awarded a concession to APM Terminals to manage, operate, and develop the Apapa Container Terminal, with the remit to increase capacity from 220,000 TEUs per year to 1.6 million TEUs. Within months of awarding this concession, delays for berthing space at the Apapa terminal had reduced significantly. Moreover shipping lines dropped their congestion surcharge from Euro 525 to Euro 75 per TEU, saving the Nigerian economy US$ 200 million a year. By early 2009, new gantry cranes had been acquired to triple the original capacity of the port.

   Nevertheless, while the port's equipment is now able to handle more than 500 containers per day for customs examinations, by the end of each day the majority are returned to stacking. By January 2009 the port was clogged with uncollected containers, and at the end of February 2009 the head of the Nigerian PA announced a temporary suspension of ship entry with immediate effect — to last until some time in mid-April to enable terminals to clear "alarming" backlogs. The controller of the Nigeria Customs Service for Apapa blamed the backlog on the need to physically examine 100 percent of containers because of the high incidence of concealment and false declarations by importers.

   However, this was not the only problem, as even cleared containers were not being collected. At the end of January it was reported that 9,741 containers were waiting in the port for delivery to the importers. Yet 851 of these had already been cleared by customs, all charges paid, and with documentation completed, but not picked up by agents. The Nigerian PA consequently proposed introducing demurrage charges of US$ 4 per TEU in a bid to force owners to move them out of the ports. However, the agents blamed a lack of trucks, arguing that many had been booked to empty containers.

   While the moratorium on the entry of new vessels was lifted in early March 2008, some backlogs and delays persisted and significant organizational and regulatory problems remain.

Source: From press reports assembled by Cornelis Kruk. Also see World Bank (2009; Chapter 12).

---

sectors — in customs, shipping, stevedoring, and handling companies. All these issues need to be factored into the decision to move toward a more privatized form of port management.

   The complementarities across reforms make it difficult to isolate and measure the impact of port privatization and performance. However, as shown in the case of the Apapa Container Terminal in Lagos (Box 3.2), privatization alone is not enough to achieve maximum efficiencies — it must be accompanied by regulatory reform.

Regulatory Framework

An appropriate regulatory framework, covering labor management and the regulation of the fleet, is a prerequisite for the maritime sector to function efficiently and competitively as it creates the conditions for a contestable market structure for port and maritime services. This framework should cover various functions: the functioning of markets and the setting of tariffs, revenues, or profits; controlling market entry or exit; and maintaining fair and competitive behavior and practices within the port subsector (World Bank,

2007). As ports evolve into landlord port authorities, for example, liberalization and deregulation reduce monopoly power for certain port services, allowing free entry by private service providers. On the other hand, in activities where there is a risk that private operators might adopt monopolistic practices, oversight of pricing practices by a regulator will help to scale up efficiency.

Regulatory institutions are also needed to exert some degree of control over the infrastructure assets used by private firms. The task of the regulator is a difficult one as it takes place under asymmetric information conditions, in that firms know their costs and market conditions better than the regulator does.

For contestable activities, services previously provided by the public port authority such as pilotage, tug assistance, vessel stevedoring, cargo handling, storage, and yard services may fall under the responsibility of private operators. Private participation in this regard reduces subsidies and costs, and helps achieve full cost recovery from users directly (Notteboom and Wilkelmans, 2001). However, the profit maximization objectives of private operators need to be checked by regulatory oversight to control the exercise of market power, to ensure that the public goods characteristics of many port sector activities are not undersupplied and, more broadly, to ensure that the public interest is upheld.

Regulatory Institutions

Typically, the Ministry of Transport oversees the development of transport and port policies and the preparation and implementation of transport and port laws,

national regulations, and decrees. Before the ratification of national laws and regulation, the Ministry makes sure that they (i) incorporate relevant elements of international conventions,[7] and (ii) represent the country in bilateral and multilateral port and shipping forums and during the negotiation of agreements concerning waterborne or intermodal transit privileges. The Ministry also prepares financial and economic analyses to evaluate the socioeconomic and financial feasibility of projects, taking the context of national policies and priorities into account.

As to implementation, in many countries, independent bodies such as the transport directorates are hosted within a ministry to carry out executive functions. A typical list of duties performed by a maritime and ports directorate is long (indicating the power of the regulatory body) and includes: the inspection and registration of ships and shipping companies; the protection of the marine environment; the implementation of traffic safety measures; compliance with the International Ship and Port Facility Security Code; the maritime education and training of merchant officers and seafarers through maritime academies, exams and licenses; the execution of the national port policy; the construction of protective works, sea locks, port entrances, the control of port state (based on the terms of the Paris and Tokyo MoUs); in the case of a maritime incident,

---

[7] For example, the International Convention of Safety for Life at Sea (SOLAS), the United Nations Convention on the Law of the Sea, the International Convention for the Prevention of Pollution from Ships (MARPOL). (See World Bank, 2007.)

the investigation and adjudication; the regulatory and licensing functions; and the construction and maintenance of the vessel traffic systems and aids to navigation and the search and rescue functions.

In an environment where competition across ports and across modes of transportation is increasing, it is important for port regulators to be given autonomy to carry out their regulatory functions. In Africa there is no evidence of the independent regulation of ports outside of South Africa[8] (Cameron, 2008). Nigeria has plans to set up an independent regulator as part of its port reform package, but has not moved beyond the planning stage. The regulatory function is therefore undertaken by other bodies in such cases, typically the Ministry of Transport or other government agency, such as a national or local port-management body, or public port authorities. Of the 13 countries featured in Table 3.2, four are regulated at the Ministry of Transport level and the rest by port authorities or port management bodies that are directly or indirectly under government control.

A sound and transparent legal framework is therefore necessary to ensure credibility, openness, and transparency in the reform process and to define PPPs. Moreover, to ensure the success of the reform process, it is essential to establish procedures for reducing the workforce in a socially acceptable way. This is important in the context of a shift toward containerization, which involves more capital-intensive techniques and a substitution of capital for labor. In a number of ports in developing and developed countries, overstaffing has been a contentious issue that has to be addressed in port reorganizations (see Nigerian and Tunisian experiences detailed in Box 3.3). In numerous cases, the workforce in ports is bloated and the success of reforms rests on a downsizing of the labor force.

Regulation of the African Shipping Industry

As the world shipping industry has become more capital-intensive and more technically demanding, it has witnessed strong concentration. For example, in 2009 the top 10 service operators controlled 51 percent of the worldwide containership TEU capacity (UNCTAD, 2009; Table 32). The number of active African shipping lines has decreased and they are being marginalized. At the global level in 2009, 35 countries controlled over 95 percent of the world merchant fleet (UNCTAD, 2009; Table 12). This list did not include any African countries.

For container shipping, regulations pertaining to issues such as capacity and quality of shipments have a large impact on maritime transport. Reforms aimed at harmonization would reduce costs and since maritime transportation is international,

---

[8] When the National Ports Act came into effect in 2006 in South Africa, a *Ports Regulator* was established, becoming operational in 2008. The Ports Regulator fulfills the following functions: (i) it regulates the port systems in line with the government's strategic objectives, including the annual approval of National Ports Authority tariffs; (ii) it promotes an equitable access to ports and facilitates and services provided by ports; and (iii) it monitors the activities of the National Ports Authority to ensure that it perform its functions in accordance with the Act.

Box 3.3: Integrating labor force reforms into port reforms: the cases of Tunisia and Nigeria

Tunisia

Tunisia has awarded 21 port concessions since 2000. The country has moved very cautiously along the path of labor force reform since the concessioning process was legalized in March 1999, which led to the establishment of the Code for Trade Maritime Ports. The principal objectives of the Code were to introduce new work schedules, allowing the port to operate 24/7, in a drive to increase the efficiency of handling activities, and create an incentive for manufacturing companies to ensure adequate training of the workforce.

Discussions between the *Office de la Marine Marchande et des Ports* and labor unions and delegates of the dockers' corporation lasted several years until the parties finally reached an agreement in 2004. The agreement made provision for the non-replacement of retiring dockers, indemnity by the government, extension of social benefits until 60 years old, and gradual diminution of the powers of the dockers' corporations.

(*Source*: Discussions with the *Office de la Marine Marchande et des Ports*, Tunisia)

Nigeria

The Nigerian port subsector has witnessed one of the most vigorous concessioning processes in Africa. From 2003 to 2006, 21 concessions were granted to 15 different local and international terminal operators. The government had to reach an agreement with labor unions on severance packages and to secure funding for the retrenchments and pensions, and also had to prevent labor unions from calling widespread strikes. Negotiations with labor unions lasted several months until agreement was finally reached on a severance package in February 2006.

these reforms need to be carried out at a regional or global level. However, obtaining cooperation across different jurisdictions, regions, and countries is no easy task. This is particularly the case in Africa where, in spite of many regional trade agreements, little devolution of national powers to supranational entities has taken place. However, some progress is being made at the international level. Following many years of negotiations, a new set of international rules to increase the security and ease the growing volume of containerized trade has been drawn up and ratified by over 20 countries (see Box 3.4).

Despite the progress made in African shipping from the viewpoint of deregulation, the industry still labors under a number of constraints. One is largely historic and dates back to 1983, to the entry into force of the UN Convention on the Code of Conduct for Liner Conferences, popularly known as the "40-40-20 Rule." This states that 40 percent of freight should be allocated to shipowners established in the country of origin, 40 percent to owners established in the country of destination, and 20 percent to shipowners of any country (cross-traders) (Teravaninthorn and Raballand, 2009). The Rule was established to encourage the development of the shipping industry in developing countries, and to counteract the application of cartel-type arrangements by liner conferences. In fact, some have argued that this Rule led to market distortions and increases in maritime costs, which had a negative effect on the development of domestic fleet industries for several countries in Africa (Harding *et al.*, 2007; Teravaninthorn and Raballand, 2009).

In 1992, the European Court ruled that "liner conferences" were illegal monopolies. Despite this, they are still regularly used to service many ports in Africa. For example, West and Central Africa countries are served by four conferences: COWAC (Continent — West Africa Conference) covering trade between North Europe and West Africa; UKWAL (UK — West Africa Lines) for trade between UK and West Africa; CEWAL (Central — West Africa Lines) for trade between North Europe and Central Africa; and MEWAC (Mediterranean — West Africa Conference) for trade between the Mediterranean region and West Africa (Harding *et al.*, 2007).

Box 3.4: Convention on Contracts for the International Carriage of Goods Wholly or Partly by Sea

After exhaustive negotiations between 2001 and 2008, a new Convention on Contracts for the International Carriage of Goods Wholly or Partly by Sea ("the **Rotterdam Rules**") was approved by the United Nations Commission on International Trade Law (UNCITRAL) in July 2008 and was adopted by the UN General Assembly on December 12, 2008. On September 23, 2009, 16 countries officially expressed their support for the Convention by becoming signatories during an official signing ceremony in Rotterdam. As at January 6, 2010 the number of signatories had risen to 21, namely: Armenia, Cameroon, Congo, Denmark, France, Gabon, Ghana, Greece, Guinea, Madagascar, Mali, the Netherlands, Niger, Nigeria, Norway, Poland, Senegal, Spain, Switzerland, Togo and the United States of America.

This new international Convention provides a legal framework for a truly global industry across all the applicable jurisdictions in order to provide legal certainty and uniformity for all stakeholders, shippers, and carriers. The new Rotterdam Rules address the challenges of modern shipping trade: namely, the growth in e-commerce; faster and bigger ships; the massive growth in containerization; quicker port turn-arounds; and modimodal transportation whereby the operator undertakes the entire transport of goods from receipt from shipper's premises to final delivery. The Convention replaces the unimodal maritime liability regimes in the Hague, Hague Visby, and Hamburg Rules.

Although the Convention will lead to increased liability for shipowners, it enshrines many valuable provisions that seek to facilitate and regulate modern shipping practices. In particular it addresses the lacuna that previously existed for maritime transport, where there is also multimodal carriage (both land and sea legs). It clearly demarcates responsibility and liability during the whole transport process. The Rules will apply not only to outgoing maritime transport but also to incoming. Furthermore, the Convention puts in place the infrastructure for the development of e-commerce in maritime transport, to reduce documentation costs and boost efficiency.

Sources: UNCITRAL website; also see Rotterdam Rules website at: http://www.rotterdamrules2009.com/cms/index.php

A further feature of the shipping industry, which acts as a deterrent to any small, nascent shipping line, is the enormous cost of building ships (mega-carriers cost over US$ 100 million). This is a massive barrier to market entry and is exacerbated by the growth of container-ization. This impact was strongly felt after 2004, as the number of line services and companies has decreased in several African countries. In Egypt, the number of international companies providing services to the country's ports fell from 61 in 2004 to 47 in 2009, while in South Africa there are now 30 companies, compared to 38 in 2004 (Viohl and Hoffmann, 2009).

This trend raises concerns about the impact of the continuing process of concentration in liner shipping, especially for countries with a low connectivity. Typically, East Asian ports use vessels in the 8,000–11,000 TEUs range, while most African ports cannot handle efficiently vessels above 2,000 TEUs. Furthermore, the poor connectivity of many African ports, resulting from their small container capacity (see Chapter 2, Map 2.1), means that large international shipping lines are forced to use regional operators for transshipments, which increases shipping costs.[9] Eritrea, Seychelles, and Somalia, for example, only record services from one single international shipping line. Liberia is served by two providers, while Cape Verde and Sierra Leone are served by three liner companies.

The experience of the Caribbean reported in Chapter 1 (Figure 1.5c) shows that freight costs for a standard-size container are much higher when a port is served by only one or a limited number of ships. Figure 3.6 shows that delays are another factor contributing to high freight costs in Africa.

Privatization of maritime transport in Africa is one way to improve efficiency and should lower costs. In the case of North Africa, maritime transport between Mediterranean countries is carried out by national shipping lines which are subject to multiple, sometimes conflicting regulatory systems (such as the Code of Conduct rule described above). In this environment, the existence of a major national public shipowning concern was considered to be a precondition for any liberalization of the maritime transport subsector. However, these countries' fleets are very old (see Table 3.3), very expensive to run, and their performance is mediocre. Moreover, new provisions regarding security and safety (deriving from the International Maritime Organization [IMO], the EU, the International Ship and Port Facilities Security Code [ISPS Code], etc.) have significantly raised the cost of renovating the fleets. As a result, North African countries are now considering a regulatory framework which should enable private North African shipping lines to compete on the northern shore of the Mediterranean.

In the current environment of increasing competition in international maritime transport, regulatory efficiency of the African fleet has nonetheless improved. For example, port state control has become increasingly efficient in Africa. This

---

[9] For example, Maersk uses Salah (Oman) to serve East Africa and Algeciras (Spain) and Tangier (Morocco) to serve West African trade in small vessels.

Table 3.3: Age distribution of merchant fleets as at January 1, 2008

Type	World Total	Developed Economies	Transition Economies	Developing Economies	African Countries including Open Registry*	African Countries excluding Open Registry*
Bulk carriers	12.7	11.9	17.8	12.7	14.0	18.0
Containerships	9.0	8.6	10.6	8.9	6.9	12.3
General cargo	17.1	13.4	20.0	17.6	17.3	22.1
Oil tankers	10.1	7.5	11.2	11.0	11.2	21.4
Other types	14.7	13.1	11.8	15.5	17.2	21.2
All	11.8	9.7	15.5	12.3	11.8	20.5

Source: UNCTAD (2006; 2008).

* Open registry: National ship registry under a national flag, which is open to ships of all nations regardless of nationality.

concerns the control of foreign ships in ports and was originally conceived to back up flag state implementation in order to detect substandard ships. The authorities verify whether the condition of the ship and its equipment comply with international requirements. Port state control has proved to be very effective, as ships usually visit several countries during a single voyage. In this way, ships are regularly controlled without being delayed by unnecessary red-tape (IMO, 2003).

In SSA, three Memoranda of Understanding have been signed in recent years: the Abuja MoU for West and Central Africa; the Mediterranean MoU for Northern Africa and other Mediterranean countries; and the Indian Ocean MoU covering Southern and East Africa (IMO, 2003). The Abuja MOU was signed in 1999 by 16 countries from West, Central, and Southern Africa. However, in their last annual meeting the participants reported weakness in its

implementation, due to the lack of necessary infrastructure and to insufficient political commitment to carry out proper flag state administration and port state control (African Union, 2008).

One may turn to Liberia for an example of a successful fleet regulatory system. The government has set up an open maritime registry, which allows the country of registration to differ from the country of ownership.[10] This is the second largest registry in the world, and includes 3,100 ships of more than 96 million gross tonnes, representing 10 percent of the world's

---

[10] Traditional reasons for choosing an open register and running a "flag of convenience" vessel include: protection from burdensome income taxes, wage scales, and regulations. Liberia is the second open registry at the global level after Panama, and the national fleet in this registry is virtually nonexistent. In 2009, over 90 per cent of the ships registered in Liberia were foreign-owned, principally by German and Greek companies.

oceangoing fleet.[11] The registry has been administered since 2000 by LISCR (the Liberian International Shipping and Corporate Registry), a US-owned and operated company. The LISCR uses a worldwide network of nautical inspectors to conduct annual safety checks in order to safeguard the quality of the shipping registry. Consequently, the Liberian registry is "white-listed" by international safety organizations, indicating above-average safety performance. The open registry generates approximately US$ 18 million per year in government revenues.

Assessing Reforms

The standard reform package for the infrastructure sector calls for market restructuring through divestiture and for private sector involvement, to include the establishment of independent regulators. This package applies to the port subsector as well as to the other subsectors (utilities, water, roads, railroads, and airports). The expected results from implementing this package of reforms are enhanced competition and increased efficiency. However, although some progress has been made in Africa, it has been uneven. Consequently, Africa still lags behind other regions in terms of efficiency indicators for the trade logistics chain.

Institutional Reforms

A comparison of the quality of infrastructure across global regions reported from aggregate indicators is provided in *Global Competitiveness Report* (World Economic

---

[11] See the LISCR website: www.liscr.com.

Forum, 2009). These indicators are collected from opinion surveys administered to executives in multinational enterprises and were collected for 101 countries over the period 2004–2007. Figure 3.2 reports the average value over the period for each of the four infrastructure subsectors (ports, roads, railroads, and airports) as well as providing an overall infrastructure indicator.

The regional averages are ranked in descending order. In general, there is a strong correlation across regions for each indicator (exceptions being Latin America and the Caribbean, which have a high value for airport infrastructure partly because of tourism). North Africa ranks fourth, close behind the East Asia and Pacific region. Africa as a region ranks last, particularly for the landlocked countries in SSA. The landlocked countries are further handicapped by the low values for the quality of the ports they use, and also for the quality of the road and airport infrastructures, possibly reflecting their small size. The difficult predicament of landlocked countries is further examined in Chapter 4.

Figure 3.3 is a scatter plot showing the relation between the quality of port infrastructure and income per capita. The strong correlation suggests two-way causality, since high income per capita is as much caused by good port infrastructure (and other factors) as the overall quality of port infrastructure is determined by per capita income (and other factors). The strong correlation is evidenced by the positioning of the low-income SSA countries in the bottom left-hand corner of the figure. This positive association between a composite index of infrastructure quality

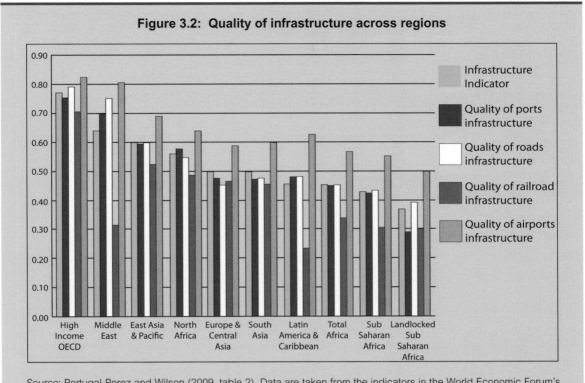

Figure 3.2: Quality of infrastructure across regions

Legend:
- Infrastructure Indicator
- Quality of ports infrastructure
- Quality of roads infrastructure
- Quality of railroad infrastructure
- Quality of airports infrastructure

Source: Portugal-Perez and Wilson (2009, table 2). Data are taken from the indicators in the World Economic Forum's *Global Competitiveness Report* 2008–2009. The aggregate infrastructure index is constructed by factor analysis. *Notes*: Regions ranked by decreasing quality of overall infrastructure . The infrastructure indicator is a simple average of the 4 sub-indicators in the figure. The maximum value taken by the index is unity.

and income per capita will also be analyzed in Chapter 4. The figure also shows that there is quite a lot of variation in infrastructure quality after controlling for differences in income per capita. This spread is particularly evident for the high income per capita countries, but it is also present among the North African countries.

A more complete assessment of factors determining performance can be obtained by comparing objective indicators of institutional quality across infrastructure categories, and by examining specific institutional reforms.

A first objective indicator of the efficiency of port services that takes into account both "hard" and "soft" infrastructure is the time it takes to handle cargo at port. Table 3.4 decomposes this indicator into four components (pre-arrival documents; port and terminal handling; customs and inspections; inland transport to warehouse). For all components except "inland transport to

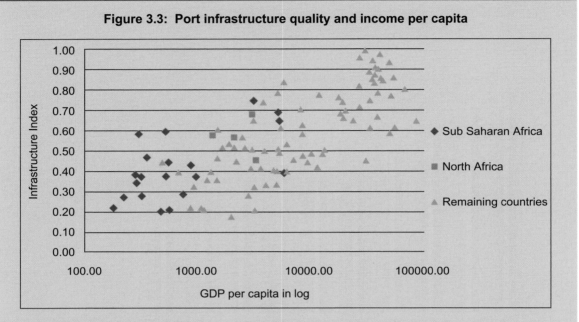

Figure 3.3: Port infrastructure quality and income per capita

Source: Portugal-Perez and Wilson (2009, table 2). Data are taken from the indicators in the World Economic Forum's *Global Competitiveness Report, 2009–2010* and the aggregate infrastructure index is constructed by factor analysis. *Note*: The index is for the sample of countries used in the regional averages reported in Figure 3.3a. Income per capita is expressed in logarithms and maximum value for the index is unity when a score of unity is obtained for each component.

warehouse," the SSA region evidences the longest delays. If, as a rough indicator, one takes the cost-equivalent of one day lost in transport cited in Chapter 1 (one day saved in shipping being equivalent to a 0.8 percent reduction in tariffs), then if SSA were to improve from its present level of 59 days' clearance time to East Asia's average clearance time of 28 days, the cost saving would be equivalent to around 2 percent. (To this, one should add the gains in time if the percentage of cargo inspection were reduced.)

More comprehensive evidence can be gleaned from a recent review of the infrastructure sectors in 24 countries in SSA, accounting for 85 percent of GDP. This suggests that the relative weakness of African practices and institutions resulting in poor governance could contribute to the low perceived score on overall infrastructure quality shown in Figures 3.2 and 3.3.

To establish any links between institutional factors related to infrastructure performance outcomes across countries, a scorecard was developed to cover the three key institutional dimensions: (i) sectoral policy reforms (legislation, restructuring, policy oversight, and private sector involve-

Table 3.4: Port cargo-handling times across regions (days)

Region	Pre-arrival Documents	Port and Terminal Handling	Customs and Inspections	Inland Transport to Warehouse	Total Time	% of Cargo Inspected (import)
OECD high income	8	2	2	2	14	5
East Asia & Pacific	18	3	4	3	28	31
Latin America & Caribbean	24	4	5	3	36	51
Middle East & North Africa	25	5	9	4	43	63
Europe & Central Asia	25	4	7	7	43	18
South Asia	24	6	7	10	47	69
Sub-Saharan Africa	**33**	**8**	**10**	**9**	**59**	**67**
World	23	5	6	5	40	43

Source: Hoffmann (2009) adopted from *World Bank Doing Business 2006*

ment); (ii) amount and quality of regulation (autonomy, transparency, accountability, tools); and (iii) enterprise governance (ownership and shareholder quality, managerial and board autonomy, accounting disclosure, labor and capital market discipline, outsourcing). Indicators that were easy to measure and deemed pertinent by infrastructure experts were then selected to cover each element of the corresponding institutional dimension. These are reported in Figure 3.4, where each indicator takes a maximum value of 1 when "best-practice" status is achieved.[12]

The individual and average scores for each component show most progress in the sectoral reforms, with much less progress on the regulatory and governance fronts.

Overall, the telecommunications subsector — which is of great importance in the overall trade logistics chain — has witnessed the most progress. It is notable that little progress has occurred on the quality of governance, particularly for ports where, as noted earlier, the regulatory bodies are still not autonomous from governance interference.

The lack of progress on governance does not necessarily imply a lack of progress on performance, where private sector participation has ushered in greater efficiencies. Figure 3.5 looks at two transport subsectors — ports and railroads — and breaks down average values of performance according to whether or not services have been concessioned out to the private sector. However, the sample is small (20 observations in ports and 13 in railroads). This explains why the differences in mean performance are not always statistically significant. Nonetheless, overall

---

[12] See World Bank (2009, Box 4.1). The discussion that follows is largely drawn from chapter 4 of that report.

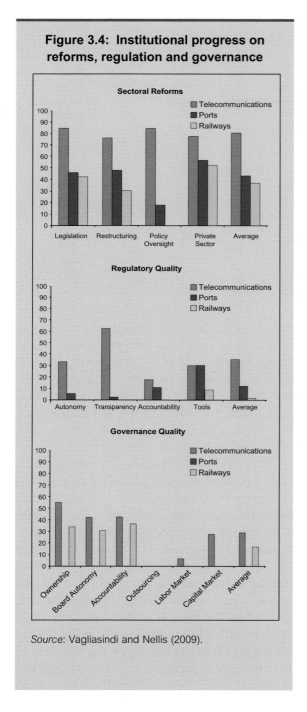

Figure 3.4: Institutional progress on reforms, regulation and governance

Source: Vagliasindi and Nellis (2009).

one can conclude that private sector participation has been associated with improved performance in both subsectors.

Efficiency of the Transport Logistics Chain

Several examples help to show what progress has been made and what remains to be done to overcome the remaining shortcomings in the "soft" component of infrastructure. Customs procedures in Africa in general, but especially in SSA, are lengthy and cumbersome and act as a bottleneck to port efficiency, thereby raising trade costs. The introduction of modern customs procedures would help to relieve this bottleneck and would contribute to the delivery of efficient port and freight transportation systems (Ocean Shipping Consultants, 2008).

Reforming customs is necessary and the major steps that need to be carried out are indicated in Box 3.5. At the same time, three characteristics of the low-income countries of SSA make this task difficult. First, a large share of government revenue is raised at customs. Because the tax base is small, tax rates are high, which encourages tax evasion. Second, customs is where the rents are to be obtained, so this is where extortion is likely to occur when governance is weak. Third, customs officials must fulfill two objectives that are at times conflicting: to raise revenue and to facilitate trade.

Delays at the customs level contribute to high transaction costs. This is clear from regional averages for the number of documents and the number of days needed to import or export a 20-ft container, reported in Figure 3.6. The difference

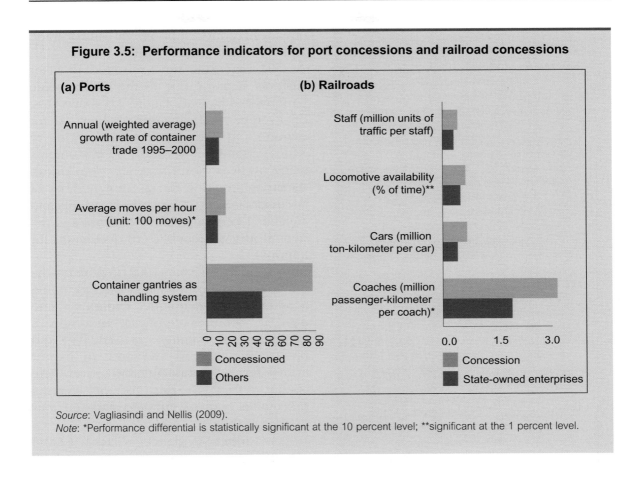

Figure 3.5: Performance indicators for port concessions and railroad concessions

Source: Vagliasindi and Nellis (2009).
Note: *Performance differential is statistically significant at the 10 percent level; **significant at the 1 percent level.

between developed countries and Africa is striking. In North America it takes on average 7 days to export and 8 days to import goods, compared to 34 days and 40 days in Africa. These delays heavily constrain the trade of fragile and perishable products, in particular agricultural commodities. The situation is worst in Central Africa and African landlocked countries, where it takes 55 days and 56 days respectively to clear import procedures.

A similar pattern emerges from Figure 3.6, which shows that in 2008, North Africa was the best performing subregion in the continent for cross-border trade fluidity indicators. For example, in Morocco in 2008 it took about 14 days for exports to clear customs procedures and 19 days for imports, compared to Central African Republic's record of 57 days for exports and 66 days for imports. However, more recent data indicate that in 2008–2009, 14 Sub-Saharan African countries were rated as "most active" in the World Bank's global *Doing Business* league for cross-border trade policy reforms. This was in part due to

Box 3.5: Customs regulatory framework — key issues and questions

The following questions indicate what needs to be done to improve the efficiency of customs:

- Have customs laws, regulations, administrative guidelines, and procedures been reviewed, harmonized, and simplified to reduce unnecessary duplication and red tape?
- Has a process of continuous review and improvement of systems and procedures been introduced?
- Have tariff rates been moderated and the number of different rates of duty rationalized?
- Has a formal process for the review and rationalization of exemptions and concessions been introduced?
- Has a program of consultation and cooperation with other government agencies been established to examine a means of rationalizing regulatory requirements?
- Have international conventions, instruments, and accepted standards including the Revised Kyoto Convention, the WCO HS Convention, the WTO Valuation Agreement, the ATA Carnet Convention, and the WTO TRIPS Agreement, been implemented?
- Do regional customs unions and economic groups adopt internationally agreed standards and work toward regional harmonization of systems and procedures?
- Does the administration actively participate in international benchmarking and information-sharing initiatives?

Source: De Wulf and Sokol (2005).

enhanced donor support for aid-for-trade initiatives (World Bank, 2010).

The extensive time required to clear customs is partly due to the cumbersome paperwork involved. Figure 3.6 shows that, on average, 8 documents are needed for exports and 9 documents for imports in Africa, against 4 and 5 documents respectively in North America. The African countries requiring the greatest number of documents to be completed are: Angola and Malawi (12 documents for exports) and the Central African Republic (18 documents for imports).

Nathan Associates (2002) report on the multiplicity of documents needed to export products in Mozambique. Exporters there need to obtain a certificate of origin, a certificate of quality, a sanitary and phytosanitary certificate, and an export license for each transaction. Moreover there is uncertainty in this list of clearing procedures, which vary across transactions (Clarke, 2005).

As further evidence, Clarke (2005) reports the outcomes of a survey which evaluates the impact of trade and customs regulation on private sector operations. The survey reported that 40 percent of the enterprises involved in exporting claimed that customs and trade regulation represented a serious obstacle in the eight African countries surveyed. By comparison, only 28 percent of exporters in Asia claimed that customs and trade regulations were a serious obstacle. As a result, most importers/exporters have to use clearing agents to clear customs procedures in Africa. Clarke notes that 85 percent of the surveyed importers in Africa use the services of a

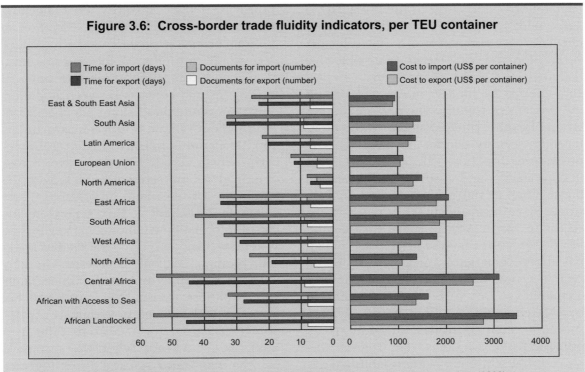

Figure 3.6: Cross-border trade fluidity indicators, per TEU container

Source: Time, number of documents, and costs computed from World Bank *Doing Business* data (2008).
Note: To ensure comparability across countries, these figures represent the official fees levied on a dry-cargo, 20-ft, full container load expressed in US dollars and associated with completing the procedures to export or import the goods. Costs include the costs of documents, administrative fees for customs clearance and technical control, terminal handling charges, and inland transport, and exclude tariffs as well as other trade-related taxes.

clearing agent. He estimates that in Zambia, the median cost is about 1 percent of the shipment value and that 70 percent of the enterprises reported needing licenses for each imported consignment.

African countries have taken steps to improve other aspects of trade and customs administration and regulation. For example, Ghana, Mozambique, and Uganda reduced average processing times from weeks to only a few days but other links in the logistics chain have not followed this trend.

Similarly, North African countries are making serious efforts to reform their customs systems in conformity with the Kyoto Convention and the agreements on international road transport, precisely in order to diminish these obstacles. Operators in North Africa unanimously agree that the major trade barrier can be found at the borders of the Maghreb countries. These steps will make a positive contribution to the World Trade Organization (WTO) negotiations on Trade

Facilitation[13] and Free Trade Area (FTA) agreements. Morocco runs physical spot-checks on goods, using a selective verification approach based on an objective risk analysis technique. In Algeria, physical spot-checks are almost an integral part of the customs procedure. The problem comes when health, phytosanitary and, more recently, security checks are involved. The procedures for these checks are weighty, uncoordinated, and costly. Notwithstanding these inherent difficulties, several success stories have been identified in the customs sector in North Africa. These include the Moroccan customs system reform, which has made remarkable progress (reducing clearance time on average from 1 hour and 45 minutes in December 2001 to 37 minutes by March 2003), and where advance submission of customs declarations is possible for all products.[14] In Tunisia, this procedure is currently being established.

The development of information systems, information technology, and modern customs practices should help to improve the governance of the African ports. Application of this type of "soft" infrastructure reduces clearance and dwell times,[15] while also improving the quality of checking procedures and also removes discretion in the administration process. Steps to reduce delays and corruption at the customs level also include the minimization of physical inspections and contacts between importers or exporters and the customs administration.

Another example of soft infrastructure is the "Transports Internationaux Routiers" (TIR), which allows goods to travel across one or more international borders with the minimum of customs involvement and delays (see Chapter 4, Box 4.4). Here the use of information technology is key for the system to function. For countries that apply TIR, prompt payment of customs dues by logistics companies on behalf of their clients and paperless transit have increased tax revenues and reduced government corruption. It is harder for a customs official to hold out for a bribe when the system is computerized and tracked by a logistics company's bar code. However, it is reported that information technology still offers extortion opportunities for corrupt customs officials — with the customs official refusing to press the "enter" key if importers and exporters do not pay up. Nonetheless, TIR does offer substantive improvements; for example, the average processing time in Ghana was reduced from weeks to a few days after its introduction (Clarke, 2005; *The Economist*, 2008).

Another example is the Cameroonian customs administration, which underwent a major reform in 2006 following the World Customs Organization (WCO) Columbus program. The purpose of the reform was to increase transparency and defeat corruption. The heart of the reform was internal control,

---

[13] The gains from trade facilitation measures for African countries, particularly landlocked ones, are covered in Chapter 4.

[14] See De Wulf and Sokol (2005) and De Wulf and Finateu (2002) for more detailed information on the customs reform in Morocco.

[15] "Dwell time" is the time cargo remains in a terminal's in-transit storage areas, while awaiting shipment (for exports) or onward transportation by road/rail (for imports). Dwell time is one indicator of a port's efficiency: the higher the dwell time, the lower the efficiency.

through the creation of indicators auto-matically and regularly implemented and disseminated by electronic mail to opera-tions managers and the director general. The objective was to strengthen the chain of command by holding each of its links accountable. Since then, three major results have been achieved: the development of a culture of performance-based personal management; "better practices" notifica-tions; and an increase in the productivity of controls (Libom *et al.*, 2009).

Conclusions

A review of the evolution of port management structures around the world shows a shift toward the landlord port model, where all but the hard infrastructure is placed in private sector hands. With a lag, Africa is joining the trend with an increase in concessioning across ports. At the same time, the extent of private investment in physical port infrastructures has been low, reflecting a variety of factors, ranging primarily from the small size of the market to weak institutional support. As a result, many ports are visited by small regional ships which undertake transshipments for the final ocean leg. Both these factors contribute to higher freight costs in the Africa region.

Evidence suggests that reform packages that include regulatory reform and inde-pendence of the regulator from government interference will allow the other ongoing policy reforms a greater chance of success. Such measures will encourage private shipping companies to call on African ports. Furthermore, private operators in the ports will be more inclined to make the

investments in physical infrastructure needed to relieve the bottlenecks identified in Chapter 2.

Overall, the shift to a more privatized environment has not made the same progress in Africa as in the rest of the world. In pursuing reforms, several precautionary steps should be taken by governments. First, before the privatization process is initiated, the government needs to have a clear vision of the objectives that the public sector is trying to achieve. Second, close coordina-tion between the different institutions involved (port institutions, customs, trans-port ministers, labor unions, etc.) is needed to define how their respective roles and interactions should evolve, for the benefit of all parties involved. Third, other efficiency-enhancing factors need to be promoted, such as pro-competitive policies and arrangements, better coordination of the various agencies that intervene at ports, and a reduction in documentation requirements and single-window processing. Finally, beyond ensuring autonomy for the ports regulator, countries should aim at achieving simplification and harmonization in their procedures, which will lead to better coordination and increased efficiency at regional and international levels.

References

AfDB. 2001. *Review of the Bank Group Operations in the Maritime Sub-Sector.* Central Operations Department. Tunis: AfDB.

African Union. 2008. "West and Central Africa Memorandum of Understanding on Port State Control (Abuja MoU)."

Presentation at the First Session of the Conference of Ministers of Transport, Algiers, Algeria.

Al-Eraqi, A.S., C. Pestana-Barros, A. Mustaffa, and A.T. Khader. 2007. "Evaluating the Location Efficiency of Arabian and African Seaports Using Data Envelopment Analysis (DEA)." WP 019/2007/DE/UECE. School of Economics and Management, Technical University of Lisbon.

Baird, A. 2000. "Port Privatization: Objectives, Process and Financing." *Ports and Harbors,* 45: 14–19.

Brooks, M.R. and K. Cullinane. 2006. "Devolution, Port Governance and Port Performance." *Research in Transport Economics,* 17: 631–60.

Cameron, S. 2008. "Africa Infrastructure Diagnostic Study — Port Sector." Mike Mundy Associates, Ocean Shipping Consultants, Ghana, February.

Clark, X., D. Dollar, and A. Micco. 2004. "Port Efficiency, Maritime Transport Costs and Bilateral Trade." NBER Working Paper No. 10353. Cambridge, MA: National Bureau of Economic Research.

Clarke, G.R.G. 2005. "Beyond Tariffs and Quotas: Why Don't African Manufacturers Export More?" Policy Research Working Paper No. 3617. Washington, DC: World Bank.

De Wulf, L. and E. Finateu. 2002. "Best Practices in Customs Administration Reform — Lessons from Morocco." World Bank PREM notes, (67). Washington, DC: World Bank.

De Wulf, L. and J.B. Sokol (eds). 2005. *Customs Modernization Handbook.* Washington, DC: World Bank.

***Economist.* 2008.** "Network Effects: Connectivity and Commitment Pay Dividends in African Transport", October 16.

Estache, A. and L. Trujillo. 2008. "Privatization in Latin America: The Good, the Ugly and the Unfair." In G. Roland and E. Stiglitz (eds), *Privatization. Successes and Failures.* New York: Columbia University Press.

Foster, V. 2008. "Africa Infrastructure Country Diagnostic. Overhauling the Engine of Growth: Infrastructure in Africa." Washington, DC: World Bank.

Gillen, D.W. and D. Cooper. 1995. "Public versus Private Ownership and Operation of Airports and Seaports in Canada." In F. Palda (ed.), *Essays in Canadian Surface Transport.* Vancouver: Fraser Institute.

Gonzalez, M. and L. Trujillo. 2009. "Efficiency Measurement in the Port Industry: A Survey of the Empirical Evidence." *Journal of Transport Economic and Policy,* 43 (2): 157–92.

Guasch, J.L. 2007. *Granting and Renegotiating Infrastructure Concessions: Doing It Right.* Washington, DC: World Bank Institute.

Harding, A., G. Palsson, and G. Raballand. 2007. "Port and Maritime

Transport Challenges in West and Central Africa. Sub-Saharan Africa Transport Policy Program." SSATP Working Paper No. 84. Washington, DC: World Bank.

Hoffmann, J. 2009. "Trade Facilitation: An Introduction." UNCTAD Virtual Institute (May).

International Maritime Organization (IMO). 2003. "Port State Control." London: IMO.

Kandiero, T. and S. Wadahwan. 2003. "Institutional Quality, Openness, and Investment in Africa." *South African Journal of Economic and Management Sciences*, 6: 346–67.

Kostianis, D. 2005. "Main Issues and Challenges for Ports and Port Operations." Presentation at the Training Seminar on Port Reform, Euromed, Marseille.

Libom, M., L. Likeng, T. Cantens, and S. Bilangna. 2009. "Gazing into the Mirror; Operational Internal Control in Cameroon Customs." Sub-Saharan Africa Transport Policy Program (SSATP) Working Paper No. 47919. Washington, DC: World Bank.

Matto, A., C. Fink, and C. Neagu. 1999. "Trade in International Maritime Services: How Much Does Policy Matter?" World Bank Policy Research Working Paper No. 2522. Washington, DC: World Bank.

Nathan Associates. 2002. *Mainstreaming Trade: a Poverty Reduction Strategy for Mozambique.*" Maputo, Mozambique: USAID.

Notteboom, T.E. and W. Winkelmans. 2001. "Reassessing Public Sector Involvement in European Seaports." *International Journal of Maritime Economics*, 3: 242–59.

Ocean Shipping Consultants. 2008. "Beyond the Bottlenecks: Ports in Sub-Saharan Africa." AICD Background Paper No. 8. Washington, DC: World Bank.

Portugal-Perez, A. and J. Wilson. 2009. "Revisiting Trade Facilitation Indicators and Export Performance." Mimeo, World Bank.

Teravaninthorn, S. and G. Raballand. 2009. *Transport Prices and Costs in Africa: A Review of the Main International Corridors.* Washington, DC: World Bank.

Trujillo, L. and G. Nombela. 1999. "Privatization and Regulation of the Seaport Industry." Policy Research Working Paper No. 2181. Washington, DC: World Bank.

Trujillo, L. and G. Nombela. 2000. "Seaports", in A. Estache. and G. De Rus (eds), *Privatization and Regulation of Infrastructures: Guidelines for policymakers and regulators.* Washington, DC: World Bank Institute.

Trujillo, L. and B. Tovar. 2007. "The European Port Industry: An Analysis of its Economic Efficiency." *Journal of Maritime Economics & Logistics*, 9 (2): 148–71.

UNCTAD. 2003. *African Ports: Reform and the Role of the Private Sector.* New York and Geneva: UNCTAD.

———. **2009.** *Review of Maritime Transport 2009.* New York and Geneva: UNCTAD.

Vagliasindi, M. and J. Nellis. 2009. "Evaluating Africa's Experiences with Institutional Reform for the Infrastructure Sectors." Working Paper No. 23, Africa Infrastructure Country Diagnostic. Washington, DC: World Bank.

Valentine, V.F. 2000. "A Comparison of African Port Performance." Paper presented at the 2001 National Maritime Conference, held in May 2001 in Cape Town, South Africa. Available online at: http://www.maritimeconference.co.za/refer ate/ValentinePaper.pdf.

Viohl, B. and J. Hoffmann. 2009. "Liner Shipping Connectivity in Africa and in South America." UNCTAD Transport Newsletter No. 42. New York and Geneva: UNCTAD.

World Bank. 2004. *World Development Report 2005: A Better Investment Climate-For Everyone.* Washington, DC: World Bank.

————. **2006.** *Doing Business.* Palgrave Macmillan, IFC, and the World Bank, Washington.

————. **2007.** *Port Reform Toolkit: Effective Decision Support for Policymakers.* Washington, DC: World Bank.

————. **2009.** *Africa's Infrastructure: A Time for Transformation, Part 2 — Sectoral Snapshots*, Ch. 12: "Ports and Shipping: Landlords Needed." Washington, DC: AICD, World Bank Group.

World Economic Forum. 2009. *Global Competitiveness Report 2009–2010.* Geneva.

CHAPTER 4

Connecting Ports to the Markets

It is well established that efficiency at ports is crucial to the overall efficiency of the transport logistics chain. However, a port is only as good, and its development only as viable, as the transport networks linking the ports to centers of production and consumption. As identified in Chapter 1, the links to other modes of transport are critical for the overall logistics chain to function well and fulfill its objective of facilitating trade. The importance of well-functioning links to ensure the efficient transit of goods across borders is even more critical for the 15 landlocked countries of Africa.

In Africa, the efficiency of the transport chain and of the maritime services is hampered by poor connectivity to markets, resulting from the poor quality and high cost of land transport infrastructure. In addition to the inadequacy of "soft" infrastructure examined in Chapter 3, poor connectivity results from the underdevelopment and poor condition of "hard" physical infra-structure along the overland transport chain. Typically, the development of road and railroad transport corridors — and in some cases inland waterways — has been limited (often one main line with various feeders of low quality). Lack of proper maintenance of roads and railroads aggravates the problem. In the case of river transport, the absence of navigable rivers into the hinterland limits the use of such a mode of transport.

This poor connectivity raises freight costs at destination, particularly for landlocked countries who have to rely on interstate transit corridors to access ports. The low quality of inland transport contri-butes to the bottlenecks at the ports, as identified in Chapter 2. As a result, port services such as containerization and intermodalism[1] are underdeveloped across the continent. In addition, land transport costs in Africa tend to be higher (per unit distance) and more important (as a share of total transport) than in other regions. According to recent estimates, transport costs for most African landlocked countries range from 15 to 20 percent of import costs — which is three to four times higher than in most developed countries (Teravanin-thorn and Raballand, 2009: 2).

However, the transport problems for business and traders in Africa do not relate solely to the hard infrastructure. They are also about the soft component of infrastructure, relating to the efficiency of customs and other border agencies, and to the affordability of arranging international shipments. And for the 15 landlocked countries in Africa, they are also about the costs related to transshipment. The weakness of the logistics systems in Africa raises overall trade costs and impacts landlocked countries the most.

This chapter deals with connectivity in Africa through transport networks and the movement of goods in and out of ports. The section that follows this introduction describes the quality of connectivity and intermodalism across the continent. It summarizes the state of the road, railroad, and inland waterway networks needed to bring the goods from the factories to the market and from the ports to the consumers. The appraisal leads to the conclusion that the entire transport network needs to be overhauled.[2] The discussion then turns to the landlocked countries that suffer most from the poor functioning of the transport corridors. Trade facilitation measures are then examined, i.e. the steps that could be taken at the national, regional, and international levels to facilitate trade; steps that would benefit greatly the landlocked countries. The analysis then moves on to evaluate the overall costs of the poor connectivity of African countries by comparing recent end-to-end freight quotes from different African countries to a European port (Rotterdam). Suggestive estimates of the ad-valorem tariff equivalent of the poor performance of the logistics chain are also provided. The chapter concludes with policy recommendations.

---

[1] Intermodalism implies the use of two or more modes of transport in an integrated manner in a door-to-door transport chain (OECD, 2001).

[2] Much of the analysis in this chapter draws on the recent AICD report (World Bank, 2009).

The Quality of Connectivity and Intermodalism in Africa

Ports constitute the main nexus for the bulk of African international trade; however, the transport of goods involves several modes of transport to connect producers and consumers in Africa to foreign markets. Most African countries face a double-bind in terms of geographic characteristics: they are very large in terms of surface area yet small in terms of population, with large distances between areas of high population density and areas of production.

To connect ports to the markets, there are three principal modes of transport: roads, railroads, and inland waterways. All three demonstrate low network densities, mirroring the low population density across the continent. In this respect, Africa fares worse than low-income countries in other global regions. As emphasized by the literature on economic geography (Krugman, 1991), the low population density also explains the lack of industrial agglomeration, as it is often cheaper to supply the sparse African population with goods from abroad, in spite of high transport costs.

Links to the hinterland — both railroads and roads — are weak, for the reasons indicated in Figure 4.1. In these circumstances, there develops a "vicious circle" of underinvestment, delapidation of the physical condition of rails/roads, and low trade volumes. First, the low level of hinterland and interregional trade does not justify investments (including investments for maintenance) in infrastructures like roads and railroads, which carry high fixed costs. This then leads to the dilapidated condition of much of the infrastructure,

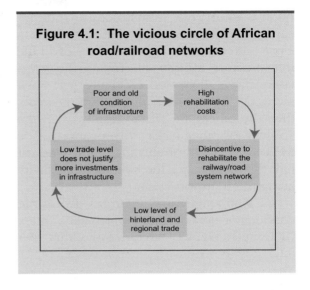

Figure 4.1: The vicious circle of African road/railroad networks

resulting in high rehabilitation costs. The substandard state of the road and railroad networks results in delays, the slow movement of goods, and to high maintenance costs for the rolling stock on the railroads, and the trucks on the road. All of these characteristics contribute to high trade costs, which in turn lead to a low volume of trade and low per capita income. Yet, in a number of countries, the asset value of the road network exceeds 30 percent of GDP and road density is high relative to the continent's income and hence its ability to pay for maintenance (World Bank, 2009).

Figure 4.2 shows an index of the overall quality of infrastructure drawn from opinion surveys administered to multinational enterprises. It gives a breakdown between North African, SSA and remaining countries. This composite index adds airports, railroads and roads to the port index presented in Chapter 3. As in the case of the port index, it shows a close link between the quality of overall infrastructure and per capita income. Across countries, there is a close correlation among the values of all the infrastructure indices, illustrating the inter-connections illustrated in Figure 4.1. So if along the transport chain one link is weak, then the others are weak. Moreover, in the absence of other modes of transport (as is the case in most of SSA), it is the weakest link that determines the overall connectivity along the transport chain.

A similar picture emerges from the rankings of the Logistics Performance Index (LPI) in Table 4.1, which shows that SSA countries have a low ranking according to this index as well. The LPI ranks the quality of the logistics environment for 150 countries, based on data obtained from a web-based questionnaire administered to professionals in logistics service companies. The LPI has the advantage of providing measures of logistics and trade facilitation costs gathered from the same source.

South Africa has the best score in Africa with a ranking of 28 and a value of 3.46, followed by Senegal (2.86) and Tunisia (2.84) (see Annex 4.1 for all the LPI rankings by country). The quality of customs services

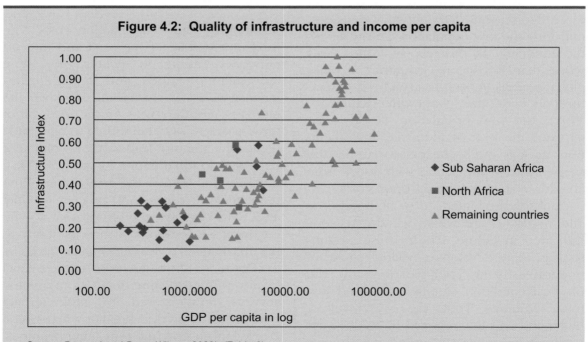

Figure 4.2: Quality of infrastructure and income per capita

Source: Portugal and Perez Wilson, 2009b (Table 2).
Note: The index is for the sample of countries used in the regional averages reported in Figure 3.3a. Income per capita is expressed in logarithms and maximum value for the index is unity when a score of unity is obtained for each component.

Table 4.1: Logistics Performance Index by region, 2010

Region	LPI	Customs	Infra-structure	International shipments	Logistics competence	Tracking & tracing	Time-liness
Europe & Central Asia (regional average)	2.74	2.35	2.41	2.92	2.60	2.75	3.33
Latin America & Caribbean (regional average)	2.74	2.38	2.46	2.70	2.62	2.84	3.41
East Asia & Pacific (regional average)	2.73	2.41	2.46	2.79	2.58	2.74	3.33
Middle East & North Africa (regional average)	2.60	2.33	2.36	2.65	2.53	2.46	3.22
South Asia (regional average)	2.49	2.22	2.13	2.61	2.33	2.53	3.04
Sub-Saharan Africa (regional average)	**2.42**	**2.18**	**2.05**	**2.51**	**2.28**	**2.49**	**2.94**

Source: World Bank (2010).

and of infrastructure are an integral part of the logistics chain. This poor logistics performance affects adversely the connectivity and transit of goods between the ports and the hinterland.

Roads

Roads are the predominant mode for freight and passenger transport in Africa and comprise the main connections from a port to the rest of a country (Map 4.1). The national road densities in SSA are lower than in low-income countries in other global regions. According to recent estimates (see Figure 4.3), 80 percent of the main road network is in good or fair condition and the current value of the national road network is at least 70 percent of its potential (World Bank 2009: Chapter 10).

With the institutional reforms introduced across a large number of African countries in recent years, most African countries now have road funds supported by fuel levies. Many others have autonomous road agencies that contract out to specialist maintenance agencies. Yet, more remains to be done in the 24 countries surveyed for the African Infrastructure Country Diagnostic (AICD): fuel levies are often too low and road funds and agencies do not meet

Map 4.1: Road network in Africa

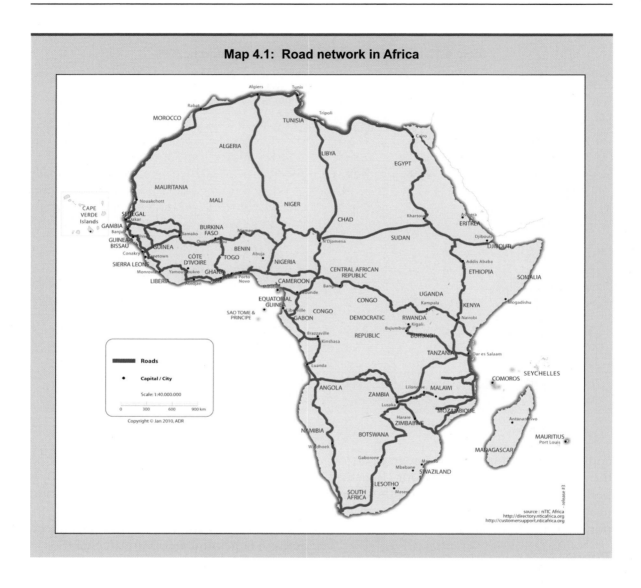

international best-design criteria. For example, fuel levies vary enormously across countries from US$ 0.16 to US$ 0.3 per liter (the latter considered to be the minimum for adequate road maintenance). Evasion, extortion, and delays contribute to low collection rates. Toll roads only operate in 0.1 percent of the region's classified road network, and almost all of these are in South Africa. Even though two-thirds of the 24 countries in the sample have a road agency, only one-third of the agency boards have private representation (World Bank, 2009: Chapter 10).

Most of the reforms have sought to improve the urban road networks and have failed to tackle rural areas, consequently the transport infrastructure gap is daunting in rural hinterlands. One of the Millennium Development Goals (MDGs) transport-related targets, endorsed by the African heads of state through the African Union in 2005, is to halve the proportion of the rural population living beyond 2 km of an all-weather road. Currently only 34 percent of the rural African population (bearing in mind

that 70 percent of the African population is rural) meets this target. Furthermore, out of 2.1 million km of roads in Africa, only 21 percent are paved, compared to the world average of 50 percent paved. This situation isolates people from basic services, transport corridors, trade hubs and economic opportunities, and of course from ports. Given that African exports consist principally of primary commodities, poor road networks that fail to link production areas to ports constitute a major barrier to trade.

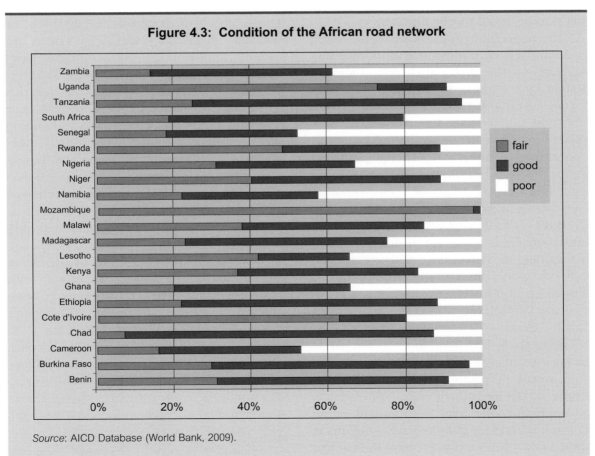

Figure 4.3: Condition of the African road network

Source: AICD Database (World Bank, 2009).

Even in towns and cities, where there has been greater progress, the development of road networks has not kept pace with the rapid urbanization witnessed since the 1970s. In 2007, 40 percent of the African population was living in urban areas and this ratio is expected to increase to 61 percent by 2050 (United Nations, 2008). To avoid congestion problems and to capture the expected economic benefits of urbanization, sound transport infrastructures are urgently needed. In addition to the urban congestion problem, major African agglomerations are still poorly linked to one another.

The region's main trunk network, which is comprised of trading corridors that link seaports to the hinterland, only includes 10,000 km of road. According to estimates for a Trans-African Highway (TAH), between 60,000 and 100,000 km of new roads are required to provide intra-continental connectivity. This would cost about US$ 47 billion over 15 years with estimated benefits of about US$ 250 billion (see details in Annex 4.2).

Buys *et al.* (2006) investigate the potential trade benefits of investing in upgrading and maintaining this TAH network. The proposed network would link 83 major cities with a length of about 100,000 km. Buys *et al.* estimate that intra-African trade, as a whole, can be expected to increase from US$ 10 billion to about US$ 30 billion per year, while initial investments and annual maintenance costs would be relatively moderate over the course of the investment cycle. For instance, an upgrade of the road from Bangui in the Central African Republic to Kisangani in Congo DR is expected to increase the volume of trade by 7.9 percent.

However, as emphasized in Chapter 3 of this report, adequate road connectivity involves more than just hard infrastructure. Africa continues to be handicapped by high road freight tariffs driven by high profit margins rather than high costs (defective roads). For example, in Central and West Africa particularly, trucking industry cartels practice *tour de rôle*[3] traffic allocation, and dispatching practices are responsible for low vehicle mileage and poor fleet quality.

Railroads

There are approximately 89,000 km of railroads in Africa (Map 4.2). These are usually single lines going inland from coastal seaports, with few rail inter-connections. The railroad networks in Africa are historically linked to ports, as they were originally built between seaports and mining sites. For this reason they were usually state-owned, or developed and owned by mining companies. Even though concessioning has met with some success and has increased traffic volumes (see Figure 4.4) as well as labor productivity, railroads remain poorly developed across the continent.

Several factors contribute to the weak rail infrastructure. First, relations with governments have traditionally been difficult as the private operators have not received sufficient compensation for loss-making passenger service routes. Second, concessionaires have restricted expenditure of their own funds to cover day-to-day maintenance, not infrastructure as was hoped for by the governments. Third, rail

---

[3] Prioritized assignment system: transport operators are assigned by turn.

Map 4.2: Railroad network in Africa

and traffic densities are low compared to other sparsely populated countries like Australia, Canada, and China, where densities are between 5 and 7. By contrast, in most African countries the density is between 1 and 6 (excluding the 13 countries that have no operating railroad.)[4] Fourth, as pointed out in Chapter 1, there is an

[4] Spatial density is measured in route-km per 1,000 sq km. The density for European countries is in the range of 20–100, whereas it is 16 for South Africa, the country with the highest density in Africa.

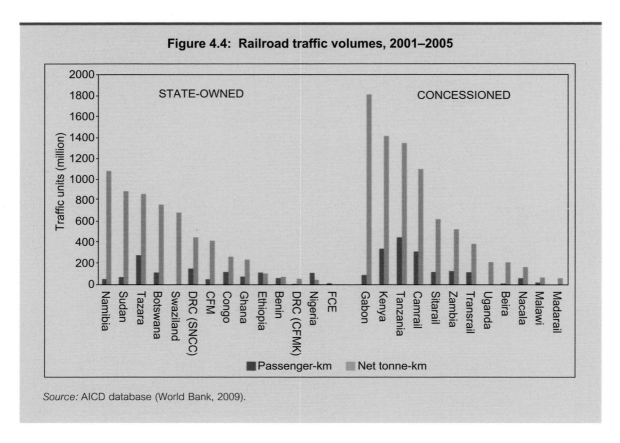

Figure 4.4: Railroad traffic volumes, 2001–2005

Source: AICD database (World Bank, 2009).

imbalance in the structure of African trade, so that it is not unusual to have a large differential between inbound and outbound freight traffic.

Few African railroads (apart from the network in East Africa and the network extending North in South Africa) traverse international borders. Almost all carry passenger traffic (there are no freight-only railways) on end-to-end traffic. Major infrastructure problems associated with aging railroads (insufficient ballast, decrepit structures, rail wear, poor rail signaling) raise the costs of rehabilitation compared with existing traffic and revenues. A further

factor contributing to poor performance is that the network (which often originated as an add-on to the mine rail lines) is disconnected and rarely lies at the center of economic activity. At the end of 2008, there were only 47 railroads operating in 32 countries in Sub-Saharan Africa, pointing to low demand.

The level and quality of the railroad infrastructure are very weak. With low demand and with competition from the road network, the vicious circle identified in Figure 4.1 translates into a perceived dwindling of the importance of this subsector other than for the transport of

Map 4.3: Major Rivers of Africa

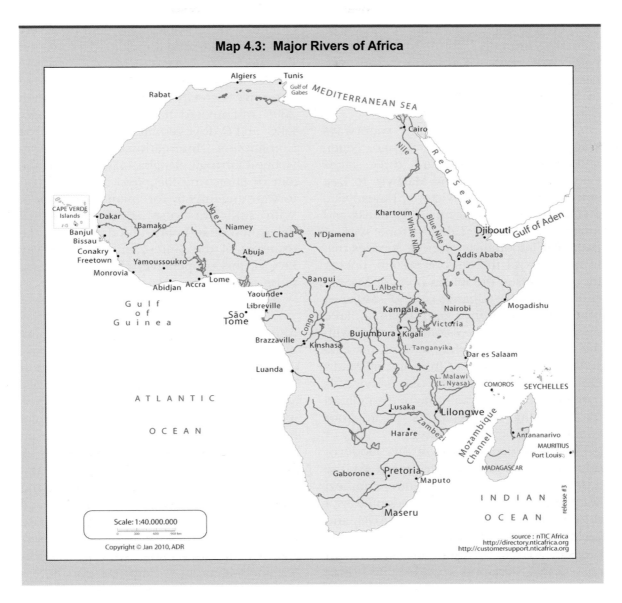

mineral goods. Without financing asset renewal and rehabilitation, competition from road networks will jeopardize the survival of railroad networks for passenger traffic and general cargo.

Inland Waterways and Inland Ports

(i) Inland waterways

This mode of transport offers an alternative for landlocked countries in terms of the transit of primary products. This is an inexpensive, energy-efficient, and environmentally friendly form of transport, particularly for the 29 African countries with navigable waterways. However, this mode of transport in Africa is in decline (World Bank, 2009).

The main African inland waterways comprise four rivers (Nile, Congo, Niger, and Zambezi Rivers) and three lakes (Victoria, Tanganyika, and Malawi). In East and South Africa, lakes Victoria, Tanganyika, and Malawi used to be crucial for transit and intraregional trade. Lake Victoria was of particular importance, offering services that formed part of the railroad system, linking the rail heads at the inland ports of Kisumu (Kenya), Bell (Uganda), and Mwanza (Tanzania). In Kenya and Uganda, lake operations were concessioned together with the railroad system, while in Tanzania lake services were separated from the railroads. On Lake Victoria, only one service is currently operating and some of the railroad track linking to the ports is in poor condition, especially in Kenya.

The renewed interest in this mode of transport in Southern Africa led to the redevelopment of the Shire–Zambezi Waterway Project, which was adopted as a priority project by both the SADC and COMESA. The overall objective of the project is to develop a waterway at the heart of regional transport corridors, to foster regional integration and open up new outlets to the sea for SADC countries (Box 4.1).

A comparable situation prevails in West and Central Africa, where the Congo basin has a navigable network of 12,000 km, covering nearly 4 million sq km across nine countries. In principle, this could be a very valuable resource in a multimodal transport network.

To tackle this missed potential, the Executive Secretary of CEMAC took action in 2005 and invited the Cameroon, Congo, DRC, and CAR governments to establish the Commission Internationale du Bassin Congo-Oubangui-Sangha (CICOS) with the aim of improving the physical and regulatory arrangements for inland navigation. With sufficient trust and supranational delegation of authority, and drawing on the example of the Shire–Zambezi Waterway Project, this cooperative effort could prove to be successful.

(ii) Inland ports

Along the transport chain, seaports are not the only nodes. Dry ports, also called inland ports, offer an important support to transport links like roads, railroads, and waterways. Many African countries have developed inland ports, which serve two broad functions: (i) as transshipment facilities from one transport mode to another and (ii) as local and regional distribution and consolidation centers. Inland terminals and logistics hubs are usually located at major rail heads or ports, and often incorporate customs facilities and bonded warehouses. Virtually all African ports require near-port terminals in order to improve port access and efficiency, but very few are being developed. Typically, the near-port hub should be close enough to the port to be linked with a trailer shuttle service, and also to expand the export stacking areas.

In principle, dry ports would be a very useful asset in a multimodal transport network and their development would accelerate the spread of containerization throughout Africa. They also facilitate in a large measure the movement of goods from point of origin to final destination without the need for customs control, or any handling en route, other than at the point of transfer between the modes.

In Africa, this waterway mode of transport is affected by outdated and insufficient infrastructure, compounded by inadequate channel markings, substandard maintenance, poor regulation, and numerous nonphysical barriers to the movement of goods. Owing to the relatively poor and declining performance of rail intermodal freight in Africa, the development of major inland terminals and hubs has not really taken off, except in South Africa and isolated locations on inland waterways and lakes, such as Port Bell in Uganda. Traffic at the City Deep terminal in South Africa,

---

Box 4.1: The Shire–Zambezi Waterway Project

Infrastructure development is high on landlocked Malawi's list of priorities to stimulate growth. The Shire–Zambezi waterway will provide the country with a crucial multimodal inland transport linkage with its neighbors and the entire region. The project is an example of successful regional cooperation, putting a waterway at the heart of regional integration and regional transport corridors. In this way, it aims to open up new outlets to the sea for SADC countries. The project will also help to reduce costs for investment in key export products.

The project comprises the following components:

- Construction of a 238-km waterway that will link landlocked Malawi's inland port of Nsanje to Mozambique's Indian Ocean port of Chinde (a reduction of transport distance to one-sixth of current levels);
- Building of berths and port buildings and the replacement of certain dysfunctional port structures, especially to allow barges and medium seagoing vessels between Chinde and Nsanje. This would open up direct waterway access to the Indian Ocean;
- Dredging and conversion of the Shire–Zambezi waterway into a more modern canal and the setting up of container stacking;
- Construction and rehabilitation of a range of interlinked roads within the corridor area (from Malawi's lakeshore town of Salima through Lilongwe to Zambia; Malawi's lake port of Nkhata bay into Zambia, Rwanda and Burundi; and Nsanje to Malawi's tea growing district of Thyolo);
- Rehabilitation and construction of the railroad from Nsanje through the Malawian cities of Blantyre and Lilongwe to Chipata, in Zambia.

The expected outcomes are:

- US$ 250 million of savings per annum on direct transport costs for Malawi, Zambia, and Mozambique and a general reduction in transport costs;
- Increase in competitiveness of exports and enhanced opportunities for diversification.

Source: Standard Bank (2008).

which is the prime intermodal hub in the Southern Africa subregion, has gradually declined over the past 20 years, carrying only 20 percent of the container traffic on the main Durban corridor. However, the implementation of new terminal operating procedures and new investment during 2008/09 have resulted in a dramatic improvement from 5 to 19 trains per day.

African Infrastructure: The Pressing Need for Rehabilitation and Maintenance

Typically, per capita expenditures on infrastructure increase in parallel with income per capita. In absolute terms, per capita expenditure on infrastructure is low, at around US$ 20–40 per year (Briceno-Garmendia *et al.,* 2008). Yet once external finance — which accounts for about 35 percent of all expenditures — is taken into account, expenditures amount to 6–8 percent of average GDP in SSA. This breaks down into US$ 20.5 billion on operation and maintenance of infrastructure and another US$ 24.9 billion on capital expenditure (Table 4.2).

Nonetheless, maintenance expenditures are insufficient, contributing to the deterioration of African hard infrastructure. Like port infrastructure, the construction and maintenance of national road and railroad networks are usually funded from the public sector. Where concessioning has occurred, investments have been for maintenance rather than capital expenditures. The only exceptions are for the ICT and power sectors, which have been more successful in attracting private infrastructure expenditures (see Table 4.2). Overall, less than 9 percent of capital expenditures in the transport sector has come from the private sector.

Table 4.2: Current infrastructure spending in Sub-Saharan Africa (US$ billion)

Sector	Operation & Maintenance of Public Sector	Capital Expenditure					Total Spending
		Public Sector	ODA OECD	Non-Finance	PPI*	Total Cap. Exp.	
ICT	2.0	1.3	0.0	0.0	5.7	7.0	9.0
Power	7.0	2.4	0.7	1.1	0.5	4.6	11.6
Transport	7.8	4.5	1.8	1.1	1.1	8.4	16.2
WSS	3.1	1.1	1.2	0.2	2.1	4.6	7.6
Irrigation	0.6	0.3	—	—	—	0.3	0.9
Total	20.5	9.4	3.6	2.5	9.4	24.9	45.3

Source: World Bank (2009, table 4).
* PPI = Private Participation in Infrastructure.

According to the recent estimates of the AICD report (World Bank, 2009), a financing gap of around 5 percent of GDP (split equally between maintenance and capital expenditures) needs to be bridged for all the infrastructure sectors. About 40 percent of rural roads and railroads plus 25 percent of main highways are in need of rehabilitation. This situation reflects a legacy of under-funding for maintenance, which is attributable to two main factors. First, there is the competition for government funds from other social sectors (health, education, etc.). Second, there is the under-collection of revenues, especially in the power and utilities subsectors.

To give an example, Nyangaga (2002) estimated that by the end of the 1980s, almost 2 million km of road in SSA (with a replacement cost of at least US$ 170 billion) were in need of repair, requiring an annual expenditure of between US$ 2–3 billion for routine and periodic maintenance. In response to this challenge, UNECA and the World Bank launched the Sub-Saharan Africa Transport Program (SSATP). This is a unique partnership of 35 African countries, 8 Regional Economic Communities (RECs), 3 African institutions (UNECA and AU/NEPAD), national and regional organizations, as well as international development partners, all seeking to ensure that transport plays its full part in achieving the development goals of SSA. One of the components of SSATP is the Road Maintenance Initiative (RMI), which aims to "commercialize" the road sector by charging user fees.[5]

In response to the RMI, many countries earmarked selected road-related taxes and charges and deposited them into a special off-budget account, or *road fund*, to support spending on roads. The performance of such funds was generally quite poor. Common problems were: inadequate financial management; absence of independent audits; extensive use of funds for unauthorized expenditures; diversion of funds; and weak oversight. As a result, most of the "first-generation" road funds have been closed down and replaced by "second-generation" road funds.[6] Second-generation road funds are now a significant feature of sector reform programs and strategies for improving road maintenance. Today 27 SSA countries have established road funds and this number is likely to increase in the

---

[5] The success of the "first-generation" road funds was thought to be dependent on four prerequisites: (i) creating ownership by involving road users in funding and management of roads to generate support for adequate road funding and also to control national agencies' monopoly power; (ii) securing an adequate and stable flow of funding based on dedicated user charges; (iii) securing a clear delimitation of all responsibilities and their appropriate assignment with matching authority; and (iv) strengthening management of roads by introducing sound business practices to obtain value for money.

[6] The characteristics of "second-generation" road funds are: (i) a sound legal basis, i.e. a separate road fund administration, clear rules and regulations; (ii) strong oversight, i.e. a broad-based private/public board; (iii) an agency that is a purchaser and not a provider of road maintenance services; (iv) revenues incremental to the budget and coming from charges related to road use, like fuel levies, and channeled directly to the Road Fund bank account; (v) sound financial management systems, lean efficient administrative structures; and (vi) regular technical and financial audits.

coming years as a result of ongoing reforms in West and Central Africa. Despite the creation of autonomous entities responsible for the management of road networks, most SSA countries still face difficulties in fully commercializing the road sector.

For railroads, for reasons discussed above, classic concessions have been unable to attract long-term infrastructure investments from the private sector. Substantial public funding will continue to be necessary and some form of guaranteed compensation scheme is required to compensate operators on unprofitable carrier services. The main issue is to determine the level of expenditure that African railroads can afford, given the low density of traffic and the competition from roads. According to the recent estimates in the AICD report (World Bank, 2009), long-term maintenance requires an investment of US$ 3 billion to rehabilitate tracks; this could be spread over a 10-year period. Excluding South Africa, once the rehabilitation has taken place, a steady-state ongoing budget of US$ 100 million per annum is needed for track reconstruction. As to the rolling stock, a freight charge of US$ 0.04 per tonne-km or passenger-km (close to the average rates in current practice) would be sufficient to replace the depreciated stock (World Bank, 2009: Chapter 11).

The Plight of Landlocked Countries

Africa is the continent with the highest concentration (15) of landlocked developing countries (LLDCs). According to the gravity model estimates of Limão and Venables (2001), the median landlocked country's transport costs for a standard 20-ft container are 46 percent higher than the equivalent costs for a median coastal economy. They also find that distance explains only 10 percent of the change in the transport costs. Poor road infrastructure represents 40 percent of the transport costs predicted for coastal countries and 60 percent for landlocked countries.

These estimates are corroborated by the freight charges from different countries to a European port (Rotterdam), as posted on the Internet in 2008 by Maersk, a global shipper (Figure 4.5). Being landlocked imposes a large premium on overall freight costs, for a standard 20-ft container. For example, Mali and other LLDCs pay large premia above ocean freight costs.

Both sets of estimates confirm that global market access for landlocked countries depends heavily on regional infrastructure and links to ports. This justifies the focal areas delineated in the Almaty Program of Action,[7] among them: (i) transport infrastructure at the national level; (ii) international laws and treaties; and (iii) cross-border cooperation. In addition, as shown in the examples developed here, transit logistics costs need to be improved. In particular, improvements call for the development of transit corridors.

Transit and Trade Corridors in Africa

A corridor is the geographical concentration of transport infrastructures and transit activities between two or more economic centers, linking them to one another and to

---

[7] The Almaty Program of Action was established in 2003 and a roadmap was drawn up by the UN-OHRLLS specifically to address the needs of landlocked countries.

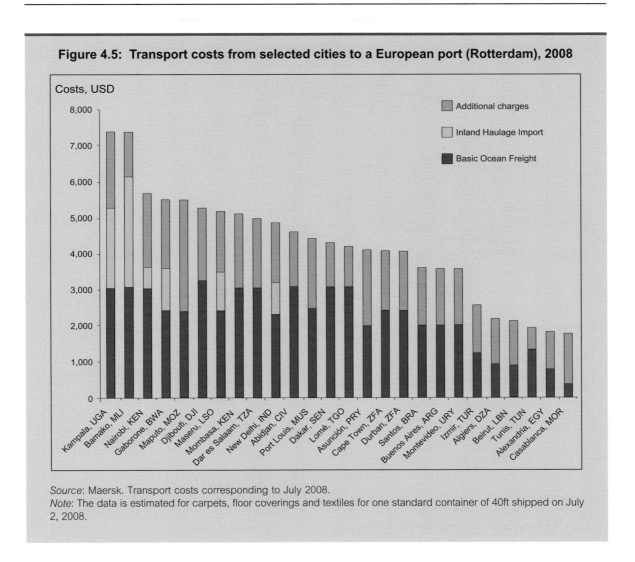

Figure 4.5: Transport costs from selected cities to a European port (Rotterdam), 2008

Source: Maersk. Transport costs corresponding to July 2008.
Note: The data is estimated for carpets, floor coverings and textiles for one standard container of 40ft shipped on July 2, 2008.

international markets (Figure 4.6). Ports are one of the gateway nodes on corridors, as they constitute a direct link to external markets. The corridor approach to improving connectivity is gaining momentum and most of the transport sector strategy in Africa is based on the development of transport corridors.

The major transport corridors in Africa are:

- *Africa-wide*: the Trans-Africa Highway (TAH) project;
- *West Africa*: the Abidjan–Lagos and the Bamako–Ouagadougou–Lomé Corridors;
- *Central Africa*: the CEMAC Corridor;

Map 4.4: Major African Corridors

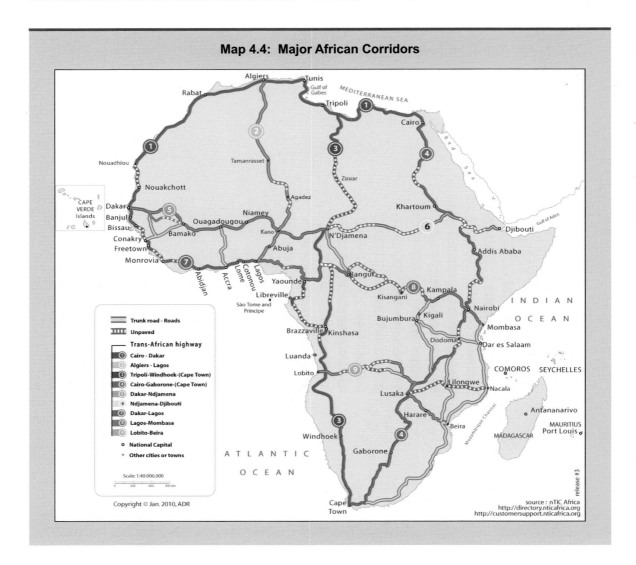

Copyright © Jan. 2010, ADR

source : nTIC Africa
http://directory.nticafrica.org
http://customersupport.nticafrica.org

- *East Africa:* the Northern Corridor;
- *Southern Africa:* the North–South Corridor, the Maputo Corridor, and the Wallis Bay Corridors.

Annex 4.2 provides detailed information on these corridors, while Table 4.3 lists the main corridors linking African LLDCs to a seaport.

Regional corridors are vital for Africa's landlocked countries, as they provide them with access to the sea and to export markets; but benefits from transit traffic through corridors can be as substantial for coastal countries. For example, in Kenya in 1990, transit traffic yielded a net value added of US$ 53 million, while Tanzania could

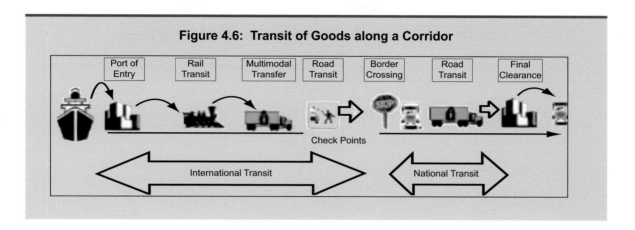

Figure 4.6: Transit of Goods along a Corridor

increase its annual foreign exchange earnings by 12–18 percent if it were to improve the management of its transit traffic system.

All corridors face the same kind of barriers to transit: long transport delays, high costs, poor infrastructure level, and a lack of institutional harmonization between the countries involved. The users along the corridor may also be subject to extortion along the multiple roadblocks and checkpoints. Table 4.4 indicates the large number of checkpoints on selected road corridors in West Africa. The Lagos–Abidjan highway, in particular, has a very high number of checkpoints (7 per 100 km).

The North–South Corridor

The busiest traffic occurs on the North–South Corridor (NSC), which is the most efficient in Africa. The NSC serves as an example for other subregions (in particular West Africa) of the gains that can be

Table 4.3: Corridors linking landlocked countries (LLCs) and ports

	Regional Corridors			
	West Africa	**Central Africa**	**East Africa**	**Southern Africa**
Main ports of entry	Abidjan, Tema, Lomé, Cotonou, Dakar	Douala	Mombasa, Dar-es-Salaam	Durban, Maputo, Bera, Dar-es-Salaam
LLC served	Mali, Burkina Faso, Niger	Chad, CAR	Uganda, Rwanda, Burundi, East of DRC	Botswana, Malawi, Zambia, Zimbabwe, South of DRC

Source: Teravaninthorn and Raballand (2009).

Table 4.4: Checkpoints on selected road corridors in West Africa

Highways	Distance (km)	No. of Checkpoints	Checkpoints per 100 km
Lagos–Abidjan	992	69	7
Cotonou–Niamey	1,036	34	3
Lomé–Ouagadougou	989	34	4
Accra–Ouagadougou	972	15	2
Abidjan–Ouagadougou	1,122	37	3
Niamey–Ouagadougou	529	20	4

Source: ECOWAS Official Site (2003).

anticipated from "deep" regional integration (i.e. regional integration that goes beyond establishing free trade by taking measures to reduce behind-the-border costs). In spite of the need for further improvements, the North–South Corridor (NSC), linking Kolwezi in DR Congo to the southern ports (mainly the port of Durban in South Africa) more than 3,500 km away and to the port of Dar es Salaam, serves as an adequate connector for all the southern and east Africa regional transport corridors and ports. Success in achieving further improvements rests on more extensive harmonization at the regional level (see Annex 4.2).

The efficient and improved performance of the NSC is considered to be a key economic driver for the region and has been developed as a pilot Aid for Trade (AfT) program by the COMESA–EAC–SADC Tripartite (see Box 5.7). As such, it has attracted considerable donor and institutional financial commitments for infrastructure improvements and upgrades.

Yet, as can be seen from Figure 4.7, delays along the NSC are still important.

Figure 4.7 gives travel times and border-crossing times between main towns on the corridor. However, it should be borne in mind that these are only averages. Travel times vary considerably according to a number of factors: type of cargo (whether break bulk, containerized, tankers, perishable goods, etc.); the direction of travel; whether the cargo is in transit or not; and by the quality of the "soft" infrastructure (i.e. whether the computerized systems are functioning and papers are cleared rapidly).

It can be seen that the journey from Kolwezi to City Deep (in Johannesburg which is an Inland Container Depot) takes on average 15–20 days, with 10–15 days of downtime at the border crossings. To give an example of the trade-offs involved, and of the uncertainties faced by transporters, if a transporter chooses to use the route through Botswana, his payload will be restricted because the ferry at Kasungula across the Zambezi has a maximum gross vehicle mass (GVM) of 45 tonnes, compared to the maximum GVM of 56 tonnes for the road network as a whole. In addition, the journey time is longer and the time saved at border crossings is minimal, if any. The same is true if a transporter chooses to cross into Botswana at Kasungula and into South Africa at Labatse (Gaborone) instead of Martins Drift.

The easiest and quickest way to reduce transport costs along the North–South Corridor is to reduce the time taken at border posts by converting them into one-stop border posts (OSBPs). If all the necessary steps were to be carried out (infrastructure upgrades, systems upgrades, streamlining of procedures [see Box 4.3]), waiting times at borders could be cut by at least half. Upgrading the road and bridge infrastructure along sections in disrepair

would save additional time. Likewise, new bridges are needed at river crossings (at Kasungula and at Tete in particular). These upgrades would produce multiple benefits: savings brought about by reducing queues (since there are long queues at both the ferry crossing at Kasungula and the bridge at Tete) and savings in running times for trucks, lower costs for truck maintenance, and less accidents. In contrast, reducing informal payments would have a marginal impact on transport costs and prices.

Trade Facilitation Measures

Trade facilitation measures reduce trade costs. Some trade facilitation measures, such as the introduction of information and

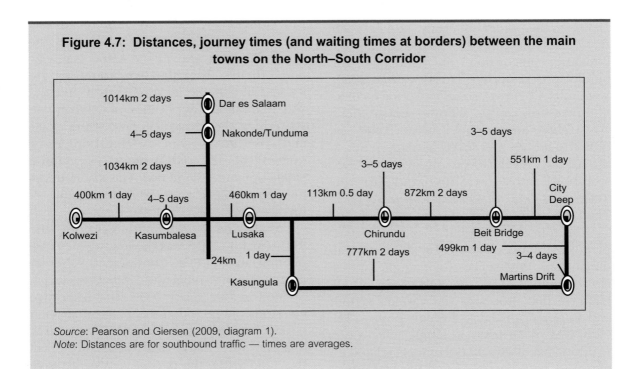

Figure 4.7: Distances, journey times (and waiting times at borders) between the main towns on the North–South Corridor

Source: Pearson and Giersen (2009, diagram 1).
Note: Distances are for southbound traffic — times are averages.

communications technology (ICT) systems to replace paperwork at customs, can be taken at the national level. For most costs relating to international trade, trade facilitation requires some kind of cooperation either at the regional or multilateral level. Effective cooperation to improve trade facilitation at the international level is the hardest to achieve because agreement must be reached among many parties, who often have conflicting interests. This section gives examples of trade facilitation measures that can help to reduce trade costs, starting with national and regional measures, and then discussing measures that could be taken multilaterally.

National and Regional Measures

(i) Customs — time at borders

Delays at the border are costly. In Asia, each day costs around US$ 370 for a 40-ft container according to estimates for landlocked countries (Arvis *et al.*, 2007; Appendix 4). However, several trade facilitation measures can be taken to reduce these costs. Three are described here: (i) the use of ICT to reduce and speed up paperwork at the national level; (ii) establishment of one-stop-border-posts (OSBPs) and (ii) the *Transports Internationaux Routiers* (TIR). The latter two require regional cooperation.

The introduction of ICT and electronic platforms reduces trade costs along several dimensions. One successful example of this is Tradenet (TTN), an IT-based virtual platform that processes the various export and import formalities through ports. TTN (see Box 4.2) uses a single electronic window that allows all documents related to transit to be accessible to all the operators:

companies, banks, forwarding and commissioners' customs agents, carriers, and shipping agents. The introduction of this single electronic window has reduced the cost of doing business by allowing all the procedures to take place with no paper, no displacement, and no personal contact, all of which significantly diminishes the risk of corruption. The electronic form also ensures the consistency of all documents, since they can be updated online and are visible to all operators instantaneously. This increases the transparency of the processes and the traceability of all operations.

Other trade facilitation measures, such as one-stop-border posts (OSBPs), require regional cooperation. This is a border post shared by two adjacent countries to conduct jointly cross-border and security clearance procedures. Practically, an OSBP relates to a situation where the goods moving in the same direction are on the same gateway, and officials from the two countries are located in a single location. It is a practical way to minimize duplication of controls and so reduce the clearance processing times and costs involved in crossing borders by unifying border control processes within a single operating sequence. This also reduces the opportunity for a fraudulent exchange of invoices (Box 4.3).

Along the North–South Corridor, the RECs (with COMESA as the lead agency) are piloting an OSBP at Chirundu, the border post between Zambia and Zimbabwe, which opened in December 2009. The respective governments provided the political support needed to implement an OSBP under a bilateral agreement. With assistance from JICA and DfID, the two governments have

---

Box 4.2: Trade facilitation at the port: the case of Tradenet, Tunisia

Tradenet (TTN) was launched in 2000 with an original investment of US$ 80.26 million. It is a public–private entity under the supervision of the Minister of Finance, with 30 percent private ownership. TTN has proved to be very successful: it received the Technology in Government in Africa (TIGA) Award 2009 and is being replicated in other African countries.

TTN has developed two sub-entities: a "service bundle" and a "transport bundle." The transport bundle handles all the documents related to the movements of ships at the port. So far, all the formalities related to the ship entry at the port have been implemented. Tunisian exports increased by close to 30 percent per annum over the period 2000–2008, with the highest growth rates in 2007 and 2008, soon after the implementation of the TTN transport bundle. Implementation of TTN in Tunisia has reduced the time required to complete export and import procedures by 2 days. The time required is now 15 days, which is similar to Egypt but still 3 times higher than the US and 4 times higher than Singapore.

With regard to future prospects for trade facilitation, "Motorways of the Sea" is a project instigated by the European Union aiming at creating maritime trade and transport corridors between Europe and its neighboring countries. TTN has been involved and is now in discussion with the ports of Marseilles in France and Genes in Italy, to harmonize their systems of data processing.

In November 2003, the TTN technology was introduced in the port of Douala in Cameroon and discussions are ongoing with Togo, Algeria, and Libya to export the same system. A successful implementation requires a sufficient level of IT infrastructure and capacities, and the existence of a basic set of transit procedures and documents, which have to be compliant with international trade agreements.

Source: Discussions with TTN.

---

constructed new buildings and a new bridge over the Zambezi River. They have also passed national legislation to allow an OSBP to operate[8] and a single operating procedure that permits all exit and entry documentation to be submitted in a consolidated manner at one time.

The time saved at a fully functioning OSBP creates economic and social benefits. The economic benefits include a reduction

---

[8] Including national legislation to allow extra-territorial exercise of powers by officials from both countries to perform their functions in a foreign country and allowing the declaration of common areas of control and harmonization of roles, powers and responsibilities of officials with an interest in border control.

in red tape and transport costs. The social benefits include a reduction in the infection rates of HIV/AIDS and other sexually transmitted diseases, as truck drivers spend less time at border posts.

However, OSBP implies the harmonization of customs procedures and legislation, and hence cooperation. Even if the principle is simple, the planning and procedures are complex. To speed up the processing of documentation, it is necessary for governments to jointly take a number of measures:

- to harmonize customs practices, facilities, ICT systems, procedures and legislation, such as signing up to the GATT valuation system;

- to ensure that countries are on the same version of the Harmonized System of Customs Classification;
- to simplify and harmonize temporary admission, re-exportation and transit procedures;

Box 4.3: Basic One-Stop-Border Post (OSBP) operating principles

- The country of entry hosts officers carrying out exit procedures so that the entire exit and entry process occurs in one common control zone.
- Entry procedures cannot begin until all exit procedures are completed and jurisdiction has formally passed from the exit state to the entry state. This is to avoid any conflict over jurisdiction within the OSBP.
- Officers carry out their own border control laws, even when acting in the adjoining country, but only within the common control zone established by a bilateral agreement between the border countries.
- A law establishing extra-territoriality authorizes officers to carry out exit procedures in the adjoining country.
- Wherever possible, inspections and other procedures are carried out jointly to increase effectiveness and save time.
- Working in close proximity encourages cross-border risk assessment of persons and goods.
- Simplification of documents and procedures as well as harmonization of regulations occur more readily in an OSBP and increase its benefits.
- Sequencing of procedures and minimizing distance between them will reduce the time spent by officers and border users.

- to harmonize exemption and other duty relief measures;
- to dispense with all pre-shipment inspections; and
- to adopt regional antidumping and countervailing duty regulations.

To fully carry out such procedures, it is necessary for countries to delegate some authority to a supranational entity, which may occasionally entail relinquishing some national priorities. Up to 15 different government agencies on both sides may be involved. In addition, the private sector needs to be kept apprised of the prevailing procedures and measures, and agree to conform to the OSBP system.

A second example of a trade facilitation measure that involves even greater regional cooperation is the seamless Transports Internationaux Routiers (TIR) (see Box 4.4). Implementation of TIR recognizes that freedom of transit rests on guarantees provided by operators against potential fiscal loss. Transit is a public–private partnership involving a chain of (preferably) harmonized national procedures. To be operational, a high degree of professionalism is required of the logistics operator organizing the sequence of operations for the consignee/shipper (this is often helped by affiliation to an international network). It is clear that the success of this implementation of GATT Article V on freedom of transit requires a robust institutional setting, which is usually lacking in Africa.

(ii) Harmonization of safety regulations

Safety regulations relating to international transport require regulations at the regional level. One important example is road safety, which is still a big issue in Africa. The Sub-Saharan Africa Transport Program (SSATP) estimates that Africa has the highest per capita traffic-related mortality rate in the world, at 28.3 deaths per 100,000 of population. The annual road crash cost in Africa is estimated at US$ 3.7 billion. Studies indicate that the rate of return on investment to reduce crashes is very high. Improvement of road safety and a reduction of accidents on the road network will help to lower insurance costs, improve predictability of transport time, and enhance overall connectivity.

Harmonization of axle loads presents an interesting example of the benefits of cooperation, but also of the difficulty of achieving the necessary collective action. Axle loads are specified by the gross vehicle mass (GVM) by type of vehicle (vehicle and trailer and the combined number of axles). In Southern and East Africa, for example, the maximum GVM allowed is 56 tonnes. Although African RECs have agreed to harmonize axle loads and vehicle dimensions, on some routes axle loads are *de facto* restricted because of the poor quality of the infrastructure. Moreover, the incentive for transporters to operate trucks with greater axle loads than officially permitted is high because of the fierce competition among carriers. However, excessive axle loads will

---

Box 4.4: Transports Internationaux Routiers (TIR)

Transit procedures seek to implement the "Freedom of Transit," Article V of the GATT, while at the same time safeguarding the interests of the transit country from potential fiscal loss. Any transit operation rests on three core principles; (i) the consignee provides a guarantee to the transit country's customs; (ii) customs affix seals on the vessel; (iii) customs implement documentary and information systems at borders to reconcile inflows and outflows.

The Transports Internationaux Routiers (TIR) is an example of a trade facilitation mechanism used throughout Western Europe. Goods that are moved under TIR can pass through these countries with customs duties and other taxes suspended and without the need for unloading/reloading at frontiers. The simplification achieved by the TIR regime rests on the following pillars:

- the use of secure vehicles or containers;
- the international guarantee chain;
- the TIR carnet (a single harmonized manifest);
- the mutual recognition of customs controls; and
- controlled access to use the system and integrity guaranteed by the United Nations Economic Commission for Europe (UNECE) and the International Road Transport Union (IRTU).

As of 2005, there were 66 Contracting Parties to the TIR Convention, including the European Community. It is, however, only possible to establish a TIR operation with 55 of these countries, as the rest do not have an approved guarantee association. The TIR system has been underused in African countries for various reasons. In Morocco, TIR carnets are rarely used, and in Tunisia TIR traffic represents a very small percentage of Tunisian transport companies' operations. In Algeria the system has been suspended (El Khayat, 2005).

accelerate the deterioration of roads that are already under stress, which will increase travel times, as well as road maintenance and freight costs (hence overall transport costs).[9]

Other ways to reduce the cost of surface transport in Africa include harmonizing road transit charges, using a regional carrier's license that would allow vehicles to operate with a single license, and using regional third-party vehicle insurance schemes.

Multilateral Measures

The issue of port safety, together with anti-pollution and other environmental aspects, is effectively carried out through obligatory membership of the International Maritime Organization (IMO), a specialized United Nations agency. When the IMO was established in 1948, its main concern was to develop the international machinery to improve safety at sea. This international body is a public good necessary to control the threat of marine pollution from ships, particularly by oil carried in tankers.

The IMO's intervention in Africa consists mostly in supporting NEPAD's activities through an Integrated Technical Cooperation Program. Technical advisory and assessment missions, workshops, training sessions, and seminars are organized in the countries concerned on a variety of themes: governance, peace and security, environment, urbanization, human resources development, employment, and HIV/AIDS. Recent achievements include: agreement by the CEMAC countries on a package of merchant marine regulations that embody IMO's principal maritime safety/security and marine environment instruments; the signing of an MoU on the establishment of a subregional integrated coastguard network in West and Central Africa; the adoption of a Code of Conduct concerning the Repression of Piracy and Armed Robbery against Ships in the Western Indian Ocean and the Gulf of Aden.

There are other examples where harmonization at the international level would yield large gains, but are difficult to achieve because of the lack of international cooperation. For instance, there are hundreds of different sizes of pallets. The costs resulting from a lack of harmonization in this area are especially heavy for developing countries, which have to comply with destination markets' standard requirements while they lack rental and exchange markets for pallets (see Raballand and Aldaz-Carroll, 2005).

The ongoing negotiations on trade facilitation at the WTO, especially those around Article V on Freedom of Transit, are

---

[9] A similar debate is taking place about super single tires (which are wider than normal tires). If used instead of dual tires, these will result in a reduction in the vehicle tare weight (the unladen vehicle weight). However, at present, axle load limits are set according to the number of axles on a vehicle and the number of tires on an axle. Therefore, there would need to be a change in legislation to allow the use of super single tires on an interlink (or double semi-trailers), which is the main vehicle combination for heavy vehicle transport in Southern and East Africa. It is generally agreed that super singles should be given a higher load limit than for normal tires but agreement needs to be reached on what exactly that load should be. The main objective is to ensure that the vehicle does not damage the road, while at the same time allowing it to carry a higher payload.

of great interest to LLDCS. Implementation of these principles is one way to overcome "landlockedness."[10] Article V requires each WTO member to allow free movement of goods, vessels, and other means of transport through its territory, destined to or coming from any other WTO member. Such transit must be allowed via the routes most convenient for international transit. GATT Article V also requires equal treatment of traffic in transit, independent of the flag of the vessel, the point of origin or departure, entry, exit, destination, or ownership of the goods and vessels. Traffic in transit must not be subject to unnecessary delays or restrictions, and must be exempted from customs and transit duties (countries can charge fees for administrative expenses incurred by the transit).

The Freedom of Transit is, however, limited by the right of the State to set the conditions or requirements for granting transit rights. LLDCs are especially concerned about Article V, which recognizes that Freedom of Transit is compromised by burdensome and lengthy procedures. Article V rules have never been interpreted by a WTO panel, so the current trade facilitation negotiations at the WTO represent an opportunity to clarify and improve the provisions "to further expedite the movement, release and clearance of goods, including goods in transit." The negotiations aim to make Article V operational and to address the special needs of the LLDCs adopted in the 2003 Almaty Program of Action. A successful outcome to these negotiations would offer an opportunity for LLDCs and transit countries to benefit from technical assistance, capacity building, and in some cases support for infrastructure development, which will assist members to comply with new WTO commitments.[11]

The Costs of Deficient Trade Logistics in Africa

Time is a barrier to trade, specifically in the context of shipping costs. More time in transit imposes inventory-holding costs, including holding buffer stocks, and depreciation in the value of time-sensitive products (e.g. spoilage or overripening of foods; fashion goods where design has to be changed regularly, etc.).[12] Time delays also reduce the probability that a country can export to major markets and are costly, as the following estimates suggest. On average, each extra day a product is delayed prior to being shipped reduces trade volumes by 1 percent. For agricultural goods, an additional delay of one day reduces exports on average by 6 percent.

In this regard, transport chains are no stronger than their weakest links. And in

---

[10] The legal aspects of trade facilitation are covered in GATT 1994 under Article V (Freedom of Transit), Article VII (Fees and Formalities Related to the Import and Export) and Article X (Publication and Application of Rules Related to International Trade).

[11] See AITIC "Trade Facilitation Briefs — Facilitating Transit Procedures: Evolution of Proposals on GATT article V in the WTO Trade Facilitation Negotiations". http://www.acici.org/aitic/documents/TFBriefs/download/TFBrief1_eng.pdf

[12] Hummels (2001) estimates that each extra day in transit for the average length of shipment to the US is equivalent to a 16 percent ad-valorem tariff. Also see Djankov *et al.* (2008).

Figure 4.8: Worldwide distribution of trade costs and Ease of Trading Index

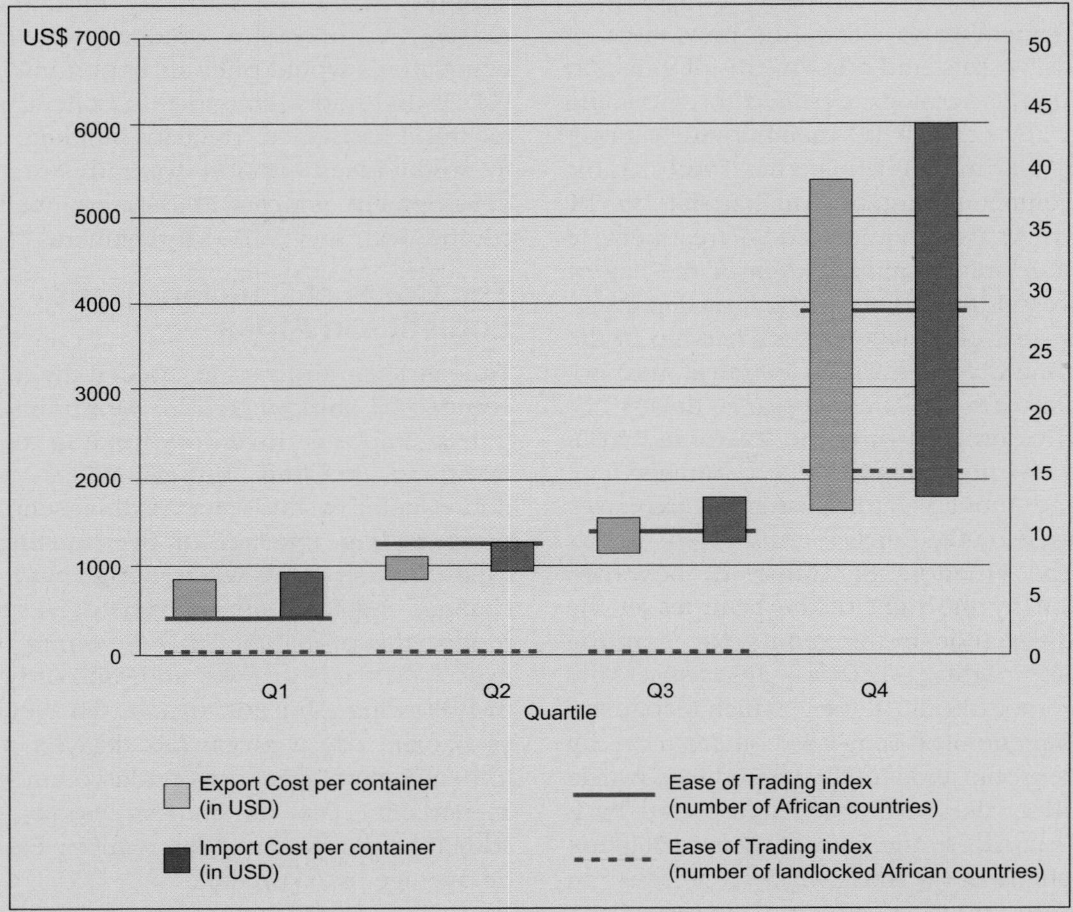

Source: World Bank (2009).
Notes: Sample of 180 countries with 45 countries per quartile; quartiles ranked by increasing importing and exporting costs per TEU. Left scale indicates the range in costs within each quartile (the range in costs per import container in Q1 is US$500 to US$1000 and in Q4 from US$1900 to US$6000). Horizontal broken line indicates the number of landlocked African countries in that quartile (i.e. 15 in Q4 and none in the other quartiles). The number of African countries per quartile is indicated on the right-hand scale.

Africa, port–rail is the weakest link, as inland transport and facilities are poorly aligned with port development. Multimodal transport is also weakly developed because the railroad links are often poor, in spite of some progress since concessioning has taken hold. The end result of poor logistics is high trade costs for African countries.

Figure 4.8 displays the distribution by quartile of export and import costs for a standard container for 180 countries, along with the values of an Ease of Trading index. The range of costs for the countries with the best logistics in quartile 1 (Q1) is between US$ 500 and US$ 1,000, while the corresponding range in the bottom quartile (Q4) is US$ 1,900 to US$ 6,000. There are only three African countries in Q1, while 29 are in Q4, which includes all the landlocked African countries. With 45 countries per quartile, almost two-thirds of the countries in the lowest quartile are African.

Comparing the costs of logistics with those of tariffs in terms of their impact on the volume of trade is another way to assess the costs of poor infrastructure and poor logistics. Chapter 1 decomposed trade costs into (i) those that are the result of trade policies and (ii) those that can be reduced through other channels, notably trade facilitation. Gravity model estimates provide an indication of the importance of unfriendly logistics relative to the trade costs imposed by trade policy. To this effect, the Tariff Trade Restrictiveness Index (TTRI) estimates presented in Table 1.3 of this report can be coupled with the costs of trading a standardized container of goods (as measured by *Doing Business* (DB) data) into a gravity model of trade that includes

the usual control variables (distance, common border, common language, and landlocked). The estimated coefficients then serve to compute a counterfactual ad-valorem TTRI that would otherwise be generated by a variation in DB trade cost figures for a given country. Portugal-Perez and Wilson (2009a) computed this "ad-valorem equivalent" of improving the business environment in their sample of 104 countries by calculating the ad-valorem tariff-cut in importing countries if each country were to move halfway to the level of Mauritius (the African country with the lowest costs along these DB measures).

Figure 4.9 provides estimates from this "tariff-cut equivalent" or "ad-valorem equivalent" for each African country in the sample. For most countries, the tariff-equivalent is higher for exports than for imports, which suggests that the poor logistics impact exports more than imports. The highest costs, about equivalent to a 70 percent tariff, are for three landlocked countries: Central African Republic, Uganda, and Rwanda. These countries also have high ad-valorem costs for imports due to poor logistics indicators. Among the lowest ad-valorem equivalent costs are the coastal countries of Gambia, Ghana, Tanzania, and Togo.

These estimates are only approximate. They depend on the validity of the gravity model augmented by trade policy barriers and other trade costs, as captured by the DB and LPI indicators as an adequate description of bilateral trade between countries. In any case, the magnitudes of the estimates are large compared to the barriers to trade due to restrictive trade policies. The pattern of

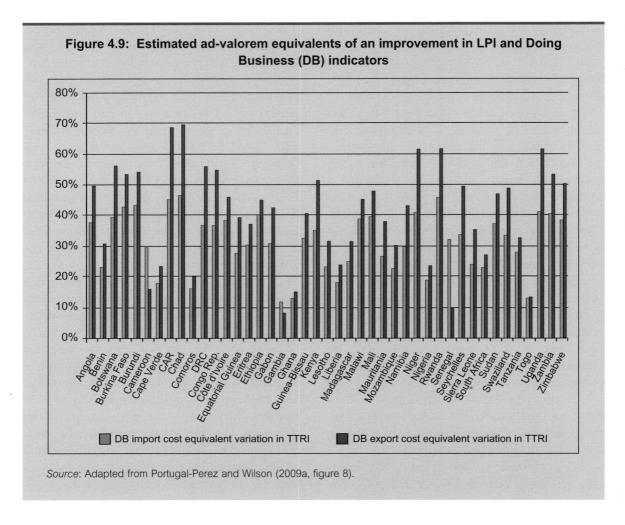

Figure 4.9: Estimated ad-valorem equivalents of an improvement in LPI and Doing Business (DB) indicators

Source: Adapted from Portugal-Perez and Wilson (2009a, figure 8).

results confirms the preliminary conclusions reached in Chapter 1, namely that African countries' high trade costs are more the result of logistics costs rather than trade barriers in destination countries or direct transport costs.

Conclusions and Policy Implications

For ports to operate efficiently and reduce transport costs, good connectivity to producers and consumers in the hinterland is essential. This in turn requires adequate road and railroad physical infrastructure. With the spread of containerization, the state of transport-related costs is becoming the most important element of overall costs along the logistics chain. This is particularly important for the 15 LLDCs in Africa that have to deal with transit through third-countries before the goods can reach their destinations.

For all African countries, but especially those in SSA, the efficiency of ports is hampered by poor connectivity with the hinterland due to the substandard condition of roads, railroads, and waterways, delivering a poor-quality service. As a result, and especially because there is little competition across modes of transport, ports can be "held hostage" to deficient infrastructure. A major financing gap, estimated by the World Bank (2009) to be in the region of US$ 31 billion per annum, is required to overhaul the infrastructure sector (including power). In addition, as shown in this chapter and in Chapter 3, the soft component of the infrastructure also needs to be improved to lower trade costs.

An improvement in the transport sector in Africa necessitates a combination of hard and soft infrastructure development measures. Most projects in the infrastructure sector funded by the International Financial Institutions take this into account and have a mix of components to address both hard and soft infrastructure deficiencies.

For landlocked countries, transit corridors need to be improved. This improvement can only be made effective by deep regional integration. The North–South corridor is functional and provides an example of the gains in connectivity that can be made from some harmonization at the EAC–COMESA–SADC level. Yet, there are many more areas where cooperation at the regional level would yield further reductions in trade costs. OSBPs and single electronic customs windows are examples of cost-reducing trade facilitation measures. Regional integration efforts are still to be developed in West Africa in particular. The

examples discussed in this chapter show that progress in regional integration is taking place but, at the same time, they also illustrate the difficulty in obtaining the necessary full cooperation to carry out the projects.

One challenge in trade facilitation is the interrelated nature of the transport logistics chain; if weak links in the chain are not addressed, reforms elsewhere may have limited impact. Seaport services are an area of local logistics competence which involve a myriad of complementary services. The movement of freight traffic through a port includes berthing activities, piloting, towing, and cargo handling. In port, vessel services are required for bunkering, repairs, and maintenance. Meanwhile, to facilitate trade, the services include customs clearance, storage, and warehousing. Many of these markets are dominated by the State and greater benefits could be derived from some liberalization with regulatory reform.

Improvements in services such as haulage, customs brokerage, insurance, declarations, advance notifications, and general supply chain performance would reduce trade costs. Often problems in developing countries in local logistics services stem from lax regulations and lack of competitiveness. The latter is difficult to address through measures in individual countries. There tend to be a small number of large agents; often part of or associated with multinational companies, with market power in international logistics services. However, the domestic market is characterized by a large number of small agents. The large agents will tend to have a dominant position in international transport. Measures taken by national governments can support local agents but will have little effect on global players (especially shipping companies). Domestic regulatory reforms and facilitation measures may support improvements, while international logistics service providers can be encouraged to influence best practice by entering the market on a competitive basis.

While domestic reforms lie at the heart of trade facilitation, some issues cannot be addressed by domestic investment or trade facilitation measures. International shipping costs, especially maritime transportation, are largely determined by three factors beyond the control of African policymakers: fuel prices, capacity utilization, and shipping cartels. However, governments can improve costs at the margin by removing policies that distort competition, such as cargo reservation schemes or "national flag requirements," and by accepting the need for regulatory institutions to monitor anti-competitive practices (although this requires regional cooperation and coordination).

Trade facilitation measures are the single most important policy action to reduce transport costs. However, without international coordination and consensus on the need for an appropriate regulatory environment, they cannot achieve their full potential. This is particularly the case for the trade facilitation negotiations currently underway under the auspices of the WTO. If successful, these negotiations, which aim at implementing the Freedom of Transit obligation of Article V, would go some way toward removing the constraints faced by the 15 landlocked countries in SSA.

References

AfDB/UNECA. 2003. *Review of the Implementation Status of the Trans-African Highways and the Missing Links.* Vol. 2: "Description of Corridors."

African Union. 2008. "State of Transport Sector Development in Africa." First Session of the Conference of African Ministers of Transport, Addis Ababa.

Arvis, J.F., G. Raballand, and J.F. Marteau. 2007. "The Costs of Being Landlocked: Logistics Costs and the Supply Chain." Working Paper Series 4258. Washington, DC: World Bank.

Behar, A., P. Manners, and B. Nelson. 2009. "Exports and Logistics." Oxford University Working paper. Oxford, UK: Oxford University Press.

Briceno-Garmendia, C., K. Smits, and V. Foster. 2008. "Financing Public Infrastructure in Sub-Saharan Africa: Patterns, Issues and Options." AICD Background Paper. Washington, DC: World Bank.

Buys, P., U. Deichmann, and D. Wheeler. 2006. "Road Network Upgrading and Overland Trade Expansion in Sub-Saharan Africa." World Bank Policy Research Working Paper 4097. Washington, DC: World Bank.

COMESA–EAC–SADC. 2008. "North–South Corridor Pilot Aid for Trade Program: Surface Transport." North–South Corridor High Level Conference, Lusaka, April 2008.

Djankov, S., C. Freund, and C.S. Pham. 2008. "Trading on Time." *Review of Economics and Statistics*, November.

El Khayat, M. 2005. "Les enjeux majeurs des transports au Maghreb 2003–2004." *Économie et territoire/Territoire et transports*. Available online at: http://www.iemed.org/anuari/2005/frarticles/felkhayat.pdf.

Global Transport Knowledge Partnership website, "One Stop Border Posts — Design & Implementation." See GTKP website: http://www.gtkp.com.

Hummels, D. 2001. "Time as a Trade Barrier", Global Trade Analysis Project Working Paper No. 18.

Krugman, P. 1991. "Increasing Returns and Economic Geography." *The Journal of Political Economy*, 99 (3): 483–99.

Limão, N. and A.J. Venables. (2001). "Infrastructure, Geographical Disadvantage, Transport Costs, and Trade." *World Bank Economic Review*, 15: 451–79.

Nyangaga, F. N. 2002. "Overcoming Obstacles to Implementation: Reforming road management in Sub-Saharan Africa." Africa Technical Note No. 32, SSATP, World Bank.

OECD. 2001. *Intermodal Freight Transport: Institutional Aspects*. Paris: OECD, Road Transport and International Linkages Research Program.

Pálsson, G., A. Harding, and G. Raballand. 2007. "Port and Maritime Transport Challenges in West and Central Africa." SSATP Working Paper No. 84. Washington, DC: World Bank.

Portugal-Perez, A. and J. Wilson. 2009a. "Why Trade Facilitation Matters for Africa." *World Trade Review*, 1: 1–38.

Portugal-Perez, A. and J. Wilson. 2009b. "Revisiting Trade Facilitation Indicators and Export Performance." Mimeo, World Bank.

Raballand, G., and E. Aldaz-Carroll. 2005. "How Do Differing Standards Increase Trade Costs? The Case of Pallets", Policy Research Working Paper No. 3519. Washington, DC: World Bank.

Raballand, G., C. Kunaka, and B. Giersing. 2008. "The Impact of Regional Liberalization and Harmonization in Road Transport Services: A Focus on Zambia and Lessons for Landlocked Countries." Policy Research Working Paper No. 4482. Washington, DC: World Bank.

Raballand, G., C. Kunaka, J.F. Marteau, J-K. Kabanguka, and O. Hartmann. 2008. "Lessons of Corridor Performance Measurement." SSATP Discussion Paper No. 7, Regional Integration and Transport — RIT Series. Washington, CD: World Bank.

Regional Trade Facilitation Program website: http://www.rtfp.org/overview_border.php

Standard Bank. 2008. "African Infrastructure Survey — Harnessing Local Opinion and Insight." Research Economics, Africa Hardcover.

Sub-Saharan Africa Transport Policy Program (SSATP). 2006. Road Maintenance Funds Matrix: Country Policy and Reform Status, SSATP website.

Teravaninthorn, S. and G. Raballand. 2009. *Transport Prices and Costs in Africa: A Review of the International Corridors.* Washington, DC: World Bank.

United Nations, 2008. *World Urbanization Prospects: The 2007 Revision.* Executive Summary. Department of Economic and Social Affairs, New York.

World Bank. 2007. "CEMAC: Transport — Transit Facilitation Project." Report No. 38463-AFR, Project Appraisal Document. Washington, DC: World Bank.

———. **2009.** *Africa's Infrastructure: A Time for Transformation, Part 2 — Sectoral Snapshots.* Flagship Report: AICD Study. Washington, DC: World Bank Group.

———. **2010.** "Connecting to Compete, Trade Logistics in the Global Economy, The Logistics Performance Index and Its Indicators", World Bank Group, Washington, DC.

Annex 4.1: Logistics Performance Index (LPI) across African countries, 2010

Country	LPI Rank	LPI	Customs	Infra-structure	International shipments	Logistics competence	Tracking & tracing	Timeliness
South Africa	28	3.46	3.22	3.42	3.26	3.59	3.73	3.57
Senegal	58	2.86	2.45	2.64	2.75	2.73	3.08	3.52
Tunisia	61	2.84	2.43	2.56	3.36	2.36	2.56	3.57
Uganda	66	2.82	2.84	2.35	3.02	2.59	2.45	3.52
Benin	69	2.79	2.38	2.48	2.65	2.64	3.07	3.49
Mauritius	82	2.72	2.71	2.29	3.24	2.43	2.57	2.91
Congo, Dem. Rep.	85	2.68	2.60	2.27	2.56	2.93	2.43	3.20
Madagascar	88	2.66	2.35	2.63	3.06	2.40	2.51	2.90
Egypt	92	2.61	2.11	2.22	2.56	2.87	2.56	3.31
Tanzania	95	2.60	2.42	2.00	2.78	2.38	2.56	3.33
Togo	96	2.60	2.40	1.82	2.42	2.45	3.42	3.02
Guinea	97	2.60	2.34	2.10	2.43	2.68	2.89	3.10
Kenya	99	2.59	2.23	2.14	2.84	2.28	2.89	3.06
Nigeria	100	2.59	2.17	2.43	2.84	2.45	2.45	3.10
Cameroon	105	2.55	2.11	2.10	2.69	2.53	2.60	3.16
Niger	106	2.54	2.06	2.28	2.66	2.42	2.45	3.28
Cote d'Ivoire	109	2.53	2.16	2.37	2.44	2.57	2.95	2.73
Gambia, The	113	2.49	2.38	2.17	2.54	2.37	2.27	3.15
Chad	115	2.49	2.27	2.00	2.75	2.04	2.62	3.14
Congo, Rep.	116	2.48	2.02	1.62	2.33	2.42	2.33	4.00
Ghana	117	2.47	2.35	2.52	2.38	2.42	2.51	2.67
Comoros	120	2.45	1.96	1.76	2.56	2.26	2.79	3.23
Gabon	122	2.41	2.23	2.09	2.29	2.31	2.67	2.87
Ethiopia	123	2.41	2.13	1.77	2.76	2.14	2.89	2.65
Djibouti	126	2.39	2.25	2.33	2.50	2.17	2.42	2.67
Liberia	127	2.38	2.28	2.00	2.33	2.16	2.38	3.08
Algeria	130	2.36	1.97	2.06	2.70	2.24	2.26	2.81
Libya	132	2.33	2.15	2.18	2.28	2.28	2.08	2.98

cont.

Annex 4.1 (cont.)

Country	LPI Rank	LPI	Customs	Infra-structure	International shipments	Logistics competence	Tracking & tracing	Timeliness
Botswana	134	2.32	2.09	2.09	1.91	2.29	2.59	2.99
Mozambique	136	2.29	1.95	2.04	2.77	2.20	2.28	2.40
Zambia	138	2.28	2.17	1.83	2.41	2.01	2.35	2.85
Mali	139	2.27	2.08	2.00	2.17	2.13	2.31	2.90
Angola	142	2.25	1.75	1.69	2.38	2.02	2.54	3.01
Burkina Faso	145	2.23	2.22	1.89	1.73	2.02	2.77	2.77
Sudan	146	2.21	2.02	1.78	2.11	2.15	2.02	3.09
Guinea-Bissau	149	2.10	1.89	1.56	2.75	1.56	1.71	2.91
Rwanda	151	2.04	1.63	1.63	2.88	1.85	1.99	2.05
Namibia	152	2.02	1.68	1.71	2.20	2.04	2.04	2.38
Sierra Leone	153	1.97	2.17	1.61	2.33	1.53	1.73	2.33
Eritrea	154	1.70	1.50	1.35	1.63	1.88	1.55	2.21
Somalia	155	1.34	1.33	1.50	1.33	1.33	1.17	1.38

Source: World Bank (2010).

Annex 4.2: Overview of the Major African Trade and Transport Corridors

(i) Trans-Africa Highway (TAH)

The Trans-Africa Highway is the most ambitious road program in Africa. It was formulated in the early 1970s by the African Union (AU), the African Development Bank (AfDB), United Nations Economic Commission for Africa (ECA), and Africa's Regional Economic Communities. Its aim was to establish a network of all-weather roads of good quality which would: (a) as much as possible provide direct road links between capitals of the continent; (b) contribute to the political, economic, and social integration and cohesion of Africa; and (c) ensure road transport facilities between important areas of production and consumption.

The Trans-Africa Highway network is conceived of as nine interlinked highways with a total length of 56,683 km (see Box 4.5).

The sponsors estimate that completing the Trans-Africa Highway will cost about US$ 47 billion over 15 years (expenditures of approximately US$ 35 billion for upgrading and maintenance and an additional US$ 12 billion for administration, monitoring of road conditions, and programs that compensate abutting settlements for loss of revenue from barricades). The economic benefits are estimated at about US$ 250 billion and the project is expected to generate around 14 million person-years of employment.

A study was jointly conducted by ECA and the AfDB in 2002 to review the existing

---

Box 4.5: The Trans-Africa Highway network: nine interlinked sections

TAH 1: Cairo–Dakar Highway: 8,636 km. TAH 1 joins with TAH 7 to form an additional north–south route around the western extremity of the continent.

TAH 2: Algiers–Lagos Highway: 4,504 km.

TAH 3: Tripoli–Windhoek–(Cape Town) Highway, 10,808 km. This route has the greatest number of missing links and requires the greatest amount of new construction.

TAH 4: Cairo–Gaborone–(Pretoria/Cape Town) Highway, 10,228 km.

TAH 5: Dakar–Ndjamena Highway: 4,496 km. Also known as the Trans-Sahelian Highway, this links West African countries of the Sahel.

TAH 6: Ndjamena–Djibouti Highway: 4,219 km: contiguous with TAH 5, continuing through the eastern Sahelian region to the Indian Ocean port of Djibouti.

TAH 7: Dakar–Lagos Highway: 4,010 km. This highway joins with TAH 1 to form an additional north–south route around the western extremity of the continent.

TAH 8: Lagos–Mombasa Highway: 6,259 km.

TAH 9: Beira–Lobito Highway: 3,523 km.

Source: AfDB/UNECA (2003)

---

physical condition of the TAH network, to highlight problems and prospects of the non-physical barriers to road transport operations, as well as the institutional framework for the development and harmonization of the TAH network (AfDB/UNECA, 2003). The total funding requirement for completion of missing links was estimated at about US$ 4.3 billion. The study proposed the next steps to be taken for TAH implementation should include financial and technical feasibility studies of the sections deemed to be in need of improvements. However, it would appear that little progress in this area has been made in the intervening seven years.

(ii) The Northern Corridor

Countries linked

The Northern Corridor is the transport corridor linking the Great Lakes countries of Burundi, DRC, Rwanda and Uganda to the Kenyan seaport of Mombasa. The corridor also serves Northern Tanzania, Southern Sudan, and Ethiopia.

Corridor administration

The Northern Corridor is administered by the Northern Corridor Transit Transport Coordination Authority (NCTTCA), created in the mid-1980s, following the signing of the Northern Corridor Transit Agreement by Burundi, Kenya, Rwanda, and Uganda. The Democratic Republic of Congo became a contracting state of the NCTTCA in 1987 after ratifying the Treaty.

Corridor characteristics

The corridor includes the Mombasa port, which is the largest and busiest port in eastern Africa.

The main roads network totals nearly 7,000 km, of which only 60 percent is paved. The main axis is the Mombasa–Nairobi–Kampala–Kigali–Bujumbura road. Eastern DRC links extend from Kigali through either Goma or Bukavu to Kisangani. From Uganda, Eastern DRC is linked via Bunagana, Mpondwe, Ishasha, Goli and Aru border posts, with the main axis going through Kasindi, Beni, Komanda, and Niania to Kisangani.

The railroad network comprises the Kenya/Uganda sections from Mombasa through Nairobi, Nakuru, Eldoret, Malaba, Jinja, and Kampala to Kasese in western Uganda (a distance of approximately 1,660 km). A branch line runs from Nakuru to Kisumu on Lake Victoria (217 km), where there is a wagon ferry link with Jinja and Port Bell in Kampala.

There are inland waterways on Lake Victoria, Lake Albert, Lake Kivu, the River Nile, and the River Congo.

The landlocked countries of Uganda, Rwanda, Burundi and Eastern DR Congo access their fuel supplies from the oil pipeline, initially between Nairobi and Mombasa but then extended to Kisumu and Eldoret.

Investment opportunities

There are a number of investment opportunities along the Northern Corridor, as outlined by NCTTCA. In addition, the World Bank has initiated a support project on the Northern Corridor that seeks to increase efficiency of road transport; to facilitate trade and regional integration; enhance aviation safety and security to meet international standards; and to promote private sector participation in the management, financing, and maintenance of road assets.

Table 4.5: Estimated interregional trade volume effect of road network upgrading[1] (US$ million) in SSA, 2006

Regional Pair[2]	Current Network Trade	Upgraded Network Trade	Change
West West	2,838	9,062	6,224
West Central	647	1,252	605
West East	23	93	70
West Southern	4	24	20
West South	870	1,540	670
Central Central	200	1,551	1,351
Central East	308	348	40
Central Southern	127	194	67
Central South	1,390	2,374	984
East East	724	1,182	458
East Southern	101	124	23
East South	871	1,378	507
Southern Southern	72	99	27
Southern South	1,868	6,753	4,885
Totals:			
Within Regions	3,834	11,894	8,060
Across Regions	6,209	14,080	7,871
West, Central East Africa with South Africa	3,131	5,292	2,161
West, Central, East Africa with Southern Africa	1,210	2,035	825
Southern Africa with South Africa	1,868	6,753	4,885

Source: Buys et al. (2006).

Notes: [1] The road network upgrade is simulated by increasing all link quality indices to a minimum level of 45. The quality indices have been elaborated by Buys *et al.* (2006) based on a mildly increasing-returns function and which captures "percent paved" roads, but also government revenues supporting road maintenance. Values by country have been normalized to 100 for the highest-quality road transport (in South Africa).

[2] Because of data issues, the following countries are not included: Botswana, Lesotho, Namibia, Swaziland, Liberia and Somalia. The other countries are grouped into regions as follows:

West: Benin, Burkina Faso, Chad, Côte d'Ivoire, The Gambia, Ghana, Guinea, Guinea-Bissau, Mali, Mauritania, Niger, Nigeria, Senegal, Sierra Leone, Togo

Central: Angola, Burundi, Cameroon, Central African Republic, D.R. Congo, Gabon, Rep. Congo, Rwanda, Zambia

East: Djibouti, Eritrea, Ethiopia, Kenya, Malawi, Sudan, Tanzania, Uganda

Southern: Mozambique, Zimbabwe

South: South Africa

Table 4.6: Rehabilitation and upgrading of the Northern Corridor's existing railroad network

Section	Rehabilitation/Upgrade Requirements	Estimated Cost (US$ million)
Mombasa–Nairobi (530 km)	This section, laid with 95 lb rails, requires spot improvement and replacement of rails and sleepers	5
Nairobi–Malaba (550 km)	Upgrading to 110 lb rails, replacement of sleepers and reconstruction of culverts	62
Nakuru–Kisumu (217 km)	Upgrading from the Nakuru to Mau Summit, a distance of 60 km, from 60 to 80 lb rail occurred between 2002 and 2004. Remaining section requires the upgrade	47
Malaba–Kampala (250 km)	Emergency repairs of bad spots, culverts and bridges are being undertaken with financing from the EU. Permanent railway rehabilitation and improvement of the signaling and telecommunications systems is required	38
Kampala–Kasese (330 km)	Major rehabilitation, including the strengthening of the basement, realignment, reconstruction of culverts and bridges, and replacing rails and sleepers	42–100
Tororo–Mbale–Soroti –Gulu–Pakwach Line (502 km)	Insecurity in Northern Uganda led to frequent closures of this line. When it opens, only freight services operate up to a certain point on the line	–

Source: Northern Corridor Transit Transport Coordination Authority (NCTTCA).

Table 4.6 details areas where railroad network rehabilitation and upgrading are need for the Northern Corridor.

(iii) The North–South Corridor (NSC)

Countries linked

The North–South Corridor (NSC) links the ports in South Africa to the port of Dar es Salaam in Tanzania, through Botswana, the copperbelts of Zambia, Mozambique, Malawi, DRC, Zimbabwe and Tanzania. It also links with the port of Wallis Bay in Namibia and Lobito in Angola.

Corridor administration

The NS Corridor is administered by three RECs: the COMESA, EAC and SADC, through the North–South Corridor Pilot Aid for Trade Program. The Program is aimed at enabling the RECs, their member states, and the international community to implement an economic corridor-based approach to reduce costs of cross-border trade in the region. It takes a holistic approach to enable producers and traders to be more competitive, thereby creating higher levels of economic growth, employment creation, and reducing poverty.

Corridor characteristics

The regional transport sector is characterized by the busiest traffic in the region in terms of values and volumes of freight but also by poor road and rail infrastructure and long waiting times at borders and ports. Those delays create significant costs and hamper regional producers' ability to access regional and international markets. The road transport system is highly competitive, deregulated, and competes openly with rail services.

The railroad network in the corridor is characterized by inflexibility, in relation to schedules and poor intermodality, resulting in delays and unreliability. The level of hard infrastructure railroad is low, as sections require refurbishment and upgrading and improvement in operations, and consequently suffer from poor efficiency and capacity constraints, including speed restrictions, shortage of operational railroad wagons, availability of locomotives, and lack of operating capital for the purchase of spares and fuel.

Investment opportunities

Some of the most effective cost-reducing measures on the corridor would be road rehabilitation; reduction in fuel costs; and, to a lesser extent, reduction in journey times and harmonization of national rules and regulations.

(iv) The Maputo Corridor

Countries linked

The Maputo Corridor links Zimbabwe, Swaziland, Botswana, and Mozambique, although it only runs through South Africa and Mozambique.

From as far east as the deep seaport of Walvis Bay in Namibia, the Trans-Kalahari Corridor connects Namibia's capital, Windhoek, with landlocked Botswana's capital, Gaborone, via the vast expanse of the Kalahari Desert. From there, direct rail and road links connect Gaborone with the Maputo Corridor along a transport route that can rightly be called the Capital Corridor, passing through

- Mafikeng, provincial capital of South Africa's Northwest Province;
- Pretoria, South Africa's executive capital located in the greater Tshwane Metropolitan Municipality;
- Johannesburg, capital of Gauteng Province;
- Nelspruit, capital of Mpumalanga Province; and
- Mozambique's capital, Maputo.

Corridor administration

The Maputo Corridor is administered by the Maputo Corridor Logistics Initiative (MCLI). It was established as a nonprofit organization consisting of infrastructure investors, service providers, and stakeholders from Mozambique, South Africa, and Swaziland to focus on the promotion and further development of the Maputo Development Corridor (MDC) as the region's primary logistics transportation route.

Corridor's characteristics

The Maputo Corridor is part of a greater transport axis linking the Atlantic and Indian Ocean via the subcontinent of Southern Africa, and runs through the most highly industrialized and productive regions of Southern Africa.

Unlocking the landlocked regions of the Mpumalanga, Gauteng, and Limpopo Provinces, the Maputo Corridor is a true transportation corridor, comprising road, rail, border posts, port and terminal facilities. The corridor is also characterized by poor road conditions between Johannesburg and Maputo, insufficient rail capacity and long journey times, long border crossing times, limited direct shipping opportunities, and limited port access.

Investment opportunities

The initial strategic focus of MCLI is to engage with the governments of South Africa, Mozambique, and Swaziland to reinforce the public–private partnerships in the arena of logistics, to ensure that the Maputo Corridor is the first choice for regional importers and exporters alike.

The governments of South Africa and Mozambique have promoted the revival of the Maputo Corridor as part of a greater Spatial Development Initiative, with bilateral policies and substantial public and private sector investments, designed to stimulate sustainable growth and development in the region. Now private businesses are needed to ensure full optimization of the Maputo Development Corridor.

The following have been identified as priority areas:

- Continuous improvement of border procedures and operational hours;
- Increased scope and competitiveness of transport services: additional capacity, higher service levels, and more competitive rates for road, rail, port, terminals and shipping lines;
- Creation and continuous enhancement of information services; and
- Coordination and acceleration of promotion of investment zones.

These challenges have been addressed by the Maputo Corridor Logistics Initiative and there is now a new, high-quality toll road, concessioned to a private operator, Maputo Railway Services. As a result, the rail has been rehabilitated and new rolling stock purchased. Waiting times at the border have been reduced and border opening times have been extended, with plans to make the border a one-stop border post. Direct container shipments have been introduced; and significant investments have been made to improve access to the port.

(v) Walvis Bay Corridors

Countries linked

The Walvis Bay Corridors comprise a network of transport corridors including the Port of Walvis Bay, the Trans-Kalahari Corridor, the Trans-Caprivi Corridor, the Trans-Cunene Corridor, and the Trans-Oranje Corridor.

Corridor administration

These corridors are managed by the Walvis Bay Corridor Group, a public–private partnership that allows it to pool resources and authorities of both transport regulators and transport operators, thus effectively serving as a facilitation center and one-stop shop coordinating trade along the Walvis Bay Corridors and linking Walvis Bay port to the rest of the Southern African subregion.

Corridors' characteristics

According to a report in the Namibian press[13] in January 2009, trade volumes along the Trans-Kalahari, Trans-Caprivi and Trans-Cunene corridors have increased from 174,299 tonnes to 282,031 tonnes, representing a growth rate of more than 61.8 percent on tonnage shipped between 2007 and 2008. The estimated revenue generated by the transport sector along the corridors increased by N\$ 45.9 million from the N\$ 73.5 million in the 2006/2007 financial year to N\$ 119.5 million in 2007/2008 and volumes on the Trans-Kalahari Corridor (TKC) increased by 19.1 percent from 4,917 to 5,857 tonnes. Volumes on the Trans-Caprivi Corridor (TCC) increased by more than 76.7 percent from 27,521 to 48,627 tonnes. Volumes on the Trans-Cunene (TCuC) increased by 60.4 percent from 141,861 to 227,548 tonnes.

The Walvis Bay Corridors, in particular the Trans-Caprivi, are seen as providing an alternative route to the Zambian and DR Congo's Copperbelt. The Trans-Kalahari Corridor route has seen a significant shift whereby road transporters and traders have moved from the traditional trade route via southern Namibia into South Africa. More than 40 percent of road transporters are now utilizing the route from Johannesburg, South Africa via Botswana into Namibia.

Walvis Bay could also be regarded as the most convenient and nearest port for a large part of Angola and the Trans-Cunene Corridor reached record levels in cargo movement in 2008 with the redevelopment of the Angolan economy, as more and more consumables, vehicles and construction materials were ordered and supplied via the Port of Walvis Bay.

The Group's main competitive strength is its setup of transport and logistics stakeholders from both the public and private sectors. This allows for the pooling of resources, expertise and authorities from both the regulators and the operators.

(vi) West African Transport Corridors

Countries linked

The West African Transport Corridors link six coastal countries (Ghana, Benin, Côte d'Ivoire, Senegal, Guinea, and Togo) and three LLCs (Burkina Faso, Mali, and Niger).

Corridors' characteristics

The landlocked countries of West Africa have traditionally been dependent on the ports to their south. According to the Web Atlas on Regional Integration in West Africa,[14] between 1999 and 2003, transport operations to and from Mali, Burkina Faso, and Niger rose by nearly 70 percent, from 2.0 to 3.4 million tonnes of goods, which represents approximately 7.5 percent of total traffic at the ports of Dakar, Abidjan, Takoradi, Tema, Lomé, and Cotonou. These transactions consisted principally of imports of consumer products and exports of agricultural products (mainly cotton).

In 1999, more than 50 percent of the transit traffic with these countries was through the port of Abidjan. The rest was

---

[13] http://www.economist.com.na/content/view/10571/70/

[14] http://www.atlas-ouestafrique.org/spip.php?article45

shared between Cotonou (19 percent), Lomé (17 percent), Dakar (11 percent), and Tema (1 percent). However, between 2002 and 2003, the traffic of goods in transit between Abidjan and the landlocked countries declined fivefold. The operations with Burkina Faso have declined from 390,000 to 15,000 tonnes. While in 1998, Burkina Faso exported 80 percent of its cotton through Abidjan, by 2003 no exports from Burkina Faso were going through the Ivorian port.

Nouakchott, in Mauritania, built with Chinese assistance in the 1980s, is growing in importance and size and is now providing competition to Abidjan, Dakar, and Tema. Nouakchott is increasingly used by Malian exporters and importers because traffic from landlocked Mali to Nouakchott has become easier and cheaper owing to less bureaucracy and fewer checkpoints on the road. Although the ports to the south of Mali are closer, the 1,500-km Bamako–Nouakchott route is considered to be a practical alternative by many. The road from Bamako to Néma (in the southwest of Mauritania) is in poor condition but the Néma–Nouakchott "Trans-Mauritanian highway" of about 1,000 km in length, is in good condition.

There have been significant improvements in connectivity in West Africa resulting from improved road links between Bamako–Conakry and Bamako–Nouakchott, and the privatization of the railroad between Dakar and Bamako and the Abidjan–Ouagadougou lines. The more traditional north–south transport and transit corridors are now facing growing competition from east–west corridors, notably from Dakar, Nouakchott, Banjul, and Conakry.

The Ivorian crisis has demonstrated the ability of regional actors to swiftly adapt transit activity to circumstances and opportunities. The closing of international road and rail routes from Abidjan resulted in a rerouting of freight to other ports in Togo, Benin, and Ghana (Teravaninthorn and Raballand, 2009). In the future, the big transport flows could again experience such pendulum swings; not only in order to bypass areas of political instability, but also to make use of the most competitive ports as well as the fastest and least expensive roads.

(vii) The CEMAC Trade and Transport Corridor

Countries linked

The CEMAC Trade and Transport Corridor links all the CEMAC country members: Cameroon, Central African Republic (CAR), Chad, the Republic of Congo, Equatorial Guinea, and Gabon.

Corridor's administration

A Trade and Transport Facilitation Program was adopted in March 2006 by the CEMAC member states. It is aimed at implementing a regional institutional framework; harmonizing national regulations; fostering customs interconnectivity and information technology systems within the region; and implementing a pilot trade and transport facilitation project on the N'Djamha–Douala (about 1,850 km) and Bangui–Douala (about 1,450 km) surface transport corridors.

Corridor's characteristics

Intraregional trade among the six countries represents less than 5 percent of the total trade in the subregion. This is primarily due to the dominance of oil, and forestry, mineral and agricultural commodities in all countries' trade mix, as well as the similarity in production structure of goods and services in the subregion. Furthermore, the current inefficient transit system which hinders regional integration, and the poor condition of road, and to a lesser extent rail infrastructure, keep the share of intra-regional trade at a very low level.

The major international trade routes in the CEMAC area consist mostly of the N'Djamha–Douala and the Bangui–Douala corridors, which link the port of Douala by road or by a combination of rail and road to landlocked CAR and Chad. Alternative corridors carry only limited traffic. Some of the road sections are currently being rehabilitated by other development partners (EC, Arab donors, France, Japan, etc.). However, the committed funding remains insufficient to secure an all-weather road network between the main CEMAC trade centers, which was one of the stated objectives of the "Réseau Intégrateur CEMAC 2000."

Table 4.7: Main characteristics of the African transport corridors

Corridor	Administrative Body	Bottlenecks	Investment Needs
Trans-African Highway	African Union	• Non-physical barriers • Institutional framework harmonization	• Technical and financial feasibility studies of the remaining sections.
Northern Corridor	Northern Corridor Transit Transport Coordination Authority	NA	• Increase efficiency of road sector • Facilitate trade and regional integration • Enhance aviation safety and security to meet international standards • Promote private sector participation in the management, financing and maintenance of roads assets
North–South Corridor	North–South Corridor Pilot Aid for Trade Program	• Poor road and rail infrastructure • Long waiting time at borders and ports • High rail tariffs and unpredictability because of poor management, inadequate use of assets and poor costing practices	• Need for an effective regional economic transport regulator to regulate competition • Road rehabilitation • Reduction in fuel costs • Reduction of border-crossing delays

(cont.)

Table 4.7: cont.

Corridor	Administrative Body	Bottlenecks	Investment Needs
		• High road maintenance costs due to permissible gross vehicle mass (GMV)	• Aligning and harmonizing sequentially countries' trade and transport policies, procedures, and regulations • Ensure that adequate power supply is available to industrial, commercial and domestic consumers
Maputo Corridor	Maputo Corridor Logistics Initiative	• Poor road conditions • Insufficient rail capacity • Long journey times, long border crossing times • Limited direct shipping opportunities • Limited port access	• Reinforcement of PPPs in the arena of logistics • Improvement of border procedures and operational hours • Increased scope and competitiveness of transport services: additional capacity, higher service levels and more competitive rates for road, rail, port, terminals and shipping lines • Implementation and enhancement of information services • Promotion of investment zones
Walvis Bay Corridors	Walvis Bay Corridor Group	NA	NA
West African Transport Corridors	NA	NA	NA

(cont.)

Table 4.7: cont.

Corridor	Administrative Body	Bottlenecks	Investment Needs
CEMAC Corridors	CEMAC Trade and Transport Facilitation Program	• Current inefficient transit system which hinders regional integration • Poor condition of road, and to a lesser extent rail infrastructure • Committed funding remains insufficient to secure an all-weather road network	NA

CHAPTER 5

Contribution of the AfDB to Infrastructure Development

Drawing on the key findings from the previous chapters, this chapter shifts focus to assess activities that the African Development Bank Group (AfDB) has undertaken specifically in the areas of ports and related logistics. It points to critical areas of intervention where the Bank can consolidate its leadership role and best direct its support. The positive news is that the Bank places a very high level of importance on infrastructure development in its lending strategy, as emphasized by its Medium-Term Strategy 2008–2012. Indeed, the AfDB considers the lack of adequate infrastructure and, in particular, the lack of transport infrastructure, as one of the main constraints threatening the growth momentum in Africa. This vision is supported by an internal policy framework which has been a driver of the Bank's activities in developing transport logistics including roads, railroads, and ports at both national and regional levels. The main activities that have been undertaken in this area fall under the following broad functions: *policy formulation*, *operations* (both public and private sectors), *regional integration,* and *partnership activities with development finance institutions (DFIs) and donors.* Each of these areas of Bank intervention is analyzed below.

From the viewpoint of its investment program in ports, between 1973 and 2000 the Bank invested US$ 804.39 million through 27 lending operations. Furthermore, the Bank's Private Sector Department (OPSM) has been instrumental in the course of the last decade in supporting the ports concession process in several African countries (see Annexes 5.1 and 5.2). This approach enforces some of the key findings in this report, in particular the need to increase private participation in the port subsector.

Linking to other modes of transport, the Bank has also taken a major role in addressing transport infrastructure, in particular roads, which are vital for the interconnectivity of ports to the hinterland. This has been achieved through investments in both national and regional projects and programs. Nonetheless, there is still room to explore opportunities in railroad projects and other modes of transport, for example, navigable rivers and lakes (e.g. the Zambezi–Shire Waterway project between Malawi and Mozambique; see Box 4.1 in Chapter 4), to ease pressure on roads for the movement of goods across the continent. In terms of Bank strategy and policy, one area that demands increased focus is maritime transportation; here a strong policy framework is needed to guide investment decisions in ports and related logistics.

Policy Formulation

The Bank policy framework for port development in Africa is guided by its *Transport Sector Policy.* The transport sector was selected by the Bank Group's 2008–2012 Medium Term Strategy (MTS) as one of its four key sectors of focus, to benefit from a significant proportion of the Bank's new commitments to infrastructure investments. The Bank's Transport Sector Policy was approved in February 1992 and superseded its previous policy in this sector, dated October 1991. The Operational Resource and Policy Department (ORPC) in its 2010 Work Program is scheduled to update the Bank's Transport Sector Policy.

The existing Transport Sector Policy distinguishes five subsectors based on physical and economic characteristics. These subsectors generally correspond to the primary modes of moving passengers and freight, and include roads, railroads, water transport (or maritime transport), air transport, and urban transport. The Bank's policy has three specific objectives: (i) to provide guidance to sector lending; (ii) to stimulate policy dialogue; and (iii) to strengthen coordination. The Policy Guidance to sector lending provides a frame of reference for internal decision-making by the Bank Group regarding transport projects and programs formulated by its regional member countries (RMCs).

The scope of the AfDB's interventions on behalf of its RMCs includes lending for projects and programs, sector and structural adjustment loans, and technical assistance. In order to increase the amount of financing available, the Bank Group promotes cofinancing arrangements with other organizations that have complementary development objectives. These financial resources are channeled to transport projects and programs which have been carefully prepared and assessed by due diligence work carried out by the Bank. The AfDB takes into consideration the following five general priorities in its lending program: (i) investment, rehabilitation and maintenance; (ii) regional trade and transport; (iii) role of government and private sector; (iv) cost recovery and financial considerations; and (v) institutional and human resources development (see Box 5.1).

Among these objectives identified in the Transport Sector Policy and to meet the key challenges of the water transport in the continent, the Bank has identified strategic options for the promotion of maritime transport. These options are described in Table 5.1. Although this blueprint articulates the focal areas that guide the Bank in its lending policies, the strategy has not yet resulted in key interventions in the area of maritime transport. The new *Transport Strategy*, which is expected to be unveiled in 2010, will provide more information and foster a better understanding of this subsector. This should result in a better targeting of activities, given the urgent needs of the port subsector. Areas for future

> **Box 5.1: Transport sector – the AfDB's five lending priorities**
>
> - **Investment, Rehabilitation and Maintenance**: Fostering an appropriate balance of expenditures for new infrastructure and equipment, rehabilitation and maintenance, based on national investment planning and coordination.
> - **Regional Trade and Transport**: Eliminating nonphysical and physical barriers to regional and international trade and transport, particularly along major transport corridors.
> - **Role of Government and Private Sector**: Creating regulatory environments conducive to the provision of efficient and safe transport services, minimizing the intervention of government in transport operations and services, and encouraging the involvement of the private sector.
> - **Cost Recovery and Financial Considerations**: Reducing or eliminating public subsidies to transport infrastructure and operations, increasing operator revenues and decreasing costs, and strengthening financial and management systems.
> - **Institutional and Human Resources Development**: Fostering institutional reform, training, education and professional development.

investment and support, such as building regulatory institutions, management reforms, human resources development, shipping coordination, strengthening maintenance procedures, inland waterway development, and multimodal regulation, which are highlighted in Table 5.1, resonate with the findings presented in previous chapters of this report.

Table 5.1: Strategic options for the promotion of maritime transport in Africa

Focal Area	Issues	Strategy
Institutional	• Inappropriate institutional frameworks for maritime administration • Inadequate institutional support for multimodal transport	• Establish and strengthen national organization for maritime administration • Form a national trade and transport promotion group to address multimodal issues in maritime administration
Management	• Inefficient management of ports • Lack of port security • Lack of organization and application of modern management practices by African shippers	• Reform management practices to encourage decision-making freedom and accountability • Strengthening the organization and staffing of port security • Improve organizational structures and management procedures
Human Resources Development	• Inadequate training and human resource management • Hazardous working conditions on shore and at sea	• Establish and strengthen regional training programs • Review and improve work rules and regulations
Shipper Coordination	• Lack of shipper representation in port administration and management decision-making	• Strengthen the role of shippers' councils and other coordination bodies
Maintenance	• Inadequate shoreside and seaboard maintenance practices • Shortage of skilled maintenance personnel	• Establish and strengthen maintenance management procedures • Provide technical training programs for maintenance personnel
Regional Cooperation	• Lack of shipping policy coordination and cooperation	• Improve the organization and management of port associations
Inland Waterway Investment	• Lack of inland waterway facilities	• Prepare integrated investment plans for inland waterways development
Multimodal Regulation	• Inappropriate regulation of multimodal transport	• Rationalize regulations pertaining to multimodal transport

---

Box 5.2: The AfDB's environment policy for infrastructure projects

Infrastructure and port projects, although crucial for Africa's economic development, can sometimes have unintended negative environmental impacts. A Bank Group Environment Policy was first adopted in 1990, to promote environmental mainstreaming in all Bank operations. Environmental and Social Assessment Procedures and a new Environment Policy were released in 2001 and 2004 respectively.

A set of new approaches is currently adopted by the Bank in its operations in order to: (i) mainstream environmental sustainability considerations into all the Bank's operations; (ii) strengthen existing environmental assessment procedures and develop new environmental management tools; (iii) clearly demarcate internal responsibility in implementation; (iv) assist RMCs to build adequate human and institutional capacity to deal with environmental management; (v) improve public consultation and information disclosure mechanisms; (vi) build partnerships to address environmental issues, harmonize policies, and disseminate environmental information; and (vii) improve monitoring and evaluation of operations.

In this way, environmental impacts of a project are reviewed throughout the project cycle, from the conception and programming stage, through to appraisal, supervision, and monitoring. In each operational department of the Bank, environmental and social specialists provide guidance and support and follow the project's progress.

Project categorization based on four levels of risk (4 being the lowest risk, 1 the highest) is one of the tools to address environmental issues. Port and infrastructure projects are rated as category 1, covering all projects that are likely to induce important adverse environmental and/or social impacts. As such, before an infrastructure project is presented to the Board for approval, the following steps need to be taken:

- conduct a full Environmental and Social Impact Assessment (ESIA), which examines the project's potential beneficial and adverse impacts, compares them with those of feasible alternatives, and recommends any measures needed to prevent, minimize, mitigate or compensate for adverse impacts and to enhance environmental and social project benefits;
- conduct an Environmental and Social Management Plan (ESMP), which summarizes the impacts; develops mitigation and enhancement measures with quantitative and qualitative details; and provides provisions for monitoring;
- conduct a Resettlement Action Plan (RAP) if relevant; and
- allow a period of 120 days' disclosure before Board presentation.

The Bank's promotion of, and adherence to, the highest international environmental and sustainability standards in its projects serves an important demonstration effect by encouraging the participation of other investors and partners.

AfDB's Operational Approach to Infrastructure Development

This section looks at the Bank Group's investments in infrastructure and related activities, followed by specific inventions in the public and private sector related to ports and other modes of transport. The Bank recognizes that the Infrastructure Department of the Bank (OINF) and the Private Sector Department (OPSM) must continue to develop a clear understanding of the strengths and constraints of the local infrastructure networks and market potentials. In that regard, Country and

Regional Strategy Papers, which are prepared in collaboration with the respective governments of countries concerned, should continue to be used as tools to define the needs and ensure coherence and synergies between assistance to the public and private sectors.

Based on consultations with RMCs as well on economic sector work, the public sector departments develop programs to address the weaknesses and constraints in the enabling environment. This may include the provision of public goods in "hard" infrastructure, comprising the sectors of energy, water and sanitation, transport, and telecommunications as well as in "soft" infrastructure, such as regulatory and legal frameworks, which are essential for economic growth and private sector development.

The Bank's Private Sector Department takes the lead in supporting private sector operations through a variety of instruments without a sovereign guarantee, including loans, lines of credit, guarantees, equity and quasi-equity investments, and technical assistance. These interventions are undertaken with private corporations, financial institutions, or state-owned enterprises and in partnership with other development institutions. In this way, the Bank seeks to build confidence around projects, and to attract other investors by creating a strong demonstration effect. In addition to the strategic alignment above, private sector projects are often assessed on the basis of their commercial viability, development outcomes, additionality, and complementarity.

Overview of AfDB Investments to the Sector

Infrastructure development in Africa, which includes transport but also energy, telecommunications, and water and sanitation, is one of the AfDB's top priorities. This is currently reflected in the Bank's 2010 operational work program, where infrastructure will account for 49 percent of total financing.

Since 2000, the renewed emphasis on infrastructure development has led to a sharp increase in AfDB investments to the sector, both in value and relative terms (see Figure 5.1). Lending approvals in the infrastructure sector reached a record high of US$ 3.05 billion in 2007 (75 percent of total approvals), an increase of around 125 percent over the 2006 level of US$ 1.29 billion. Of this US$ 3.05 billion, 40 percent was allocated to transport infrastructure. In terms of subregional allocations to hard infrastructure, North Africa received in 2007 the largest share (Figure 5.2).

However, as shown in Figure 5.1, in 2008 Bank Group investment approvals for infrastructure decreased to US$ 2.17 billion, although this still represented 45 percent of the AfDB's total commitment for the year. Regional infrastructure projects accounted for 12 percent of the Bank's total commitment. With respect to the transport subsector, in 2008 the Bank Group contributed US$ 393.94 million of its own funds to cofinance projects in the transport subsector, and mobilized an additional US$ 114.41 million from external partners and private sector institutions, with a further US$ 243.62 million coming from governments and local firms.

In terms of the split between financing windows for approvals in the infrastructure sector in 2008, US$ 1.05 billion (48 percent) came from the ADB window, compared to US$ 1.12 billion (52 percent) from the ADF window. The development of regional infrastructure also increased from US$ 193.80 million in 2006 to US$ 213.70 million in 2007, reflecting the Bank's emphasis on regional integration (AfDB, 2008; ICA, 2008a, 2008b, 2009). As a result of its strong commitment toward infrastructure development in Africa, the Bank emerges as one of the key players in this sector. Nevertheless, much remains to be done to bridge the infrastructure investment gap in Africa, which is estimated by the Africa Infrastructure Country Diagnostic (AICD) study to stand at US$ 31 billion per annum (World Bank, 2009).

To improve resource mobilization for the development of African ports, the Bank has mainly focused on developing public–private partnerships through its Private Sector Department. The public sector arm of the AfDB has targeted the development of the hinterland interface, mainly through the construction of road networks and the creation of regional trade corridors.

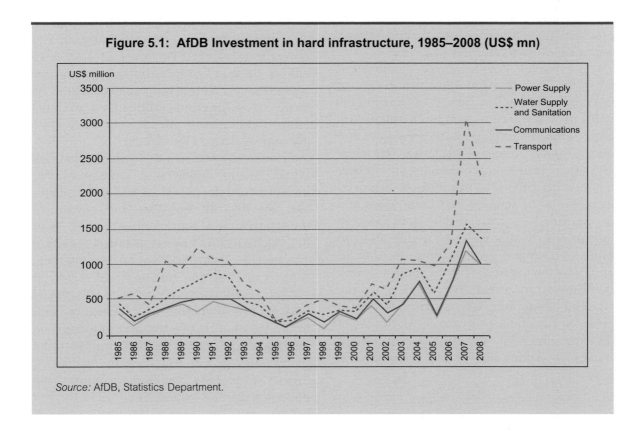

Figure 5.1: AfDB Investment in hard infrastructure, 1985–2008 (US$ mn)

Source: AfDB, Statistics Department.

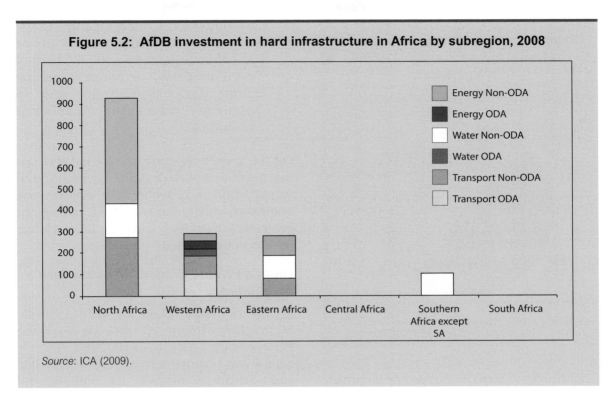

Figure 5.2: AfDB investment in hard infrastructure in Africa by subregion, 2008

Source: ICA (2009).

AfDB Investments in Ports: Lessons Learned

Between 1973 and 2000, the AfDB assumed a leadership role by carrying out substantial investment in ports, as documented in the *2001 Review of Bank Group Operations in the Maritime Subsector* (AfDB-COD, 2001). In that 17-year period, the Bank Group committed to US$ 804.39 million, representing 27 financing operations in regional member countries (see Annex 5.1). ADF financing accounted for 48 percent of the Bank Group's total maritime investments (see Figure 5.3).

The main areas of Bank Group support to the maritime sector during 1973–2000 included: (i) construction of new ports; (ii) reconstruction and rehabilitation of ports; (iii) procurement and installation of safety equipment; (iv) institutional support (e.g. capacity building, trade facilitation; enhancing the regulatory framework); and (v) maritime studies (i.e. to prepare projects or to evaluate the performance of the subsector). Within the *Maritime Review*'s timeframe (1973–2000), approximately 74 percent of the operations were implemented before 1990, while the remaining 26 percent were completed in 1997. The decline in the AfDB's pipeline of projects in the maritime subsector during this period is due to the fact that under the ADF-VII lending policy, there were no resources allocated to the ports subsector. This gave the Bank the

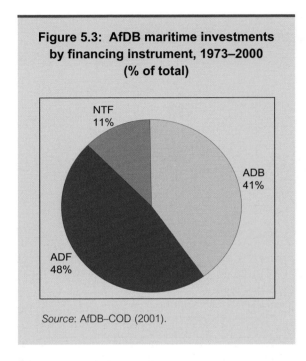

Figure 5.3: AfDB maritime investments by financing instrument, 1973–2000 (% of total)

NTF
11%

ADB
41%

ADF
48%

Source: AfDB–COD (2001).

opportunity to explore the use of its private sector window to finance port projects.

Another key finding of the *2001 Maritime Review* was the need to support regional integration, which is articulated as one of strategic areas of Bank intervention. In this respect, the Report highlighted the following critical focal areas:

- the need to finance inland waterway studies on selected lakes and rivers (such as Victoria, Chad, Niger, and Nile) that have significant regional integration impacts;
- the need to finance studies and mobilize resources to support the setting-up of inland multimodal container ports, which are required to facilitate the transit of cargo to landlocked countries; and

- to encourage RMCs and RECs, through policy dialogue, to cooperate in rationalizing their ports in terms of need and use, to adopt minimum tariffs for transit cargo, and to promote access to landlocked countries.

On the knowledge side, the Report stressed the need to conduct more economic and sector work, in order to fully evaluate the contribution of the maritime subsector projects to the overall economic development agenda.

Bank's Private Sector Infrastructure Investments

A principal objective of the Bank's Private Sector Department (OPSM) vis-à-vis the infrastructure sector is to promote PPPs by combining resources from both the public and private windows, as well as by providing technical assistance (TA) and capacity building to the Bank's RMCs. The combination of nonconcessional and concessional resources from the AfDB boosts the bankability of a project and makes it more attractive to private sector cofinanciers. Furthermore, a Public–Private Partnership Strategy is under preparation that should, among other things, define internal incentives and procedures for promoting private participation more robustly. As a result of this strategic orientation, all infrastructure projects submitted by OPSM for approval by the Board in 2007 and 2008 took the form of PPPs.

As African ports are increasingly privatizing part of their activities through

Box 5.3: AfDB's Technical Assistance support toward a feasibility study of road/railroad linkages between Kinshasa and Brazzaville

One example of technical assistance provided by the Bank to the transport sector in 2008 was to cofinance a study into a project designed to link the capital cities of the two Congos, Kinshasa (Democratic Republic of Congo) and Brazzaville (Republic of Congo) and to construct a 1,015-km railroad to connect the cities of Kinshasa and Ilebo in the DRC.

The study comprises two components: (i) feasibility and final design of the road/railroad bridge between the two capitals, including terminal facilities as well as access roads to existing road and railroad networks in both countries and (ii) the feasibility of the Kinshasa–Ilebo railroad.

These infrastructure linkages aim to increase interregional trade, reduce transportation costs and travel times between countries located along the corridor, and to fill one major missing link in the Tripoli–Windhoek corridor.

The Bank contributed an ADF grant of UA 5.0 million toward the total cost of the study (UA 5.44 million), with the remainder provided by the governments of the DRC and the Republic of Congo.

Source: AfDB (2008).

Over the past decade, the Bank has approved four major port projects: (i) a senior loan of US$ 10.0 million for the Djibouti Bulk Terminal (2003); US$ 150.0 million for the Damietta Container Terminal in Egypt (2007); US$ 80.0 million for the Doraleh Container Terminal in Djibouti (2008); and US$ 71.36 million (Euro 47.50 million) for the Dakar Container Terminal in Senegal (2009) (see Box 5.4 and Annex 5.2). All these projects were PPPs, financed by both the private and public sectors.

Private sector operations in the port subsector thrive where an enabling environment has been created by way of port reforms and the formulation of legal and regulatory frameworks. However, there are still ports in Africa that need to be deregulated, and this poses a challenge to private investment in these countries. In addition, other constraints impeding private sector involvement include: governance issues; insufficient capacity to design; contraction and regulation of the private sector participation; lack of local capital market to support private projects; the long gestation period needed for infrastructure projects; and reconciliation of recovery of cost with constraints in customers' affordability and availability of subsidies.

Given that many ports continent-wide have weak onshore and offshore infrastructure, poor management, shallow draft and low terminal capacity — and given too the advent of post-Panamax vessels (supersize ships), there is an urgent need to identify and develop hub ports along regional lines in order to attract international shipping lines. This will bring about greater economies of scale for ports, and so reduce

concessions, OPSM is also focusing on port infrastructure projects to be managed under concessional agreements. Over the last decade, about 25 percent of the cumulative approved operations emanating from the Private Sector Department have been in the transport sector, and of these, 50 percent are directly related to the development of ports in Africa.

maritime transport costs. Notwithstanding this overarching objective, there are good prospects for further development and expansion of container terminals in some ports. Indeed, OPSM is in the process of carrying out its due diligence on a number of port projects with PPP investment potential.

Public Sector Infrastructure Investments

Public infrastructure investments by the AfDB have traditionally focused on the development of the hinterland infrastructure networks through roads and, to a lesser extent, railroad projects and programs. Even though these networks may not link to a port interface, such infrastructures facilitate the movement of people and goods to markets, and ultimately boost trade.

In 2008, for example, the public sector division of the AfDB supported the development of road networks in Tunisia (Road Project V [AfDB — OINF, 2008b]) and Burkina Faso (AfDB — OINF, 2009c). In

---

Box 5.4: The Doraleh Container Terminal project in Djibouti

The Middle East has seen soaring container port volumes, and virtually all ports with privatized container operations are increasing their capacity and/or their capability to handle larger vessels. This includes the transshipment range comprising the Arabian Sea/Gulf of Aden ports. By contrast, cargo-handling facilities at most East African ports remain fairly basic.

Forecast demand in the subregion is strong for both the transit and transshipment businesses. Container port demand arising from Ethiopia's foreign trade has been increasing at around 1.5 times the rate of Ethiopian GDP growth over the last 5 years. For example, Ethiopian traffic at the Djibouti port has increased at an average growth rate of 20 percent per annum over the last 5 years and at 18 percent per annum over the last 10 years. Container port throughput in the broader region (which comprises Djibouti's potential transshipment market), increased by 218 percent over 1995–2005, reaching 32.6 million TEUs in 2005. Container transshipment demand for the Arabian Sea/Gulf of Aden port range, consisting of Salalah (Oman), Aden (Yemen), and Djibouti ports, is forecast to increase by 164–280 percent over the 2005–2015 period, to around 7.06–10.15 million TEUs.

To tap into the existing growth potential, in 2008 the Bank agreed to cofinance the construction of a new terminal at the natural deepwater port of Doraleh under a 30-year concession agreement awarded to Doraleh Container Terminal (DCT). The port is located a few kilometers from the existing Djibouti port, and will handle exclusively all container business in Djibouti. The Djibouti port will continue to operate for bulk cargo traffic only. The project will have a 1.5 km quayline length and the capacity to handle 1.55 million TEUs by 2015. The terminal will have the deepest draft in the region at 18 m and will be able to receive vessels with a capacity of up to 12,000 TEUs. The new site at Doraleh will be the first port after Suez capable of accommodating the latest generation of supersize container ships and is set to become an important transit port and transshipment hub.

The Bank agreed to invest US$ 80 million (20 percent of the total project cost). The project is co-sponsored by the Port Autonome International de Djibouti (PAID) and Dubai Port World (DPW).

Source: AfDB — OPSM (2008).

Tunisia the objectives were to support the upgrading of the classified roads network throughout the country, and to improve accessibility to the principal development poles to boost trade and economic growth. In Burkina Faso, the project aimed to reduce general transportation costs and to improve the state of roads along the main national corridor of the country. Burkina Faso is a landlocked country without a seaboard, so the diversification of its access corridors is critical to its development. The road targeted by the project was identified as the main highway corridor (among the five existing ones) to access neighboring ports located in Togo and Ghana in particular.

Nevertheless, the Bank also considers the development of public infrastructure in the broader framework of regional integration. The Bank's approach in this regard is the development of *trade corridors*, through the development of transnational multimodal transport networks, to link national economies and allow landlocked countries to access ports. The Bank considers this approach as a necessary condition of intraregional and global trade development as well as integration of national markets.

The identification of regional transport corridors is a key development strategy in a resource-constrained environment. In its recently approved *Regional Integration Strategy*, the Bank proposes to validate the identified development corridors by investigating their linkages and economic potential. This process would involve assessing individual development corridors in terms of growth, development impact opportunities, indicative infrastructure requirements, investment potential, and

ability to support regional integration. In this respect, the Bank will combine the development of the corridors with parallel investments in trade facilitation. In this regard, the Bank will promote and support private sector activities along the corridors, especially small and medium enterprises (SMEs), by promoting the implementation of favorable policy and regulatory frameworks and facilitation of trade. Support to SMEs will also help to promote economic diversification and exports.

The Bank has established itself as a leading financier of regional (multinational) operations in Africa, and this funding has traditionally come from the African Development Fund (ADF), which is the AfDB's concessionary window. However, more recently, increasing emphasis is being placed on mobilizing nonconcessionary finance for regional operations. For example, recent major AfDB regional infrastructural projects and initiatives developed with various development partners include: the North–South Corridor project (Box 5.7); the Central African Economic and Monetary Community (CEMAC) Transport and Trade Corridor project (Annex 5.3); the second phase of the Mombasa–Nairobi–Addis Ababa Road Corridor project (Box 5.5), and the Nacala Road Corridor project (see Annex 5.3). These projects aim at removing critical bottlenecks to trade and transport flows, by developing the hinterland interface and improving access to ports, which will ultimately reduce transport delays and costs.

The Bank also intends to produce a series of country reports on measures that can be taken by member governments,

Box 5.5: Mombasa–Nairobi–Addis Ababa Road Corridor Project, Phase II

The Mombasa–Nairobi–Addis Ababa Road Corridor Project, approved by the AfDB in 2009, aims at promoting trade and regional integration between Ethiopia and Kenya by improving transport communications between the two countries. The project involves the construction to bitumen standard of 438 km road sections including a 245-km Merille River–Marsabit–Turbi road section in Kenya and a 193-km Ageremariam–Yabelo–Mega road section in Ethiopia. The total cost of the project is US$ 510.31 million.

The project is to be cofinanced by the Bank Group (64 percent), the European Union (23 percent), and the governments of Ethiopia and Kenya (13 percent). The expected outcomes of the project include reduced transport and shipping costs between Kenya and Ethiopia; reduced transit time for import and export goods; and increased volume of Ethiopian transit goods using the port of Mombasa. Ultimately, transit to/from Ethiopia via the port of Mombasa should increase from zero in 2009 to 500,000 tonnes by 2014; and to over 1 million tonnes or 20 percent of total Ethiopian sea freight by 2018. The average transport cost of US$ 0.50 per veh-km on the corridor in 2009 should reduce by 20 percent by 2011 and by 50 percent by 2014. Transit and travel time of 5 days between Addis and Nairobi in 2009 should be reduced by 20 percent (1 day) by 2011; and by 60 percent (3 days) by 2014.

The development of the corridor will expand market sizes beyond national boundaries and foster an enabling environment for the private sector and for attracting foreign direct investment. In addition to enhancing trade and strengthening regional integration, the project will contribute to poverty reduction in both countries by increasing access to markets and social services for the surrounding areas, and by empowering women and other disadvantaged groups through adequate roadside socioeconomic infrastructure and services.

Source: AfDB — OINF (2009a)

individually and collectively, to accelerate integration of their economies. The first report was produced by the Bank in 2009, and focused on priority infrastructure options in Burundi (Box 5.6).

In addition to "hard" infrastructure investment, "soft" infrastructure is also crucial to an RMC's economic development. Soft infrastructure can be defined as the social overhead capital of a region or country, which enhances the commercial environment for businesses and trade — for both domestic and foreign companies who may be thinking of scaling up investment. Soft infrastructure covers a broad spectrum of areas, including: governance, regional leadership, education and knowledge, research and development, technical and business advisory services, access to capital and finance, support to business and trade associations, crime prevention, health, and social inclusion issues.

Soft infrastructure is increasingly recognized as the foundation of successful and sustainable economies (Stimson *et al.*, 2006) and for that reason has even been termed "smart" infrastructure (Smilor and Walekin, 1990). Some economists have argued that trade costs are negatively related to the existence of improvements in soft infrastructure (Khan, 2006). For example, in the first phase of the Mombasa–Nairobi–Addis Ababa Road Corridor Project, approved in 2004 by the AfDB, one of the seven components was a study of the container terminal on the Ethiopian side of the corridor. The aim of this study was to present an integrated development plan of the whole corridor into a viable trade route, taking into account all the necessary construction or improvement to the physical infrastructure, including transit infrastructure facilities. Among the facilities, a one-stop border post (OSBP), which is considered as soft infrastructure, was identified as a possible improvement to the efficiency of the corridor. The Chirundu, between Zambia and Zimbabwe (mentioned in Chapter 4), is the first OSBP along the North–South Corridor

Project. Another active OSBP financed by the Bank is between Rwanda and Burundi.

The Bank Group's Regional Integration Activities

The Bank's *Regional Integration Strategy*, approved in March 2009, articulates three principal objectives. First, it supports the establishment of an effective and efficient pan-African and subregional institutional framework to promote trade and manage the integration process. Second, the strategy aims to facilitate an enabling investment policy framework for the continent. Third, it sets out the different resources that the Bank has at its disposal, in terms of financial

---

Box 5.6: An infrastructure Action Plan for Burundi: accelerating regional integration

Burundi has badly suffered as a result of conflicts over the last two decades, which has left a legacy of substandard and poorly maintained infrastructure. The challenges that this presents are compounded by the fact that Burundi is a landlocked and densely populated country. Against this background, significant changes are underway to overhaul the regional trade and infrastructure landscape. On the one hand, Burundi has recently become a member of the East African Community (EAC), which could induce shifts in the trade structure with its partners. On the other hand, several major regional projects are in the pipeline which could deeply affect the relative competitiveness of existing transport corridors, as well as the supply of electricity and the structure of energy trade.

To address the problem of pervasive poverty in Burundi, the government is committed to accelerating the economic GDP growth of the country to 6–7 percent per annum in real terms. To support the government in meeting this objective, in 2009 the Bank conducted a study in Burundi to suggest priority infrastructure options, with a focus on transport, communications, and energy, to maximize the economic benefits of regional integration. The study produced a medium-term Action Plan to develop the proposed infrastructures. The report provides the government, the donor community, and the private sector with a detailed assessment of infrastructure investment opportunities in Burundi and the wider region. It will therefore underpin the government's ongoing dialogue with donors and the business community about these opportunities. Finally, this report contributes to a better coordinated action within the donor community.

The African Development Bank and the World Bank are collaborating on the preparation of a Country Economic Memorandum (CEM) for Burundi. The relevant findings of this report on infrastructure will be integrated into the forthcoming CEM.

Source: AfDB — OREA (2009).

investment, technical assistance, and knowledge to facilitate delivery of priority regional infrastructure.

This new strategy is expected to result in a number of benefits for its RMCs and the continent: greater economies of scale and increased competitiveness; higher levels of FDI and a more enabling environment for private sector participation; enhanced African presence in the global marketplace; a scaling-up of intraregional trade; the establishment of a more effective African "voice" on issues of development and regional integration; and a more efficient provision of regional public goods. To achieve these concrete results, the strategy is underpinned by two mutually reinforcing pillars: *regional infrastructure* and *institutional capacity building*, the latter including trade facilitation and capacity building measures.

The Bank has traditionally supported regional infrastructure, but without building into it trade facilitation programs. The new strategy, therefore, marks a shift toward a more balanced approach, and will include capacity building to the Regional Economic Communities (RECs) in the soft areas of trade facilitation, in addition to the development of trade-related infrastructure. Specifically, this support will aim to:

- Assist and build capacity to develop trade facilitation strategies and implement trade facilitation audits;
- Promote the harmonization and coordination of regional trade policies, with a view to eliminating tariff and nontariff barriers (NTBs) to the cross-border flow of production factors, goods and services;

- Harmonize environmental standards and regulations;
- Streamline cross-border infrastructure regulations and remove public procurement bottlenecks; and
- Support the implementation of customs unions.

The NEPAD Infrastructure Project Preparation Facility (NEPAD-IPPF) in 2009 funded a feasibility study on the extension of the Port San Pedro and related infrastructure in Côte d'Ivoire. The objectives of the proposed project are to stimulate economic growth and socioeconomic development, and to build an efficient regional transport system to facilitate access to reliable services for the landlocked country of Mali and some parts of Guinea and Liberia. The broad focus of the project is to support import and export-oriented SMEs by facilitating trade and contributing toward regional integration. More specifically, the project aims at extending the capacity of the port so that it can serve as a regional hub, as well as promoting multimodal transport (road/rail) for a free flow of people and goods.

The NEPAD-IPPF Special Fund contributes to these objectives by (i) reducing costs while improving the quality of transport services to improve competitiveness and (ii) supporting regional integration and the integration of markets by improving transport services. The development of road links converging to the Port, namely, Odienné (Ivory Coast)–Bougouni (Mali) and Danane–N'Nzérékoré (Guinea) forms part of the West Africa Monetary and Economic Union (UEMOA) Community Priority Road

Network articulated in the Community Infrastructure and Transport Road Action Program (PACITR). This road network, together with the bridge over the Cavally River linking Côte d'Ivoire to Liberia, seeks to (i) capture the road traffic from the southeast of Mali, Guinea, and Liberia, and (ii) to transit goods at least-cost through the port of San Pedro by land and sea routes to the markets in the regional hinterland.

The Bank has also taken into account the main issues stated in West and Central Africa Memorandum of Understanding (MoU) on Port State Control, which was signed in Abuja in 1999. The Abuja MoU regulates the implementation of port state control provisions, i.e. the inspection of foreign ships in national ports to verify that their condition and equipment comply with the requirements of international conventions, and that the ship is operated in compliance with applicable maritime laws. The aim of the MoU is to foster the eradication of substandard shipping practices, to ensure safety and security of persons on board ships, and protect the marine environment from pollution. A presentation of the MoU took place in 2008 at the African Union conference of Ministers of Transport in Algiers, which identified areas of improvement for a better implementation of the MoU, especially related to institutional commitments.

On softer issues, the Bank's Regional Integration Department (ONRI) has developed a strong trade facilitation program which is aimed at addressing cross-border transport regulations/procedures relating to the development of the corridors. These include the development and management of OSBPs, transit traffic regimes, cross-border

movement of persons and standards pertaining to vehicle size, weight and safety requirements. In this regard, ONRI has organized two consultation missions to assist members of RECs to formulate positions in the World Trade Organization negotiations on trade facilitation. The Bank aims to strengthen the capacity of ECCAS and CEMAC, within the framework of the ongoing development of a capacity-building program for the implementation of the Consensus Transport Master Plan of Central African States. The second consultations will be held with COMESA, EAC, and SADC as a follow-up to the Tripartite Summit of these three RECs, geared toward their eventual merging into one body.

In addition, the Bank continues to help shape Africa's regional infrastructure development through its knowledge products. First, it undertakes periodic reviews of the NEPAD Short Term Action Program (STAP) to identify implementation challenges and make appropriate recommendations. Technical support is provided to address shortcomings identified in the STAP process, including weak definition of projects and programs, the need for improved leadership and ownership, as well as the lack of enabling policy and regulatory frameworks. Second, by expediting the development of the medium- to long-term strategic Program for Infrastructure Development in Africa (PIDA), in collaboration with the AUC and the NEPAD Secretariat, ONRI provides support toward its eventual implementation. Third, it provides advice and technical support and collaborates with the NEPAD Secretariat, RECs, and RMCs to facilitate alignment of national, REC, STAP, and PIDA infrastructure priorities, and to prioritize

---

Box 5.7: The North–South Corridor: an Aid for Trade pilot program

The North–South Corridor (NSC) has been identified (in full collaboration with DfID) as a pilot program under the Aid for Trade (AfT) initiative to help reduce transport and transit costs, and boost trading opportunities in southern and eastern Africa. The Bank has committed to contribute US$ 600 million over 2009–2012 to support activities along the Corridor.

The Corridor traverses the vast area from the copperbelt of southern DRC and northern Zambia to the port of Dar es Salaam in the northeast, and to the South African ports in the south. Its development involves the Secretariats of COMESA, EAC, and SADC, which have already set up a joint Task Force to enhance implementation of the program and its benefits. The main objectives are to:

- Remove main bottlenecks to trade flows and target areas of intervention along the Corridor;
- Address the Corridor's development in a holistic manner, looking at regulatory, administrative and infrastructural constraints to transport and transit systems as a whole;
- Ensure that interventions to reduce costs and time are effected in a coherent and sequential manner to generate a "knock-on" effect in terms of savings along the entire Corridor;
- Allow all information to be collated and made available on a GIS database to help informed decision-making;[1]
- Support regional trade policy regulation and trade facilitation initiatives.

Significant progress has already been made, including preparation of financing proposals, identification of transport networks and bottlenecks, mapping of existing and planned investments, and strengthening trade facilitation measures. Some development partners, including DfID, are providing support. The challenge is now to take the pilot to the next phase and secure more support.

---

infrastructure projects for funding and implementation. In this regard, prioritization is based on criteria already agreed with the RECs and RMCs. Lastly, the Bank also supports the harmonization process for regulations, procedures, and standards that affect cross-border connectivity.

The AfDB is working with the WTO and UNECA to implement the WTO's Aid for

Trade (AfT) Agenda, which supports the trade liberalization agenda by addressing supply-side constraints. The North–South Corridor is one of the pilot programs in which the Bank is participating as part of the AfT agenda (Box 5.7).

Partnerships and the Infrastructure Consortium for Africa

The Bank leverages resources with development-oriented financing institutions to support projects in its RMCs. In September 2008, the Bank established a financing mechanism, namely the African Financing Partnership (AFP), which

---

[1] This was originally organized through the Regional Trade Facilitation Program website (www.rtfp.org). However, the RTFP officially came to an end in October 2009, after achieving significant success. A follow-on program, to be called TradeMark Southern Africa, is due to commence in the near future.

facilitates collaboration with some of the larger DFIs, with a provision for the eventual participation of smaller DFIs and private financiers. The principal objective of the AFP is to optimize the consolidated market knowledge and project financing skills of the DFIs, including the AfDB, and thereby mitigate financial risks for cofinanciers. The AFP focuses on very large projects that require massive capital injections — these often fall within the infrastructure sector. The AFP enables all partner institutions to avoid unnecessary duplication of efforts, lower legal and administrative costs, increase financing capacity, and achieve greater diversification and synergies, thereby maximizing project effectiveness.

The Bank has also taken steps to build a strong partnership with the African Finance Corporation, which will yield huge efficiency benefits for both institutions. Furthermore, the Bank leverages the networking opportunities afforded by its Annual Meetings to create a forum for representatives from national authorities, investors, financiers, promoters, and contractors to meet and share project ideas. All these mechanisms provide an opportunity to build synergies and catalyze additional financing for infrastructure development in Africa.

Similarly, the Infrastructure Consortium for Africa, which is hosted by the AfDB in Tunis, facilitates a more coordinated approach to infrastructure development. It has in particular promoted collaboration between the AfDB and other donors and helps to define a common approach to support policy reforms, negotiations, and the involvement of the private sector. The Consortium has also been instrumental in promoting partnerships to leverage financial support to bridge the infrastructure gap in Africa.

In 2007, the Bank successfully mobilized close to US$ 2.7 billion in cofinancing in the transport, energy, and ICT subsectors (ICA, 2008b). In 2008, the Bank Group contributed US$ 393.94 million of its own funds to cofinance projects in the transport subsector, while it mobilized a further US$ 114.41 million from external partners and private sector institutions, with an additional US$ 243.62 million of funding coming from governments and local firms.

Conclusion

Between 1973 and 1997, the Bank assumed a leadership role vis-à-vis investments in the port subsector in Africa, mainly using public sector instruments. However, more recently, public investments have declined in favor of private sector investments. To date, almost all Bank port development projects have been prepared by its Private Sector Department, including those in Egypt, Djibouti, and Senegal. Nonetheless, opportunities for a scaling-up of participation by both public and private sectors should be explored, given the substantive financial needs of the ports subsector.

The AfDB should be commended for increasing its support to transport projects and programs, which account for the bulk of its total infrastructure investments. However, there is a need to ease pressure on the road transport systems and to focus on other modes, such as rail and navigable rivers and lakes (e.g. the Zambezi–Shire Waterway Project; see Box 4.1).

Beyond hard infrastructure, the AfDB also supports soft infrastructure investments, such as OSBPs, which are essential nodes in the movement of goods in and out of ports and through transport networks and corridors. The Bank is well placed through its key partnerships with RECs, government bodies, and civil society organizations, to explore other areas where it might intervene effectively to assist its RMCs, such as in helping to streamline and harmonize customs procedures and enhance the institutional regulatory framework.

Discussions with national authorities and other partners reveal that there is room for the Bank to invest further in ports and related logistics. However, as these types of investments are expensive, the Bank should continue to leverage all the instruments at its disposal and strengthen its partnerships, in order to catalyze the participation and resources of other key players.

References

AfDB. 2008. *Annual Report, 2007*. Tunis: AfDB.

——. **2009.** *Annual Report, 2008*. Tunis: AfDB.

AfDB — CEPR. 1992. *Transport Sector Policy*. Presented to the Board of the African Development Bank on February 26, 1992.

AfDB — COD. 2001. *Review of Bank Group's Operations in the Maritime Subsector*, April 2001.

AfDB — OCIN. 2002. Project Appraisal Report: "Multinational — BCEAO: Proposal for an ADF loan of UA 6.20 million to finance the project to reform systems and means of

payment in UEMOA countries." Prepared by OCIN. Submitted to the Board of the African Development Bank on October 2, 2002.

——. **2003**. Project Appraisal Report: "Ghana: Proposal for an ADF loan of UA 18 million, an NTF loan of UA 3 million and a TAF grant of UA 0.80 million to finance the Road Infrastructure Project." Prepared by OCIN. Released on August 11, 2003.

AfDB — OINF. 2008a. Project Appraisal Report: "Ghana: Proposal for supplementary loans of UA 43.10 million to finance three (3) on-going road transport projects. Board Memorandum." Prepared by OINF. Submitted to the Board of the African Development Bank on February 11, 2009.

——. **2008b.** Project Appraisal Report: "Tunisia: Proposal for an ADB loan of Euro 174.33 Million to finance the Road Project V." Prepared by OINF. Submitted to the Board of the AfDB on May 28, 2008.

——. **2009a.** Project Appraisal Report: "Mombasa–Nairobi–Addis Ababa Road Corridor Project Phase II." Prepared by OINF. Submitted to the Board of the AfDB on July 1, 2009.

——. **2009b**. Project Appraisal Report: "Multinational — Mozambique/Malawi/ Zambia — proposal for ADF loans of UA 102,720,000 to Mozambique and UA 14,320,000 to Malawi to finance the Nacala Road Corridor — phase I." Prepared by OINF. Submitted to the Board of the AfDB on June 24, 2009.

—— **2009c.** Project Appraisal Report: "Burkina Faso: Proposal for an ADF loan of

UA 10 million and ADF grant of UA 31 million to finance the project to rehabilitate the Koupela–Bittou–Cinkanse–Togo border road and the Mogande access road." Prepared by OINF. Submitted to the Board of the AfDB on February 11, 2009.

AfDB — ONIN. 2004. Project Appraisal Report: "Mombasa–Nairobi–Addis Ababa Road Corridor Project." Prepared by ONIN. Released on November 5, 2004.

AfDB — ONRI. 2009. *Bank Group Regional Integration Strategy, 2009–2012*. Presented to the Board of the AfDB in March 2009.

AfDB — OPSM. 2003. Project Appraisal Report: "Djibouti: Proposal for an ADB loan of US$ 10 million to finance the Djibouti Bulk Terminal project." Prepared by OPSD. Submitted to the Board of the African Development Bank on December 3, 2003.

——. **2007.** Project Appraisal Report: "Egypt: Proposal for a US$ 150 million senior loan to finance the Damietta Container Terminal." Prepared by OPSM/GECL/OIVP. Submitted to the Board of the African Development Bank on December 4, 2007.

——. **2008.** Project Appraisal Report: "Djibouti: Proposal for a senior loan of US$ 80 million to finance the Doraleh Container Terminal (DCT) project." Prepared by OPSM. Submitted to the Board of the African Development Bank on September 24, 2008.

——. **2009a.** Project Appraisal Report: "Senegal: Proposal for a loan of 47.5 million Euro to finance the Dakar Container Terminal." Prepared by OPSM. Submitted to the Board of the African Development Bank on July 20, 2009.

——. **2009b**. "Information Note on the Trade Finance Initiative."

AfDB — OREA. 2009. "An Infrastructure Action Plan for Burundi: Accelerating Regional Integration."

Infrastructure Consortium for Africa (ICA). 2008a. *ICA Annual Report*, 2007.

——. **2008b**. "Questionnaire for the preparation of the 2007. Annual Report."

——. **2009**. "Questionnaire for the preparation of the 2008 Annual Report."

Khan, H.A. 2006. "Soft Infrastructure, Trading Costs and Regional Co-operation", CIRJE Discussion Paper, University of Denver.

Smilor, R.W., and M. Wakelin. 1990. "Smart Infrastructure and Economic Development: The Role of Technology and Global Networks," *The Technopolis Phenomenon*. Austin, TX: IC Institute, University of Texas.

Stimson, R.J., R.R. Stough, and B.H. Roberts. 2006. "Regional Economic Development: Analysis and Planning Strategy." New York: Springer.

World Bank. 2008. "Abidjan–Lagos Transport and Transit Facilitation Project, Report No.: AB2798, Project Information Document, Washington, DC: World Bank.

Annex 5.1: Bank Group Approvals in the Transport Maritime Subsector, 1973–2000

No.	BANK GROUP WINDOW	REGION	PROJECT NAME
	ADB		
1	Côte d'Ivoire	WST	DEEPENING OF VRIDI CANAL ENTRANCE
2	Cameroon	CEN	EXTENSION OF DOUALA SEA PORT I
3	Cameroon	CEN	EXTENSION OF DOUALA SEA PORT PHASE II
4	Comoros	EST	MUTSAMUDU PORT DEVELOPMENT
5	Gambia	WST	BANJUL PORT DEVELOPMENT PHASE 1
6	Congo, Dem. Rep.	CEN	MATADI KINSHASA PORTS DEVELOPMENT
7	Guinea	WST	CONAKRY PORT DEVELOPMENT
8	Madagascar	EST	PANGANALES CANAL DEVELOPMENT
9	Seychelles	EST	VICTORIA COMMERCIAL PORT
	ADF		
1	Madagascar	EST	PANGALANES CANAL DEVELOPMENT
2	Cape Verde	WST	MAIO PORT CONSTRUCTION
3	Burundi	CEN	BUJUMBURA SHIPYARD CONSTRUCTION
4	Cape Verde	WST	SAO VINCENT SHIPYARD IMPROVEMENT STUDY
5	Multinational	ZZMULT	NAVIGATION STUDY ON RIVER SENEGAL
6	Eritrea	EST	ASSAB PORT DEVELOPMENT PROJECT
7	Cape Verde	WST	MINDELO SHIPYARD IMPROVEMENT
8	Madagascar	EST	THE PANGALANES CANAL STUDY
9	Multinational (OMVS)	ZZMULT	STRENGTHENING OF THE RIGHT BANK DYKE OF THE DIAMA DAM PROJECT
10	Egypt	NOR	TWO CANALS STUDIES
11	Gambia	WST	BANJUL PORT II
12	Madagascar	EST	THE REHABILITATION OF THE PROTECTIVE DYKE OF TOLIARY TOWN AGAINST FLOODING BY THE FIHERENANA RIVER
13	Madagascar	EST	TOLIARY TOWNSHIP PROTECTION PROJECT
	NTF		
1	Benin	WST	COTONOU PORT
2	Cape Verde	WST	MAIO PORT CONSTRUCTION
3	Burundi	CEN	BUJUMBURA SHIPYARD CONSTRUCTION

Source: AfDB-Central Operations Department (2001).

DATE APPROVED	YEAR APPROVED	AMOUNT APPROVED (UA mn)	TOTAL COST (UA mn)
19/12/1973	1973	3.30	23.10
21/12/1976	1976	5.00	40.00
18/08/1977	1977	5.00	40.00
26/11/1981	1981	10.00	39.20
22/06/1982	1982	7.00	17.47
30/09/1982	1982	20.00	80.27
26/04/1983	1983	12.69	28.50
25/01/1984	1984	11.00	32.78
25/01/1984	1984	18.42	30.19
19/11/1984	1984	2.76	9.74
27/11/1986	1986	0.55	7.42
17/09/1987	1987	0.53	0.56
20/09/1988	1988	0.34	0.37
17/04/1989	1989	41.02	55.37
18/03/1991	1991	4.60	5.11
27/01/1992	1992	1.84	2.03
05/1992	1992	4.83	5.38
06/01/1993	1993	1.56	1.68
14/12/1993	1993	16.00	27.00
10/1993	1993	6.85	7.61
11/1997	1997	6.44	7.16
17/10/1978	1978	2.42	9.68
19/11/1984	1984	6.00	33.68
27/11/1986	1986	4.45	7.42

Annex 5.2: Examples of AfDB Private Sector Port Projects, 2000–2009

(i) Djibouti: Bulk Terminal Project (2003)

At project preparation phase, Djibouti had an acceptable level of infrastructure, although further investment was required to meet the country's growing level of economic activity. The Port of Djibouti was identified as the most significant infrastructure to kick-start its economy, and one that could benefit other countries in the subregion, since the road and rail networks link Djibouti with Ethiopia. The development of Djibouti Port was identified as having broader beneficial impacts, since by facilitating the supply of grains and fertilizers to neighboring countries (Ethiopia, Eritrea, Somali, and Sudan) it would raise living standards and mitigate the effects of famine, which is a recurrent affliction in this subregion of Africa.

The project had to be implemented on a fast-track basis in a subregion that had previously failed to generate significant investments from international commercial banks, which proved reluctant to provide the long-term financing required by capital-intensive infrastructure projects. Furthermore, the financial market perceptions (creditworthiness and sovereign risks of the country) and sector constraints (regulatory arrangements of the port and nature of the domestic financial market) also made it difficult to obtain local debt financing of the project.

Consequently, the Bank's participation was sought to build comfort and confidence around the project and thereby attract other commercial lenders. The following needs were identified: (i) to facilitate the local banks' understanding and assessment of the risks of the project; (ii) to ease discussions with prospective international lenders who had also revealed their reluctance to assume Djibouti's sovereign risks over long periods and/or were unable to participate without the Bank's involvement; and (iii) to give comfort to the private investor (sponsor) about Djibouti's sovereign risk, as the local private banking sector was not yet in a position to absorb or manage those risks. The Bank's expertise in project appraisal, supervision, and risk mitigation was also sought.

The project comprised the development, design, construction, ownership, operation and maintenance of bulk terminal facilities for cereals and fertilizers, destined for export to Ethiopia and the wider subregion. Initially, the concession granted the right to build, own, operate and transfer (BOOT) a bulk terminal project on an area of 42,000 square meters in the Port Autonome International de Djibouti for a period of 30 years. The bulk terminal has been successfully built as conceived and is now fully operational.

In terms of impact, the project has considerably improved the port turnaround time. It has also had a more far-reaching impact, by contributing to food security and poverty reduction in Ethiopia, the major user of the port. The project has improved cargo handling and reliability, and has added value to the port as a whole by increasing its competitiveness. Furthermore, new business opportunities in servicing the port operations and associated logistics have been created by the project. It has encouraged the growth of local and indigenous companies, for example by employing subcontractors who provide truck haulage services and equipment rental services, all of which are spearheaded by the private sector.

Nevertheless, delays in implementation start-up often negatively impact project costs and expected revenues. By virtue of the time delay and the nature of this particular turnkey Engineering, Procurement and Construction (EPC) contract, the contingency provision was insufficient to cover the overrun. As a result, the lesson was learned to increase the amount of contingency in similar future investments. Furthermore the proposed Operations and Maintenance Service Agreement did not materialize as planned, thereby creating an operational risk. The Concessionaire will be advised to pay closer attention to this aspect in future deals. The development of an Environmental and Social Management Plan (ESMP) was expected to be a condition precedent to first disbursement, but two years into project operations, an ESMP had still to be developed. Relaxed adherence to project conditions and covenants often increases the project's related risks; in this case, the environmental risks mitigation effort was compromised by this omission.

The total cost of the project, cofinanced by the Société Djiboutienne de Gestion du Terminal Vraquier (SDTV) and the ADB, was estimated at around US$ 30 million. In December 2003 the Board of the ADB approved a US$ 10.0 million senior loan, which represented 33 percent of the total project cost.

Source: AfDB–OPSM (2003).

(ii) Egypt: Damietta Container Terminal project (2007)

For Egypt and its neighboring countries, the container transshipment industry has grown rapidly in recent years and this trend is expected to continue. For the period 1990–2005, the average annual growth rate of container shipments in Egypt was 18.6 percent, rising to 21.2 percent since 2000. This strong demand is directly linked to the level of economic activity. In addition to direct trade-related factors and transshipments, container port demand has been boosted by the continuing containerization of general cargoes in some commodity trades and of backhaul bulk cargoes. From 1995–2005 the annual increases in container-handling demand in Egypt exceeded Egyptian GDP growth by an average of 7 percent. The total volume of containers generated by the Egyptian economy and handled via Egyptian ports is expected to increase by around 118 percent in the period to 2015 and then demonstrate a further growth of 26 percent from 2015–2020. The total range of possible import/export container port demand in 2020 is projected to be in the range 2.8–3.9 million TEUs.

In order for Egypt to capture a significant portion of the Egyptian and regional transshipments container activity, the AfDB agreed in December 2007 to cofinance the upgrading and expansion of the Damietta transshipment port under a 40-year concession agreement. The two other sponsors of the project are the Kuwaiti Gulf Links Ports International (KGLPI) and the Aref Investments Group. Together they form the Damietta International Ports Company (DIPCO), which is the SPV executing the BOOT concession.

Damietta port began operations in 1986. It is situated on the Mediterranean coast of Egypt, about 37 km west of Port-Said. The port currently handles exports of agricultural products, fertilizers, and furniture as well as the delivery of imported goods such as petrochemicals, cement, grains, flour, and general cargo with a total capacity of about 5.6 million tonnes annually. Damietta is well connected by roads and railroads; this gives the port a competitive advantage over other Egyptian terminals. However, the port's existing facilities are unable to serve the potential demand of 4.5 million TEUs, which would make it one of the largest transshipment facilities in the Mediterranean and the only one capable of handling the new generation of supersize container ships.

To take advantage of Damietta's natural comparative advantages, a new container terminal would be built and equipped with modern transshipment facilities. The project consisted of: (i) construction of quay walls; (ii) dredging of the access channel and turning basin; (iii) installing the modern transshipment equipment; and (iv) developing the terminal area and container yard. These new terminal berths of about 2,360 m will be able to accommodate the latest-generation container vessels, with a maximum draft of 16 m, a length of 400 m, and a width of 53 m. The project will occupy approximately 130 hectares of land at the port. Ultimately by 2014, the port will reach a maximum capacity of 4.5 million TEUs annually.

The total project cost was estimated at US$ 680 million. The ADB Board approved a US$ 150 million Senior Loan, which represented 22 percent of the total cost. Two other leading Middle Eastern commercial banks invested US$ 330 million (48 percent of the total), with the Sponsors providing US$ 200 million (30 percent) in equity.

Source: AfDB — OPSM (Nov. 2007).

(iii) Senegal: The Dakar Container Terminal (2009)

The Port of Dakar is the busiest in West Africa, handling 90 percent of the total value of Senegal's foreign trade. It has a natural advantage in terms of geographical position, as it is situated at the crossroads between Europe, North America, South America, and Sub-Saharan Africa. It has a dredged navigational channel and breakwater, and facilities for handling liquid and dry bulk, general cargo, and containerized cargo.

The demand for container volume is growing and expected to reach 416,000 TEUs by 2012 and 580,000 TEUs by 2016. In order to improve the port's facilities and to safeguard its competitiveness, a 25-year renewable Concession Agreement was signed in October 2007 between the Government of Senegal (represented by the

Port Autonome de Dakar [PAD]) and Dubai Port World (DPW). Under the Agreement, DPW has been awarded the concession to equip, operate, and manage the existing container terminal in the Northern Zone of the Port of Dakar ("Terminal à Conteneurs" or "TAC") under Phase 1 of the Project. The second phase is to design, finance, construct, operate, and manage the Port du Futur, when the throughput of the existing port reaches 416,000 TEUs. Port du Futur will have a potential capacity of 1.75 million TEUs.

The Bank was invited to cofinance the project, as part of its continuing effort to promote projects in the port subsector. The Bank has previously collaborated in a similar transaction, where DPW was also a sponsor. The Bank's financial backing was sought at a time of liquidity constraints for most commercial banks, in the wake of the global financial crisis. By fulfilling a countercyclical role, the Bank's participation served a demonstration effect, helping to attract other investors and lower the perceived commercial risks.

The proposed investment will cover Phase 1 of the project, which consists of upgrading the stacking areas, the improvement of other port infrastructure (railroad installations, electricity, roads and buildings) and the acquisition of equipment (mobile harbor cranes, auto-twist spreaders, reach stackers, empty handlers, tractor-trailers) and installation of additional container handling and stacking equipment (STS cranes, etc.).

The project cost for this first phase is estimated at Euro 210 million, of which the equipment (24 percent), civil works and development (24 percent), and concession fee (22 percent) comprise the most important components. The AfDB was invited to provide 50 percent of the total debt, on a par with Standard Chartered Bank. In July 2009 the Bank approved a loan of Euro 47.5 million to that effect.

Source: AfDB — OPSM (2009).

Annex 5.3: Examples of AfDB-Supported Transport Corridor Projects

(i) The CEMAC Trade Corridor project (2007)

The member countries of the CEMAC region agreed in 2006 to develop the CEMAC Trade Corridor project to improve transport and trade efficiency in the subregion. Trade in the subregion was especially constrained and transport costs were among the highest on the continent. Before project implementation, delays at the Douala Port in Cameroon could take up to 28 days and transport of goods from the port to Ndjamena (Chad) or Bangui (Central African Republic) took 15 days and 10 days, respectively.

The AfDB in collaboration with the World Bank, the European Commission, and the French Development Agency (AFD) agreed to jointly finance the CEMAC Trade Corridor project. At preparation stage the AfDB and the World Bank agreed to share technical expertise, while Cameroon, Chad, and CAR formed a steering committee using the CEMAC platform. In February 2007, the AfDB signed a US$ 67 million agreement with CEMAC and CAR. In June 2007, the World Bank approved a US$ 201 million package for the three country members of the steering committee, and in October 2009, approved additional financing for Cameroon and CAR for an amount of US$ 217 million.

(ii) Ghana: rehabilitation of sections of the Abidjan–Lagos Road Corridor

In Ghana, the AfDB has been financing rehabilitation of road sections of the Abidjan–Lagos Road Corridor since 2002. In 2008, the following amounts were approved: US$ 40.14 million for the Tema–Aflao Rehabilitation Road Project and US$ 21.18 million for the Akatsi–Dzodze–Noepe Road Upgrading Project. The targeted sections are part of the broader Abidjan–Lagos coastal corridor which connects Côte d'Ivoire to Nigeria through Ghana, Togo, and Benin via 1,028 km of coastal roads.

This regional corridor has been identified by ECOWAS and UEMOA as a priority to promote economic and social development in the region. The corridor's importance is major in terms of the daily movement of people and goods, which is one of the highest in the Africa continent on several segments. The Abidjan–Lagos corridor has the potential to become a catalyst for economic integration and subregional cooperation of UEMOA and ECOWAS member countries.

The roads targeted by the different AfDB projects are considered by the Government of Ghana to be critical international roads that need immediate attention in order to reduce poverty, especially in the Eastern Region. Consequently, the roads have been included in the current Roads Subsector

Development Program. The project is designed to facilitate regional integration activities as well as access to social services and markets. It is therefore in line with the Bank Group Policy on Regional Economic Integration, as articulated in its Regional Integration Strategy, and it conforms to the bilateral agreement between the Bank and the ECOWAS.

Several donors financed other sections of the Corridor, including the World Bank, the European Union, and the Japan Bank for International Cooperation.

On the same corridor, a project is currently under preparation by the AfDB to finance other sections in Togo.

Source: AfDB — OINF (2009).

(iii) SADC Region: the Nacala Corridor

The Nacala Corridor is one of the priority projects of the SADC region and is consistent with the NEPAD and Bank strategy for multinational infrastructure projects. The objective is to remove obstacles to the movement of persons and goods, and to support regional cooperation, integration, and trade. The Nacala Corridor comprises a total of 1,033 km of road works and two one-stop border posts (OSBPs).

To support the development of the Nacala Corridor, the Bank approved in 2009 the financing of the Nacala Road Corridor — Phase I, consisting of two ADF loans: (i) US$ 159.45 million to Mozambique and (ii) US$ 22.23 million to Malawi. The project comprises the improvement of road transport over 361 km or 35 percent of road works in Mozambique and Malawi. The next two phases will cover 360 km or 34.9 percent of road works in Zambia (Phase II) and 312 km or 30.1 percent of road works in Mozambique and Malawi. It will also include two OSBPs between Mozambique/Malawi and Malawi/Zambia (Phase III).

The project should provide Malawi, Zambia, and the interior of Mozambique with an improved road transport linkage to the port of Nacala and improve transport services along the corridor. It will improve accessibility of the communities in the zone of influence to markets and social services and contribute to the reduction of poverty.

Ultimately after Phase I, the average travel time in Mozambique will be reduced by 41 percent, from 9 hrs in 2008 to 5.3 hrs by 2014; and in Malawi by 60 percent, from 50 minutes in 2008 to 20 minutes by 2013. Furthermore, delays at the Mozambique/Malawi and Malawi/Zambia borders should be reduced from 36 hours to 6 hours by 2015, due to the establishment of two OSBPs.

Links between ports and harbors and major centers of economic activity in the hinterland should be improved. Import/export cargo handled at Nacala port should increase from 0.9 million tonnes per year in 2009 to 1.6 million tonnes per year by 2015. Mozambique's rating in the Global Competitiveness Index should improve from 3.1 in 2009 to 4.1 in 2015. Furthermore, its percentage share of transport and transit cost in cif and fob prices of import and export should be reduced by 25 percent by 2015.

Source: AfDB — OINF (2009b).

(iv) Agona Junction–Elubo Road Study: Part of the Road Infrastructure Project (Eastern and Western Regions)

As outlined above, the AfDB has financed several road projects in Ghana that are sections of the Abidjan–Lagos Corridor.

The second component of one of those projects — the Road Infrastructure Project (Western and Eastern Regions) — comprised a feasibility study on the Agona Junction–Elubo road section. The Bank agreed to finance the study in 2003.

The study was divided into two stages: the first aimed at assessing the feasibility, environmental impacts, and the impact on poverty reduction of the civil works. The second stage offered detailed engineering designs, provided cost estimates and preparation of tender documents for the approved alternative.

This study was instrumental in planning road infrastructure investments to rehabilitate and strengthen the trade corridor.

Source: AfDB — OCIN (2003).

CHAPTER 6

Going Forward:
Developing Regional Hub Ports in

Introduction

This chapter draws on the key lessons from the preceding chapters to point the way forward toward the development of regional hub ports in Africa. The emergence of such hub ports is important both for the regional economic integration of African countries and for their wider integration in the world trading system. As discussed earlier, the gradual opening up of African economies and their growing international integration have given rise to a corresponding increase in the demand for international transport services. However, few African ports are capable of handling the latest generation of post-Panamax vessels, and they are generally ill-equipped for the dramatic changes in trade and shipping patterns that are currently under way.

In response, many African countries are aiming to modernize their ports and develop them into regional hubs through large-scale investment programs, to provide transshipment services for cargo from other origins destined for third countries. The momentum of modernization is being further fueled by the growing presence and consolidation of global shipping lines, integrated multimodal operators (covering rail–road–sea transport), and international terminal operators in African ports. These operators have been engaged in these countries for some time now and see that the time is ripe for an expansion of services in the African port sector.

Indeed, many African ports have the potential to become regional hubs. However, this outcome depends on the capital injections and other related activities, including policy reforms, that governments are able to put in place toward port development and regeneration. These planned investment and related activities also offer avenues for private sector participation in African port development. In particular, the dredging of African ports, many of which are characterized as too shallow for the latest generation of container ships, could be a frontline area of intervention for the private sector and development partners alike. This issue is elaborated upon later in this chapter. The aspiration of many governments and Port Authorities (PAs) to develop their ports into regional hubs augurs well for the increased competitiveness of the African shipping industry in the future; this will boost

trade in the region and strengthening national economies generally. However, Africa can support only a few regional hubs and the key issues of *how* African ports can transform themselves into regional hubs, and *where* such hub ports should be located, is of critical importance.

This chapter examines this topic and focuses on the relevant issues facing African governments and International Financial Institutions (IFIs). The rest of the chapter is organized as follows. The next section summarizes the principal characteristics of African ports and the infrastructural conditions and policy reforms required to transform them into regional hubs. Against this background, there follows an examination of the comparative advantages of a number of key ports becoming regional hubs. The discussion then turns to the various key roles that IFIs can play in this process. The chapter ends with a summary of the key points impacting African countries in their efforts to modernize and transform their ports, to more fully integrate into the world trading system.

Developing African Ports into Regional Hubs: Physical Characteristics and Policy Requirements

A hub port can be described as an international or regional port that, in addition to the normal cargo-handling functions of import and export trade, also caters for so-called transshipment cargoes (in particular containerized cargoes) to and from major intercontinental or regional shipping routes, with the additional provision of services to a number of (usually smaller and / or shallower) African ports. An analysis of potential hub ports generally centers on their physical characteristics (TEU capacity; depth of water; berth lengths; availability of quayside gantries and container-handling equipment, etc.) and their road/rail/air linkages to the hinterland.

Practically all hub ports in the world today handle a mixture of three main types of cargo:

- **captive cargoes** (destined for and / or originating from the direct hinterland of the hub port);
- **transit cargoes** (cargoes destined for and / or originating from the more remote hinterland and / or landlocked countries); and
- **transshipment cargoes** (sea–sea cargoes).

The potential of African ports to become regional hubs is determined by several factors, including the shipping services it provides, the port's physical characteristics and location, and the types of vessel it can handle. Several characteristics facilitate the creation and successful operation of transshipment hubs (see Box 6.1). The availability of a considerable volume of captive cargo is often cited as a Critical Success Factor for a port seeking to become a hub. The reason for this is that transshipment cargo tends to be "foot loose" and may easily be shifted to another port if circumstances (e.g. facilities and tariffs) are better there.[1]

Investing in port capacity is not in itself a sufficient condition to transform a port into a hub unless it also enjoys a strategic location, adequate water depth, and the facilities and performance to ensure low handling costs. A good corridor for transit traffic is another prerequisite, and this may require measures to facilitate a fast and efficient flow of traffic on the main trade corridors from the port to the landlocked hinterland. In this respect, a port's competitiveness depends not only on its own physical capacity and the services it can offer, but also on the quality and fluidity of the land transport networks that serve it (principally the regional interstate roads). Ports that benefit the most from this emerging trade competition tend to be located in countries that also possess good roads (without roadblocks), operational rail lines, and border posts with the least administrative formalities and swift customs clearance.

In effect, the most important policy considerations for governments looking to establish hub ports are how best to foster and finance integrated port and transport facilities and associated land uses. National port plans must be developed to cover modal integration and port-specific issues. A key requirement is the allocation of enough land for integrated development in the early stages of port planning, particularly for new ports. Also, linkages between rail and port

---

[1] A well-known exception to this Critical Success Factor is the Port of Salalah in the Sultanate of Oman. Practically all containers handled in this port (3.5 million TEUs in 2009) are transshipment containers.

This relates to the function and location of this port. Salalah is located close to the convergence point where the large sea trade lane between Asia and Europe, and the North–South connection between Europe, the Middle East and Africa meet.

Box 6.1: Basic transshipment requirements of a hub port

Experience suggests that several port characteristics facilitate the creation of transshipment hubs:

- Location close to major world or regional shipping routes, leading to minimum deviation from that shipping route;
- Preferably already handling a considerable volume of base import and export cargo;
- Land area available for cargo storage and / or value adding activities;
- Access to a large hinterland, preferably with more than one transport mode;
- Sufficient depths in approach channel and the port and the possibility to increase the depth if required by the port users (shipping lines);
- Little or no queuing of ships ("the berth has to wait for the ship and not the other way around");
- Safe and secure port access from land and sea and a secured (ISPS) port area;
- Efficient ship and cargo handling operations;
- Good relations between port employers and employees (unions);
- Reasonable level of port performance;
- Active port business community;
- Banking and communication facilities;
- Limited or rather no corruptive practices;
- Stable political systems; and
- Regional role.

---

concessions should be made to provide the best incentive for multimodal integration. This requires governments of both coastal and landlocked countries to decide which transit corridors to support and develop. Coordinated system development provides the key to exploiting the major scope for traffic growth. The Ghana Gateway and the Maputo Corridor between the port of Maputo and South Africa, Swaziland, and Zimbabwe provide useful examples of this. Landlocked countries will likely want more than one alternative. Where the bottlenecks are at the seaports, the planning and development of inland ports (dry ports) warrant consideration, particularly for landlocked transit countries. The Ghana Boankra Inland Port is an example in the overall scheme of port development and trade facilitation.

Before the start of the global financial crisis, almost all major shipping lines started to order large numbers of 8,000+ and even 12,000+ TEUs vessels to be employed in the very lucrative and booming trade lane of Europe–Asia in particular. This meant that the "smaller" container vessels, mainly in the 4,000 to 6,000 TEU classes, began to be withdrawn from this route and replaced by the bigger sisters, in what is often referred to as the "cascading process," following the economy of scale principle. The 4,000 to 6,000 TEUs vessels were partly employed in the African liner services. The problem, however, was that only a few ports in Africa had sufficient depth to receive such mid-sized vessels.

Although the global financial crisis has caused some hiatus to this cascading process, there are signs (since mid-2010) that it may reemerge in areas where booming trade between the major economic and production blocs proves to be sustainable. As such, an African port aiming to become a regional hub must ensure the development of a port with sufficient depth to receive the larger vessels that are becoming more and more commonplace on African shipping routes.

Traditionally, high sea freight costs have been a major impediment to the development of ports in Africa, which have typically been served by "Liner Shipping" and "'Conference Services." Liner services have both advantages and disadvantages. One major advantage is that the tariffs are negotiated beforehand and usually maintained during the contract period, which acts as a risk mitigation factor in terms of unexpected costs. The liner contract is a guarantee that each port of the line will be called at, irrespective of the volume of cargo to be loaded and/or unloaded. Conference Service agreements have a similar effect. Sometimes a number of shipping companies enter into a Conference Agreement, meaning that ships belonging to different shipping lines will maintain very similar services, tariffs and conditions, irrespective of the shipping company calling. The disadvantage of the systems is that the tariffs are usually high.

In this context of traditionally high freight rates, a port hub in Africa should help to lower the cost of trade for shipping lines and cargo owners. This would entail the move away from Africa's current multiple gateway system of medium-sized ports, toward the model of transshipment hubs with larger gateway feeder ports. For cargo owners, hub ports would offer savings in total yearly supply chain costs through increased shipping line competition and improved service levels and delivery times, while greater maritime activity would improve access to regional and global markets. The shipping lines would see better utilization with fewer stops and increased port efficiency and speed at the hub.

The necessity for a conducive environment for the creation of port hubs enjoins African governments to determine how best to develop state-of-the-art ports, and how to equip them with appropriate technologies and management skills. This determination should certainly involve the international private sector, particularly in the container terminal business. The prevalence of state-owned service ports in Africa has long been associated with low operational efficiency as well as a low concentration of global operators. A policy of attracting major international container lines and terminal operators — who are well acquainted with the advantages of scale in terminal operations and with the benefits of an efficient hub-and-feeder structure in the deep-sea trade — will serve to increase efficiency and lower costs.

In the last 10–15 years, the African port sector has witnessed a considerable number of reforms, including a scaling-up of public–private partnerships involving some of the major international players in port development. The reforms in Africa, as elsewhere, have suggested that the landlord port model has generally enjoyed greater success than the public services port model, and is the best way to attract private sector participation.[2] On the other hand, the number of African countries that have introduced the landlord port model is very limited. The World Bank's Africa Infrastructure Country Diagnostic (AICD) Report of 2006 cites only two countries, Nigeria and Ghana, as having "comprehensively adopted the favored landlord port model."[3]

For government policies and reforms to achieve optimal efficiency in Africa's ports, they need to consider how best to introduce/incentivize competition. Over the last two decades, lessons from global port reforms have indicated the need to avoid mono-

polistic practices in ports privatization. The specific cases of Colombia, Argentina, and the United Kingdom show that building competitive environments tends to make ports more efficient and to lower costs, which benefits not just the Port Authorities, but also shipping lines, terminal operators, cargo owners, private investors, and end consumers. On the other hand, port reforms in several African countries seem to have been designed to minimize competition. Indeed, some African governments are even preserving government monopolies (Durban) or creating private ones (Tema).

Certainly, where cargo volumes are relatively low, as is the case in most African ports, inducing competition can be difficult. In such cases, an appropriate regulatory framework is essential. But again in a number of African ports, monopolies operate without there being a regulatory framework in place to monitor for anticompetitive activities (e.g., Maputo, Mozambique). Most countries in Africa lack a regulatory framework and tools to prevent anticompetitive practices on the part of port and multimodal operators. Only South Africa is currently taking steps to establish an Economic Regulator to address port anticompetitive behavior.[4]

---

[2] In Nigeria, for example, the Federal Government has made colossal savings of US$ 2.5 billion from port reforms. The Bureau of Public Enterprises (BPE) indicates that the Nigerian economy would save a further US$ 2.5 billion following the concessioning of the nation's ports over a 10-year period. This amount, which is equivalent to 5 percent of the country's Gross Domestic Product, is required by the Federal Government to maintain the ports. The successful implementation of the port reforms would quadruple cargo-handling productivity at the ports, reduce port operating costs by US$ 65–80 million yearly (about 20–25 percent) and reduce port charges by 20–30 percent, thereby saving port users between US$ 70 and US$100 million annually. The reforms would reduce the cost of Nigeria's imports by as much as 5–13 percent per annum, through increased efficiency, improved service delivery, modernized port development, and a general fall in the cost of shipping and clearing goods at the ports.

[3] Other countries engaged in the process of changing their port management system include Liberia and Sierra Leone. Also, the Tanzanian government has amended the National Port Law, while the Tanzania Ports Authority is in the process of changing from a public services port model to landlord port model.

[4] Regulation that ensures fair competition is rare. Only Peru, Australia, Colombia, and perhaps Mexico have well-established Economic Regulators to address pricing regulation. Authorities in many countries, even those of the European Union, seem unwilling to manage port anticompetitive behavior, despite their authority to do so. Given the difficulty regarding regulation, it may be essential for African governments to consider this in initial concession contracts with partners.

Comparing African Ports for Regional Port Hub Status

A considerable number of ports in Africa have the potential to develop into transshipment hubs. These are analyzed below, according to their geographical locations. On the Mediterranean coast of Africa, the main contenders are: Tangiers (Morocco), Damietta (Egypt) and Suez Canal Container Terminal (or Port Said East). In sub-Saharan Africa, the following ports have the potential to become major regional hubs: Dar-es-Salaam (Tanzania), Port Louis (Mauritius), Djibouti (Djibouti), Mombasa (Kenya), Abidjan (Côte d'Ivoire), Durban and Cape Town (South Africa), Tema (Ghana), Douala (Cameroon), Lagos (Nigeria), and Dakar (Senegal).

(i) Mediterranean Coast

Tangiers (Morocco) has already been transformed into a "Pure Transshipment Port" (PTP), which is providing regional feeder services, especially to the West African coast. Tangiers' development into a PTP exhibits most of the key criteria highlighted earlier for successful regional port hub development. The port is well positioned — sitting at the western end of the Strait of Gibraltar, which divides Africa and Europe. Container traffic lies at the heart of the strategy of the port, with container volumes reaching 1.2 million TEUs in 2009. The two container terminals already opened are each managed by a consortium of international terminal operators. The port has the physical infrastructure in place to handle more than 3 million TEUs a year, thus Tangiers will have spare capacity for some time to come. Much of Tangiers' initial

appeal lay in its lower labor costs. As well as political stability, Morocco boasts a business-friendly legal system, attractive incentives for FDI, advanced infrastructure, and a competent and highly trained workforce. This has attracted more than 2,500 foreign companies to locate their businesses in the country.

(ii) West African Coast

Along the West African coast, in terms of size and activity, the **Port of Lagos (Nigeria)** is the most important. Its annual merchandise traffic, in excess of 30 million tonnes, represents approximately 55 percent of Nigeria's port activity (excluding hydrocarbon exporting terminals) and 25 percent of the combined ECOWAS member countries' port activity. However, the Port of Lagos essentially serves the national hinterland and only the outlying areas of Niger, Cameroon and Benin, an area that accounts for more than half of the population. However, the concentration of port activity is largely on the national hinterland, which limits the port's importance as a regional hub.

The Nigerian authorities are undertaking investment programs with the aim of transforming the port into a regional hub. Under the Lagos Free Trade Zone (LFTZ) initiative, the Nigerian Ports Authority and the Lagos State Government are to build the first private deepwater port in Lekki, 60 km distant from the Lagos metropolis. The total cost is estimated at US$ 6 billion and the port is expected to be ready in 2011. The rationale behind the port is to provide a deepwater port for Nigeria, thereby allowing larger vessels to berth. It is also intended to relieve the congestion in the Lagos/Apapa ports. Also the port is located to take advantage of the future development of the new Lagos Free Trade Zone.

By contrast, the ports of **Abidjan**, **Tema**, and **Dakar** play a more regional role in West Africa. These ports do not rely solely on their national hinterland in order to thrive. The development of the West African road network, together with an increasing number of alternative transport services rendered to the landlocked regions, have increased their regional roles but placed them in direct competition with each other.

Considering the fact that regional hubs are usually established in ports with substantial cargo volumes, **Abidjan (Côte d'Ivoire)**, with a capacity of 640,000+ TEUs, appears a more likely candidate to serve as the regional hub. The Ivorian government aims to expand the port further from an import–export point to a gateway for landlocked countries in West Africa. The Port Authorities aim to develop the port's capacity to handle volumes for Burkina Faso, Niger, and Mali, which is expected to grow strongly over the next five years, as will transshipments for ports in the subregion. To this end, a bond issued by Abidjan Port has been oversubscribed by over 30 percent, raising 30 billion CFA francs (US$ 56 million) to finance port development.

However, **Tema (Ghana)**, which is a new and highly mechanized terminal, offers substantially more efficiency and berth productivity, compared to other ports on the west coast of Africa. Tema is the first to offer a terminal with the efficiency required for regional hub services. Though Tema has lower volumes (about 350,000 TEUs), this is enough to attract main regional feeder

services, thus assigning Tema regional hub status. Significantly, the port is currently expanding its berthing facilities and working on achieving greater depth in order to attract more cargo. The government is aiming to achieve 14 m depth (currently it stands at 11.5 m) and has dredged berths 1-6. The port is also focused on reducing the turn-around time for vessels which currently stands at 1.7 days and to ensure that the cost of doing business is one of the lowest in the subregion *(Otal Trade Watch, July 2010)*.

(iii) East African Coast

Along the East African coast, Dar-es-Salaam (Tanzania), Port Louis (Mauritius), Maputo (Mozambique), Durban (South Africa), Djibouti, and Mombasa (Kenya) are the major ports with the potential to become regional hub ports. The successful completion of planned investment programs in these ports will determine the extent to which they are transformed into regional hubs.

At present **Durban (South Africa)** emerges as a frontrunner in terms of size and activity. Durban is Africa's busiest general cargo port and home to one of the largest and busiest container terminals in the southern hemisphere. The port handles the greatest volume of seagoing traffic of any port in southern Africa. However, Durban's cargo-handling demand has exceeded the terminal's handling capacity, causing berth congestion and forcing carriers to impose penalty surcharges. Under the government's current program for the port, an additional capacity of 600,000 TEUs is being developed to bring the total container capacity of the port to 3.6 million TEUs by 2011. This project includes

Durban container terminal's reengineering project, which will realize the true potential capacity of this premier port.

The port of **Dar-es-Salaam (Tanzania)** is also well placed as a transshipment hub, ideally located to meet the export and import needs of Tanzania's landlocked neighbors, namely Burundi, Malawi, Rwanda, and Zambia. Also, Dar-es-Salaam has a number of inland depots for landlocked countries that import and export via the port. However, Dar-es-Salaam has not been able to take full advantage of its position due to limited capacity, which has led to the diversion of consignments to the neighboring port of Mombasa. Besides, most of the inland depots are currently located close to the port, leading to serious road congestion and pollution.

To remedy the situation, the Tanzania Port Authority is aiming to strengthen the port's container-handling capacity. A National Port Strategy Study undertaken in 2008 recommended two options: (i) development of two additional container berths in the port of Dar-es-Salaam (Berths 13 and 14); and (ii) development of a deepwater port along the coast (several locations have been identified). The expansion program to build the second container terminal is estimated to cost around US$ 400–650 million.

Furthermore, Tanzania is investigating the feasibility of the development of a dry port (also known as an inland port) facility as a solution to the problem. The major objective is to decrease the usually long dwell times of containers destined for landlocked countries by moving them by rail (under bond) to the dry port located some 40 km away from the Port of Dar-es-Salaam as soon as basic administrative procedures have been completed. Movement by rail will reduce the need for road transport which, in turn, will result in less road congestion in and around the port and the city and reduce its pollution effect. The development of the dry port opens opportunities for private investments in terms of development and/or management, as well as participation by the landlocked countries that will benefit from this initiative. Moreover, it will open the way for investment in upgrading and repairing the Dar-es-Salaam railroad, which would have large spillover effects, notably by revitalizing traffic at the port of Bujumbura.

In respect to **Mombasa (Kenya)**, the Kenya Ports Authority (KPA) has finalized a Vision 2030 that includes PPP participation in the development of port infrastructure and provision of services. The scheme provides for the dredging of the Port of Mombasa to allow larger vessels to the port and the benchmarking of facilities and services to international standards. Another element of Vision 2030 is the development of a new deepwater port at Lamu Island. In May 2010 the Kenyan government awarded a contract to Japan Port Consultants (JPC) to carry out a feasibility study for Lamu Port, which experts hope will position the country as a major transshipment hub. The first port at Lamu is being developed with assistance from the governments of Qatar and China and is scheduled for completion at the end of 2011.

The Port of **Djibouti** is creating an additional 3 million TEUs, to achieve a total capacity of 3.4 million TEUs. In June 2000 the government of Djibouti signed a management contract with Dubai Port World (DPW), to strengthen the import and export function of the port (some 90 percent of all cargo handled is Ethiopian cargo). DPW developed plans to build a large deepwater container facility at Doraleh (some 10 km from the Port of Djibouti). The maximum capacity of this terminal will be 1.7 million TEUs (compared to the 250,000 TEUs of the present terminal in Djibouti). The project will be built on the basis of a BOO (Build-Own-Operate) contract and the estimated cost of the project is about US$ 350 million. The first phase of Doraleh (Phase 1-A) was opened for business in May 2009. Phase 1-A (capacity 800,000 TEUs) was financed through equity. Phase 1-B (capacity 1.1 million TEUs) will be financed through cash reserves and bank loans. The anticipated container flows are import/export, transit and transshipment.

(iv) The Role of Public–Private Partnerships

Thus far, it is apparent that the potential does exist for a number of African ports to become regional hubs, although as indicated earlier, this will depend on the success of planned investments and related modernization of these ports. The development of Tangiers demonstrates the successful role that public-private partnerships can play toward the desired outcomes and point the way forward for other African governments and port authorities to replicate. In effect, the investment programs in those other ports call for similar partnerships in port development in Africa.

The Role of IFIs in the Development and Improvement of Ports and Related Infrastructure

As African countries contemplate strategies for transforming their ports into regional hubs, they should pay heed to the important role that IFIs, such as the African Development Bank, can play in the process. IFIs can facilitate private sector participation as well as provide finance for port development. These issues are discussed at greater length below.

Provision and /or Facilitation of Expertise, Training and Education

Expertise: As indicated earlier, port reform and the introduction of PPPs, especially leading to the establishment of landlord port management systems, are highly complex exercises. They require expertise in many disciplines such as legal, operations, finance, economy, etc. Selecting the best professional expertise is a difficult task in itself and can only be done adequately when professional insight, oversight, and market knowledge are available. IFIs can support governments and national Port Authorities to produce the requisite documents; they can also avail experts in the port reform processes. Also, the experienced and professionally qualified consultants that governments and port authorities rely on are expensive and IFIs may be prepared to contribute financially to these costs.

Training and Education: In order to create a good working relationship between the government, national Port Authority, the consultant, and the potential private sector participants, the public party should have sufficient in-house expertise to meaningfully engage in the process. If such expertise is not available, education and training are extremely important. Workshops and seminars on dedicated topics are a very good means to point out the essential stages of the processes to be followed. This is another area where IFIs may provide a useful function, either with the involvement of their own staff or in the role of a financier and/or facilitator.

Arranging /Facilitating Financing Deals

Dredging: As indicated earlier, many African ports are characterized as rather shallow. Developments in the international shipping market require ports to have sufficient water depth to allow larger vessels to call. Experience shows that initial capital and/or maintenance dredging projects are difficult to realize and can be expensive undertakings in relatively remote areas. IFIs, and the AfDB in particular, could assist African ports that have similar dredging problems to jointly enter into a dredging contract with a dredging company. The Bank could facilitate the introduction of Performance Based Maintenance (PBM) dredging contracts between the African countries and a dredging company (see Box 6.2). The cost of this to the African countries would be lower than if they were to draw up a contract on an individual country basis; moreover the ports would be assured, for the duration of the contract, that the guaranteed water depth would always be available.

Regional Investment: In the context of regional cooperation, IFIs could assist

Box 6.2: Performance Based Maintenance (PBM) dredging contract

A PBM dredging contract is an agreement between a client (for instance a Port Authority) and a dredging company. The contract stipulates that the dredging company, at all times during the contract period, guarantees that the agreed water depth is always available. The dredging company regularly surveys the depth in the contract area. If the contract depth in a certain location, due to sedimentation, is about to be reached, the dredging company dredges that area. The client also makes regular soundings (depth surveys). If these show that at a certain location the dredging company is in default (i.e., the depth is less than the contract depth), the dredging company is liable to pay a fine.

Unlike contracted capital or maintenance dredging campaigns, the dredging company is not paid for the number of cubic meters of silt it has removed. The agreement between the parties is made on the basis of a long-term estimate of the dredging quantities during the contract period. This may result in higher dredging costs per cubic meter than in case of a single dredging campaign. But the principal advantage is that the Port Authority is guaranteed that the required contract depth is always available. The costs of the bidding process of a dredging campaign may, moreover, well outbalance the possibly higher cubic meter dredging costs of the PBM contract.

countries, both coastal and landlocked, to invest, possibly through an international consortium, in major new port development investment projects. The plans of the governments of Kenya and Tanzania to build a new deepwater port on their coastline represent such an initiative. Such a facility, including efficient and sufficient hinterland connections, will require significant financial capital outlay, which the IFIs may be able to provide or facilitate.

Railroad Corridors: The importance of the railroad in Africa for freight movement has already been demonstrated (see Chapter 4). However, even though the concessioning of railroads has met with some success and has increased traffic volumes as well as increased labor productivity, this mode of transport remains poorly developed across the continent. Yet railroads are an economically sound choice for long-distance transport of large volume bulk commodities, agricultural products, and general and containerized cargoes across the continent for onward transit to African ports and beyond. In addition to helping to mobilize funding for strengthening and expanding this inland transport mode, IFIs can provide advice and expertise to countries that enter into railroad concessioning agreements.

Provision of Other Catalytic and Direct Financing for Port Development

As there is a great need to attract more external investment to the port sector in Africa, IFIs can galvanize the private sector in other ways and participate directly in port finance. IFIs may have differing aims, and this will play an important role in their choice of projects. However, these institutions have the common dual mission of "transitionality" (supporting the move from state to market economy) and "additionality" (providing "something more" than a commercial lender would on a given deal). In this context, IFIs may be well positioned to provide assistance to African governments in the reform process through the design of appropriate port frameworks; restructuring and divesting port institutions; and capacity building for port planning and regulation. In addition, IFIs can assist African governments by attracting and negotiating with private partners to assure substantial benefits for the African partner country. Another consideration is that IFIs are well experienced in the area of risk mitigation mechanisms, which acts as a further incentive to attract private capital into port projects.

IFIs could also directly finance critical elements of port infrastructure. As indicated earlier (Chapter 5), the AfDB has since 1973 successfully participated in infrastructure financing and port development in Africa. IFIs, including the AfDB, are well placed to focus directly on the private sector segment of port infrastructure in African countries, using instruments such as the traditional lines of credit to increase private investment. The long-term tenor of such lines of credit will allow borrowers to extend the maturity of their lending operations, thereby making the port development programs more commercially attractive to investors.

In addition, IFIs could use varied instruments, including equity and quasi-equity products and guarantees to increase the participation of the private sector. Through these, IFIs would bring in other investors with the capital, skills, and know-how needed for African port development. The AfDB Local Currency Project is an example of a successful mechanism that could be employed to increase private participation in ports. This project brings increased investor attention to Africa and brings visibility to African currencies and bond markets. It addresses the need for local currency loans that eliminate currency risk for borrowers and promotes international best practices. A wider application of this activity focused on African ports could be instrumental in contributing to the financing needs for port development.

Concluding Remarks

This chapter has highlighted the requirements for the development of regional hubs in Africa, analyzed the potential of specific African ports to become regional hubs, pointed to the opportunities available for private sector participation, and has outlined some of the contributions that IFIs can make in the process.

African ports are presently characterized by high sea freight rates and high levels of congestion. Their transformation into more efficient port hubs will not only reduce these rates but also contribute toward inter-African economic integration, as well as the continent's fuller integration into the world trading system. Several African governments and Port Authorities are aiming to develop their ports into hubs. Improvements planned in many other ports in the continent will also offer opportunities for private participation.

Key measures in the process to transform ports into regional hubs include fostering and financing integrated port and transport facilities and associated land use. Also, policies that introduce and/or enhance competition are necessary to increase efficiency. In both these areas, global experiences have shown that the transformation of a public services port into a landlord port model often leads to a highly successful outcome.

In this context, IFIs can play a major role through the provision and/or facilitation of expertise, training and education, whereby experienced professionals can assist African governments in the preparation of their port reforms. In addition, IFIs are well placed to assist in arranging and/or facilitating public–private financing deals that are badly needed to carry out major rehabilitation and expansion programs for African ports.

Glossary

Backhaul To haul a shipment back over part of a route that it has already traveled; return movement of cargo, usually opposite from the direction of its primary cargo destination.

Beam The width of a ship.

Berth Civil engineering structures located on a quay to allow oceangoing vessels and other floating craft to be moored or secured alongside with the purpose of loading/offloading cargoes. Berths are usually classified to the water depth in front of them. Distinction is made between dedicated container berths, dry bulk berths, liquid bulk berths and general cargo, multipurpose or neo bulk berths.

Berth dues (or quay dues or dockage) Charges for the use of a berth. Typically assessed based on the duration of a vessel's stay and length overall (LOA).

Bonded warehouse A warehouse authorized by customs authorities for storage of goods on which payment of duties is deferred until the goods are removed.

Border control services Services of the Contracting Parties competent to carry out border controls, such as frontier police, customs, plant protection and veterinary inspections services, and any other services as may be deemed necessary.

Break-bulk A loose, non-containerized cargo stowed directly into a ship's hold, to ship in small, separable units. Loose cement, grain, ores, etc. are termed "bulk cargo," whereas cargo shipped in units (bags, bales, boxes, cartons, pallets, drums, sacks, etc.) is "break-bulk".

Broker A person who arranges for transportation of loads for a percentage of the revenue from the load.

Build-operate-transfer (BOT) A form of concession where a private party or consortium agrees to finance, construct, operate and maintain a facility for a specific period and transfer the facility to the concerned government or port authority after the term of the concession. The ownership of the concession area (port land) remains with the government or port authority during the entire concession period. The concessionaire bears the commercial risk of operating the facility.

Build-own-operate-transfer (BOOT) A form of concession where a private party or consortium agrees to finance, construct, own, operate, and maintain a facility for a specific period and transfer the facility to the concerned government or port authority after the term of the concession. The ownership of the concession area (port land) vests in the private party or consortium during the entire concession period and is transferred to the government or port authority at the end of the concession period. As with the BOT, the concessionaire bears the commercial risk of operating the facility.

Bulk carrier/vessel All vessels designed to carry bulk cargo such as grain, fertilizers, ore, and oil.

Bulkhead A structure to resist water; a partition separating one part of a ship from another part.

Bunkering The act or process of supplying a ship with fuel.

Bunkers (a) A bin or tank, especially for fuel storage on board a ship; (b) Fuel used aboard ships.

Capesize vessels A very large bulk carrier between 80–150,000 dwt, which used to be unable to transit the Suez Canal and therefore forced to sail around the Cape of Good Hope to and from Europe. Now those vessels can transit through the Suez Canal as long as they meet the draft restriction (18.91 m/62 ft as at 2008).

Cargo tonnage Ocean freight is frequently billed on the basis of weight or measurement tonnes. Weights tons can be expressed in terms of short tons of 2,000 pounds, long tons of 2,240 pounds, or metric tons of 1,000 kilograms (2,204.62 pounds). Measurement tons are usually expressed as cargo measurements of 40 cubic feet (1.12 cubic meters) or cubic meters (35.3 cubic feet).

Carrier Any legal or naturalized person who, in a contract of carriage and in accordance with the national laws and regulations of the Contracting Parties, undertakes to perform or to procure the performance of carriage by sea, inland waterway, rail, road, air, or by a combination of such modes.

Clearance The size beyond which vessels, cars, or loads cannot pass through, under, or over bridges, tunnels, highways, and so forth.

Common carrier A transportation company that provides services to the general public at published rates.

Concession An arrangement whereby a private party (concessionaire) leases assets from an authorized public entity for an extended period and has responsibility for financing specified new fixed investments during the period and for providing specified services associated with the assets; in return, the concessionaire receives specified revenues from the operation of the assets; the assets revert to the public sector at expiration of the contract.

Consolidation Cargo that consists of shipments of two or more shippers or suppliers. Container load shipments may be consolidated for one or more consignees.

Container Steel or aluminum frame forming a box in which cargo can be stowed meeting International Standard Organization (ISO)-specified measurements, fitted with special castings on the corners for securing to lifting equipment, vessels, chassis, rail cars, or stacking on other containers. Containers come in many forms and types, including: ventilated, insulated, refrigerated, flat rack, vehicle rack, open top, bulk liquid, dry bulk, or other special configurations. Typical containers may be 10 ft, 20 ft, 30 ft, 40 ft, 45 ft, 48 ft, or 53 ft in length; 8 ft or 8.5 ft in width; and 8.5 ft or 9.5 ft in height.

Container berths Number of berths designated for the loading and unloading of containerized cargoes.

Container freight station A dedicated port or container terminal area, usually consisting of one or more sheds or warehouses and uncovered storage areas where cargo is loaded ("stuffed") into or unloaded ("stripped") from containers and may be temporarily stored in the sheds or warehouses.

Container handling capacity The number of containers, usually expressed in the standard dimension of TEU, that a port or terminal is designed to handle in a period of one year. A Twenty Foot Equivalent Unit (TEU) is the standard unit to express container capacity. A TEU is a representation of a container with the following dimensions: 8 ft wide; 8 ft or 8 ft 6 in or 9 ft 6 in in height; and 20 ft long. The very large portion of the world container population consists of 20 ft and 40 ft containers. A 40 ft container equals 2 TEUs.

Container pool (a) An agreement between parties that allows the efficient use and supply of containers; (b) a common supply of containers available to the shipper as required.

Container terminal An area designated for the handling, storage, and possibly loading or unloading of cargo into or out of containers, and where containers can be picked up, dropped off, maintained, stored, or loaded or unloaded from one mode of transport to another (that is, vessel, truck, barge, or rail).

Container vessel Ship equipped with cells into which containers can be stacked. Container ships may be full or partial, depending on whether all or only some of its holds are fitted with container cells.

Container yard A container handling and storage facility either within a port or inland.

Contraband Cargo that is prohibited.

Contract carrier Any person not a common carrier who, under special and individual contracts or agreements, transports passengers or cargo for compensation.

Controlled atmosphere Sophisticated, computer-controlled systems that manage the mixture of gases within a container throughout an intermodal journey, thereby reducing decay.

Corridor A geographical concentration of transport infrastructures and transit activities between two or more economic centers, linking them to one another, and often to ports/international markets.

Customs broker A person or firm, licensed by the customs authority of their country when required, engaged in entering and clearing goods through customs for a client (importer).

Customs house A government office where duties are paid, import/export documents filed, and so forth, on shipments.

Demurrage A penalty charge against shippers or consignees for delaying the carrier's equipment beyond the allowed free time. The free time and demurrage charges are set out in the charter party or freight tariff.

Dock or quay A structure attached to land to which a vessel can be moored.

Draft (or draught) The depth of a ship while in the water. Measured as the vertical distance between the waterline and the lowest edge of the keel.

Dredging Removal of sediment to deepen access channels, provide turning basins for ships, and maintain adequate water depth along waterside facilities.

Dry bulk Loose, mostly uniform cargo, such as agribulk products, coal, fertilizer, and ores, that are transported in bulk carriers.

Dry bulk berths Number of berths designated for the loading and unloading of dry bulk cargoes. Dry bulk cargoes are homogeneous cargoes that are usually transported in loose form, being loaded and unloaded in a more or less continuous way with the use of mechanical equipment and devices such as grabs, conveyor belts, section machines, etc. Examples of dry cargoes include: coal oil, liquid chemicals and liquefied gases.

Dwell time The time cargo remains in a terminal's in-transit storage areas, while awaiting shipment (for exports) or onward transportation by road/rail (for imports). Dwell time is one indicator of a port's efficiency: the higher the dwell time, the lower the efficiency.

Electronic data interchange (EDI) Transmission of transactional data between computer systems.

Feeder service Transport service whereby loaded or empty containers in a regional area are transferred to a "mother ship" for a long-haul ocean voyage.

Fixed costs Costs that do not vary with the level of activity. Some fixed costs continue even if no cargo is carried; for example, terminal leases, rent, and property taxes.

Forklift Also called a lift truck, a high/low, a stacker-truck, trailer loader, or a sideloader, it is a powered industrial truck used to lift and transport materials.

Forty-foot (40 ft) equivalent unit (FEU) Unit of measurement equivalent to one 40-ft container. Two 20-ft containers (TEUs) equal one FEU.

Free trade zone (FTZ) A zone, often within a port (but not always), designated by the government of a country for duty-free entry of any nonprohibited goods. Merchandise may be stored, displayed, or used for manufacturing within the zone and reexported without duties being applied.

Gantry crane A crane fixed on a frame or structure spanning an intervening space typically designed to traverse fixed structures such as cargo (container) storage areas or quays and which is used to hoist CONTAINERS or other cargo in and out of vessels and place or lift from a vessel, barge, trucks, chassis, or train.

Gateway A point at which freight moving from one territory to another is interchanged between transportation lines.

Grounding Contact by a ship with the ground while the ship is moored or anchored as a result of the water level dropping, or when approaching the coast as a result of a navigational error.

Harbor dues (or port dues) Charges by a port authority to a vessel for each harbor entry, usually on a per gross tonnage basis, to cover the costs of basic port infrastructure and marine facilities such as buoys, beacons, and vessel traffic management system.

Inland carrier A transportation company that hauls export or import traffic between ports and inland points.

Intermodality The use of two or more modes of transport in an integrated manner in a door-to-door transport chain.

Jetty (or pier) A structure that is perpendicular or at an angle to the shoreline to which a vessel is secured for the purpose of loading and unloading cargo.

Landlocked state A state which has no sea coast or which does not have a direct link with the sea coast through its own territory.

Landlord port An institutional structure where the port authority or other relevant public agency retains ownership of the port land and responsibility for port planning and development, as well as the maintenance of basic port infrastructure and aids to navigation.

Lender's direct agreement Agreement between parties to a concession or BOT agreement (government or port authority and special purpose vehicle [SPV] or terminal operator) and the lenders (usually banks or a consortium of banks) setting out the rights and obligations of the lenders in relation to the government or port authority regarding the facilitation of the financing of a port project. The lender's direct agreement is used in the event of a proposed termination of the concession agreement to induce the lenders to provide the debt to the SPV or operator under the financing documents. These rights and obligations usually comprise assignment rights with respect to the concession and the site lease agreement, priority rights with respect to repayment of the debt, and step-in rights in case of termination as a result of breach of contract by the SPV or operator.

Lighter An open or covered barge towed or pushed by a TUGBOAT or a pusher tug and used primarily in harbors and on inland waterways to carry cargo to or from the port.

Liner A vessel sailing between specified ports on a regular basis.

Liner conference Agreement between two or more shipping companies to provide scheduled cargo and/or passenger service on a particular trade route under uniform rates and common terms. Also called shipping conference.

Liquid bulk berths Number of berths designated for the loading and unloading of liquid bulk cargoes. Liquid bulk cargoes are liquids that are transported in tank compartments on board a vessel and stored in tanks on shore. The cargo is loaded and unloaded by means of pumps. Examples of liquid bulk cargoes are: crude oil, liquid chemicals and liquefied gases.

Loaded draught (or draft) Depth of water to which a ship is immersed when fully loaded.

Lo-lo (lift-on lift-off) Cargo-handling method by which vessels are loaded or unloaded by either ship or shore cranes.

Mixed cargo Two or more products carried on board one ship.

Mobile crane General purpose crane capable of moving on its own wheels from one part of a port to another.

Mode of transport Method used for the movement of goods or people (e.g. by sea, road, rail).

Multi-purpose berths Number of berths designated for the loading and unloading of multipurpose cargoes. These are any assortment of conventional general, unitized, containerized and/or NEO-BULK cargo. Examples of neo-bulk cargoes are: motor cars, sawn timber and steel products.

Neobulk cargo Uniformly packaged goods, such as wood pulp bales, which stow as solidly as bulk, but are handled as general cargoes.

Open Registry National ship registry — under a national flag — open to ships of all nations, regardless of nationality.

Panamax Panamax ships are the largest ships that can pass through the locks of the Panama Canal (specifically used for dry bulk and container vessels). Panamax ships can measure up to 956 ft long (for container ships), 105 ft wide, 190 ft from the waterline, and up to 39 ft below the waterline. Weight can vary, but based on these measures should average between 65,000–69,000 tons. Ships too large to transit the canal are called "post-Panamax."

Pilotage The act of assisting the master of a ship in navigation when entering or leaving a port or in confined water.

Pooling Sharing of cargo or the profit or loss from freight by member lines of a LINER CONFERENCE.

Port dues (or harbor dues) Charges levied against a shipowner or ship operator by a port authority for the use of a port (see also HARBOR DUES).

Port handling capacity The design cargo handling capacity of a port expressed in tonnes/year.

Port of registry Place where a ship is registered with the authorities, thereby establishing its nationality.

Project financing Financing wherein the lender looks to a project's cash flows to repay the principal and interest on debt, and to a project's assets for security; also known as "structured financing" because it requires structuring the debt and equity such that a project's cash flows are adequate to service the debt.

Rail-mounted gantry (RMG) or rail-mounted container gantry crane Used for container acceptance, delivery, and stacking operations in a container yard.

Reefer Refrigerated container or vessel designed to transport refrigerated or frozen cargo.

Relay To transfer containers from one ship to another.

Ro/ro A shortening of the term "roll-on, roll-off." Ro/ro is a cargo handling method whereby vessels are loaded via one or more ramps that are lowered on the quay.

Rubber-tired gantry (RTG) or rubber-tired container gantry crane Gantry crane on rubber tires typically used for acceptance, delivery, and container stacking at a container yard.

Shed Covered area for the reception, delivery, consolidation, distribution, and storage of cargo. *Note*: A warehouse usually points at longer-term storage, whereas a shed usually is used for shorter-term storage. (Also see WAREHOUSE)

Side loader A lift truck fitted with lifting attachments operating to one side for handling containers.

Stevedoring To load or unload a cargo while in port.

Sto-ro A vessel with capacity for break-bulk cargo as well as vehicles or trailer borne cargo.

Storage capacity The area in a port designated for the storage of cargo.

Stowage factor The average cubic space occupied by one ton weight of cargo as stowed aboard a ship.

Super Post-Panamax The latest generation of "super post Panamax" vessels has a width of about 22 container rows, compared to "post Panamax" vessels, which accommodate 18 container rows.

Supply chain A logistics management system that integrates the sequence of activities from delivery of raw materials to the manufacturer through to the delivery of the finished product to the customer in measurable components.

Tare weight The weight of wrapping or packing; added to the net weight of cargo to determine its gross weight.

Traffic in transit Passage of traffic across the territory of a Contracting Party with or without transhipment, warehousing, breaking bulk, leaning, repairing, repacking, assembly, disassembly, reassembly of machinery and goods, and change of mode and means of transport when any such operation is undertaken solely for the convenience transportation, provided that such passage is only a portion of a complete journey beginning and terminating beyond the frontier of the State across whose territory the traffic passes.

Transit Passage across the territory of a Contracting Party when such passage is only a portion of a complete journey, beginning and terminating beyond the frontier of the State across whose territory the transit takes place.

Transshipment A distribution method whereby containers or cargo are transferred from one vessel to another to reach their final destination, compared to a direct service from the load port of origin to the discharge port of destination. This method is often used to gain better vessel utilization and thereby economies of scale by consolidating cargo onto larger vessels while transiting in the direction of main trade routes.

Transshipment port A port where cargo is transferred from one carrier to another or from one vessel of a carrier to another vessel of the same carrier without the cargo leaving the port.

Tugboat A boat that maneuvers vessels by pushing or towing them. Tugs move vessels that should not move themselves alone, such as ships in a crowded harbor or a narrow canal, or those that cannot move themselves, such as barges, disabled ships, or oil platforms. Tugboats are powerful for their size and strongly built, some are ocean-going. Some tugboats serve as icebreakers or salvage boats. Early tugboats had steam engines; today diesel engines are used.

Turnaround time The time it takes between the arrival of a vessel and its departure from port; frequently used as a measure of port efficiency.

Twenty-foot equivalent unit (TEU) Container size standard of 20 ft. Two 20-ft containers (TEUs) equal one FEU (40-ft container). Container vessel capacity and port throughput capacity are frequently referred to in TEUs.

Variable cost Costs that vary directly with the level of activity within a short time. Examples include costs of moving cargo inland on trains or trucks, STEVEDORING in some ports, and short-term equipment leases.

Warehouse Covered area for the reception, delivery, consolidation, distribution, and storage of cargo. *Note:* A warehouse usually points at longer-term storage, whereas a shed usually is used for shorter-term storage. (Also see SHED)

This publication was prepared by the Bank's Development Research Department (EDRE) in the Chief Economist Complex (ECON). Other publications of the Complex include:

ADB POCKET BOOK
A pocketbook of data from two statistical publications: the *Compendium of Statistics* and *Selected Statistics on African Countries*.

AFRICA COMPETITIVENESS REPORT
The report presents an in-depth assessment of many aspects of Africa's business environment and highlights the key issues that hinder progress in Africa's competitiveness and job growth. The report is published by the African Development Bank, in collaboration with the World Economic Forum and the World Bank.

AFRICAN DEVELOPMENT REVIEW
The African Development Review is a professional development economics journal that provides a platform for expressing analytical and conceptual views on Africa's development challenges. It is published three times a year.

AFRICAN ECONOMIC OUTLOOK
An annual publication jointly produced by the African Development Bank, the OECD Development Center, and the United Nations Economic Commission for Africa (UNECA). It analyzes the comparative economic prospects for African countries.

AFRICAN STATISTICAL JOURNAL
A bi-annual publication aimed at promoting the understanding of statistical development in Africa.

COMPENDIUM OF STATISTICS
An annual publication providing statistical information on the operational activities of the Bank.

ECONOMIC RESEARCH PAPERS
A working paper series presenting preliminary research findings on issues of relevance to African development.

GENDER, POVERTY AND ENVIRONMENTAL INDICATORS ON AFRICAN COUNTRIES
An annual publication providing statistics on broad development trends relating to gender, poverty and environmental issues in all 53 African countries.

PRODUCT CATALOGUE FOR ICP PRICE SURVEYS IN AFRICAN COUNTRIES
This catalogue provides International Comparison Program for Africa (ICP-Africa) survey information on a series of products to be priced in Regional Member Countries of the African Development Bank.

SELECTED STATISTICS ON AFRICAN COUNTRIES
An annual publication, providing statistics on selected social and economic indicators for the 53 Regional Member Countries of the African Development Bank.

WALL CHART ON THE MDGS
The chart provides data on progress towards attaining the Millennium Development Goals in all Regional Member Countries.

Copies of these publications may be obtained from:

Development Research Department (EDRE)
African Development Bank

Headquarters	**Temporary Relocation Agency (TRA)**
01 BP 1387 Abidjan 01,	Angle des trois rues, Avenue du Ghana,
COTE D'IVOIRE	rues Pierre de Coubertin
TELEFAX (225) 20 20 49 48	et Hedi Nouira
TELEPHONE (225) 20 20 44 44	BP 323 — 1002 TUNIS BELVEDERE
TELEX 23717/23498/23263	TUNISIA
Web Site: www.afdb.org	TELEFAX (216) 71351933
EMAIL: Economics-Research@afdb.org	TELEPHONE (216) 71333511
	Web Site: www.afdb.org
	EMAIL: Economics-Research@afdb.org

DATE DUE